THE NATIONAL UNDERWRITER COMPANY

CONDOMINIUM INSURANCE COVERAGE GUIDE, 3RD EDITION

Christine G. Barlow, CPCU, Chris Kendall CPCU, AIM, AIT, ARM, ARP, ARe

Highlights of the Condominium Insurance Coverage Guide, 3rd Edition

The resource you hold in your hands contains everything that makes this guide the instant, must-have reference for professionals seeking to properly insure the various condominium risks that unit owners and associations face. It delivers the clearest possible analysis of the most important documents, including state statutes and bylaws. Available insurance policies are explained in the context of defining documents, and all relevant concepts are thoroughly clarified.

In addition, this new third edition now includes the following:

- Explanation of changes to ISO HO 00 06 Unit-owners form
- State-by-state chart of condominium regulations
- Sample policy forms
- An updated D&O chapter for directors and officers of condominium associations
- Updated claim discussions

The guide also includes sample condominium bylaws and sample insurance policy coverage forms, which, in combination with the expert analysis and guidance, enables users to correctly address the exposures faced by condominium unit owners and associations. Agents, underwriters, risk managers, and claims adjusters must comprehend these relationships in order to properly design and interpret insurance coverage for policyholders.

Additionally, a chapter is dedicated to the risks that individuals face as association directors and officers and the most effective methods for handling those risks.

Condominium Insurance Coverage Guide, 3rd Edition, comes to you from The National Underwriter Company, a division of ALM Global LLC, the leader in insurance coverage interpretation and analysis. National

Underwriter is now part of ALM | PC360. It is the same great content brought to you by the same authorities in Property and Casualty insurance. It contains the authoritative guide for insurance agents, claims adjusters, and underwriters in interpreting and analyzing condominium insurance policies.

For customer service questions or to place additional orders, please call 1-800-543-0874.

Additional Coverage Guides Available:

- Businessowners Policy
- Business Income
- Commercial Auto Program
- Commercial General Liability
- Commercial Property
- Construction Defects
- Critical Issues in CGL
- Directors and Officers Liability
- Employment Practices Liability
- Guide to Captives and Alternative Risk Financing
- Homeowners
- Insurance Claims: A Comprehensive Guide
- Mold Claims
- Personal Auto Policy
- Personal Umbrella
- Workers Compensation

3rd Edition

Condominium Insurance Coverage Guide

Commercial and Personal Lines Series

Christine G. Barlow, CPCU
Chris Kendall, CPCU, AIM, AIT, ARM, ARP, ARe

The National Underwriter Company

June 2023

International Standard Book Number: 978-1-58852-808-7

Printed in the United States of America

ABOUT THE NATIONAL UNDERWRITER COMPANY

In order to offer you more as a professional in your industry, we are under a new brand. The coverage guides that you've come to know and love from National Underwriter is now part of ALM IPC360. It is the same great content brought to you by the same authorities in Property and Casualty insurance. Your access to information is now expanded through our rebrand.

PropertyCasualty360 or PC360, is part of ALM, a global information, data, intelligence and content company with reporters and editors all over the world. In addition to the industry-leading insurance coverage you have come to expect from PC360, the ALM network of writers follows the biggest news events across a range of professional markets, including legal, commercial real estate, and investment advisory. We strive to identify trends earlier than anyone else and bring an insightful and analytical lens to our coverage that helps you excel in your field.

ALM Update Service Notification

This ALM publication is regularly updated to include coverage of developments and changes that affect the content. If you did not purchase this publication directly from ALM and you want to receive these important updates sent on a 30-day review basis and billed separately, please contact us at (800) 543 0874. Or you can mail your request with your name, company, address, and the title of the book to:

ALM
4157 Olympic Boulevard
Suite 225
Erlanger, KY 41018

If you purchased this publication from ALM directly, you have already been registered for the update service.

ALM Contact Information

To order any ALM titles, please

- call 1-800-543-0874, 8-6 ET Monday – Thursday and 8 to 5 ET Friday
- online bookstore at www.nationalunderwriter.com, or
- mail to ALM, Orders Department, 4157 Olympic Blvd., Ste. 225, Erlanger, KY 41018

About the Authors

Christine G. Barlow, CPCU, is Executive Editor of *FC&S Expert Coverage Interpretation, an ALM company.* Christine has been with The National Underwriter Company since 2006, when she began as an assistant editor. Before joining the National Underwriter Company, she was an underwriting supervisor for Maryland Automobile Insurance Fund, underwriter for Montgomery Mutual Insurance Company, senior underwriter for Old American, and an underwriter for Charter Group.

The publications Christine wrote or edited include *Personal Lines Unlocked*, the *Key to Personal Lines Underwriting, Homeowners Personal Lines Coverage Guide, Commercial Flood Insurance Coverage Guide, Personal Flood Insurance Coverage Guide, Personal Lines Endorsements Coverage Guide, Closing the Gap*, and *Condominium Insurance Coverage Guide*, all published by The National Underwriter Company. Christine also writes articles for Claims magazine. She is a speaker or presenter at various insurance related seminars and meetings.

Christine graduated cum laude from Towson University, Maryland, with a degree in Sociology/Psychology and a concentration in Gerontology.

Contributing Editor

Chris Kendall, CPCU, AIM, AIT, ARM, ARP, ARe spent the majority of his property and casualty insurance career working for the Cincinnati Insurance Companies as a commercial lines underwriter, underwriting manager, and director of commercial lines insurance operations. Among his various roles with this company, he managed underwriter education & training and served as an instructor across multiple lines of commercial insurance, including workers compensation. More recently, Mr. Kendall worked as Operations Lead for the Cincinnati office of AssuredPartners, one of the largest independent agency brokers in the United States.

Mr. Kendall earned a Bachelor of Arts degree from the University of Cincinnati. In addition to the insurance certifications listed above, he is also a licensed insurance agent. His commercial insurance instruction background includes live classroom, online teaching and textbook editing for The Institutes, one of the most respected insurance certification organizations in America. Mr. Kendall is past President of the Underwriting Executives Council, a midwestern association of insurers. He currently serves as Executive Director of the Greater Cincinnati Insurance Board, a non-profit insurance trade association and the first one in America founded in 1838. In addition to supporting the local Cincinnati area insurance industry, this organization is a provider of prelicensing classes and continuing education for both property & casualty and life, accident & health insurance agents.

Mr. Kendall can be contacted via e-mail at chris@cib-online.com or on his LinkedIn profile at www.linkedin.com/in/chriskendall.

Chris Kendall
937.999.9704

Publisher

Rosalie L. Donlon, group editor-in-chief, Reference Solutions for ALM Global LLC, has more than 20 years of professional publishing experience as a lawyer, writer, editor and content acquisition strategist. In this role, she focuses on property & casualty insurance issues as well as insurance coverage, policy interpretation, liability concerns, and insurance litigation. Her portfolio also include legal, tax and financial planning publications

Rosalie has written and edited publications on employment and labor law, safety, retirement plans, healthcare compliance and environmental law. In addition to her experience in legal publishing, Rosalie has been in private practice with a small law firm and a benefits communications consultant with Mercer Human Resource Consulting.

Before joining ALM, Rosalie was the contributing author and editor of several insurance industry and legal publications, including *Employment Practices Liability: Guide to Risk Exposures* and *Coverage and Guide to Captives and Alternative Risk Financing*, published by The National Underwriter Company, and *Connecticut Appellate Practice and Procedure, Fifth Edition*, published by Law Journal Press.

Rosalie earned her Juris Doctor degree from the University of Toledo College of Law and graduated with a Bachelor of Arts in History and Fine Arts from Fairfield University.

Social Media:
Twitter: @RosalieDonlon
LinkedIn: https://www.linkedin.com/in/rosaliedonlon/

Table of Contents

Chapter 1

Introduction

Condominiums are one of those complicated risks that aggravate insurance professionals, from agents to adjusters. The interplay of a condominium association declaration or agreement and the master policy of that association, and how they interplay with the unit owners insurance is often confusing and sorting out which policy pays for damages is essential.

The condominium concept has its genesis in ancient Rome. The term "condominium" is derived from the Latin "con" meaning "joint" and "dominium" meaning "right of ownership."

From its early beginnings, the condominium has morphed into its current forms, landing first in the Commonwealth of Puerto Rico with the passage of the Horizontal Property Act of Puerto Rico in 1948, before landing on the U.S. mainland.

The condominium concept is simple enough: to establish affordable housing for large numbers of people, allowing them property ownership that would otherwise be beyond their reach.

The housing model necessary to achieve this evolved into one with three distinct features:

(1) Dwelling units—with each unit exclusively owned by the person/persons purchasing it.

(2) Common elements—hallways, stairs, and elevators, for example, jointly owned by all unit owners as tenants in common, with each unit owner's interest measured by the proportionate value the unit bears to the total value of all units.

(3) An administrative framework or association—headed by a board of managers made up of unit owners established to manage the common areas and the assets of the association, as well as set out the rights and obligations of the unit owners.

This new form of ownership had to overcome the common law property ownership concept, which was rooted in the ownership of land. With the common law concept, boundaries could easily be set around properties, making it easy to determine ownership through surveys. Jane's property could easily be distinguished from Harry's; and as respects insurance it was easy to determine *who* was to be insured, *what* was to be insured, *where* the object of insurance was located, *when* coverage applied, and *how* coverage was to apply.

This W4H of coverage (who, what, where, when, and how) is much more difficult to apply to condominium coverage because the lines to be drawn around each are not always clear.

The key to understanding condo coverage is to be able to clearly draw lines of demarcation around ownership as well as around the W4H of coverage. Once lines are clearly drawn or identifiable, the condo coverage mystery is solved.

This coverage guide provides a roadmap to identify those boundaries, making it easy to understand how condo coverage applies in its multilayered forms.

Who should use this book? It offers critical insights to agents who struggle to determine what coverage is best for their clients. It offers underwriters a path to a better understanding of the exposures they assume, helping them to better tailor coverage at the beginning to minimize confusion, frustration, and disappointment at later stages when claims occur. It applies to claims adjusters to help them sharpen the blurred lines between losses that belong to the condo unit owner and those that belong to the condo association.

In the final analysis, this book is useful to all insurance professionals engaged in providing condominium customers with insurance value through the right balance among product, price, and service—from sale to underwriting to claims settlement.

This book focuses on examining the insurance needs of the unit owner and the condominium association, showing how the Condominium Association Form and the Unit-Owners Form work together in providing coverage. It also tackles problem issues in condominium coverage, including loss assessment, deductibles, and insurance to value.

This first Chapter of the book examines the importance of Condominium Property Acts/Horizontal Property Acts in establishing the objects of insurance as well as the scope of insurance. The Illinois Condominium Property Act is used as a template to show how to draw boundaries around condo ownership and consequently around the W4H of insurance coverage for condos. Each state has its own statutory requirements for coverage.

A review of policy coverage—specifically ISO CP 00 17 10 12 (the Condominium Association Coverage Form) and ISO CP 00 18 10 12 (the Condominium Commercial Unit-Owners Form), as well as ISO HO 00 06 03 22 (Personal Unit-Owners Form)—shows how coverage conforms to the acts Note the ISO HO 00 06 03 22 was introduced by ISO in 2022, replacing the previous 2011 edition. This form update will be discussed as well.

Condominium directors and officers coverage, given its central importance as a requirement of the condominium administrative framework, is explained.

A review of the agent's role in providing coverage and approaches to satisfying customers' coverage needs is included, as well as an examination of the roles of underwriters and claims adjusters as valued partners in the service of the condominium customer.

A series of condominium claims case studies are reviewed and the twists and turns of the cases within the context of boundaries, the act, condominium bylaws, the declarations, and the coverage issues surrounding the claims are also discussed.

The book closes with an analysis of the critical areas necessary for providing value for condominium customers.

Copies of the association and unit-owners forms from Insurance Services Office are provided at the end of the book, as well as sample condominium bylaws.

A chart outlining condominium laws by state can be found online at http://www.nuco.com/fcs/2023/05/01/condominium-statutes-by-state/

The message of this book is that the key to understanding condominium coverage is to understand the rules governing condominiums and condominium owners. Once the rules are clearly understood, the lines become highly visible around *who* is covered, *what* is covered, *where* coverage applies, *when* it apples, and *how* it applies, making the type and scope of coverage needed by insureds easily determined. Condominium Property Acts and Condominium Insurance.

Condominiums, their individual units and structures, cause a lot of confusion when placing coverage. Because the policy of the unit-owner needs to intersect with the association policy, coverage for various parts of property and liability is confusing. Add in state requirements, and the waters are even muddier.

The condominium property act is the bedrock upon which all matters pertaining to condominiums are built. Condominium acts vary by state, and provide definitions of property such as common elements, limited common elements, units, and boundaries between units, as well as insurance requirements and who is responsible for repairs on what type of property. The fact that the individual units are individually owned, and not simply rented, makes coverage for condominiums unique. The unit-owners need to cover their property, but the determination as to where the unit ends and the association property begins can be complicated.

Terms to remember:
Common elements are those elements in which all unit owners have a shared ownership interest.
Limited common elements are those elements shared between one or more units, but are not accessed by the rest of the community – a shared staircase or balcony.
Units are the portions designated for individual ownership.

The Declaration filed by the developer is subject to the condominium act as are the insurance provisions, bylaws, covenants, and rules pertaining to condominium associations. Already there are three moving pieces; the developer who constructs the condominiums and sells them; the association that develops in order to manage the complex itself, and the individual unit-owners who have interest in their unit, but also bear some liability to maintenance and upkeep of property used by all other unit-owners. It is no wonder that the journey begins with a review of the condominium property act and its importance in understanding condominium coverage. Specifically, we will review definitions of terms we often encounter in our policy wordings so that you understand the terms in context. We will review sections of the act that help define the boundaries of ownership and responsibility to sharpen your understanding of where coverage begins and ends for the stakeholders in a condominium complex. We will close this chapter with an examination of the insurance provisions stipulated in the act.

The excerpts from the Illinois Condominium Property Act that follow are for exemplary purposes only. Each state has its own act, and the acts vary from state to state. While acts change and are revised from time to time, the act remains the final authority on the division of responsibilities between the association and condominium owners. A chart of condominium statutes by state can be found online at http://www.nuco.com/fcs/2023/05/01/condominium-statutes-by-state/

The Illinois Condominium Property Act[1]

The Illinois Condominium Property Act (765 ILCS 605)—long established, tested, and refined over time—provides an excellent example of a well-crafted condominium property act. The current Act can be found online at https://www.hopb.co/illinois-condominium-property-act-765-ilcs-605

It begins with definitions of terms regularly encountered in day-to-day insurance activities. Please note that the following discussion does not include all Definitions annotated in the current Act; only those most critical to understanding how exposures and insurance apply to this unique ownership arrangement are covered.

Definitions

Section 2. of the act defines the following terms:

- Declaration (a)
- Parcel (b)
- Property (c)
- Unit (d)
- Common Elements (e)
- Unit-Owner (g) Condominium Instruments (l) Unit-Owners' Association or Association (o)
- Developer (q) Limited Common Elements (s) Building (t)

Declaration

> (a) "Declaration" means the instrument by which the property is submitted to the provisions of this Act, as hereinafter provided, and such declaration as from time to time amended. [Sec. 2. Definitions].

The condominium declaration is the constitution of the condominium corporation; it provides the structure by which the corporation is initially organized and managed. It incorporates the provisions of the act and is subject to the act in all respects. As the act clearly states, "Any provisions of a condominium instrument that contains provisions inconsistent with the provisions of this Act are void as against public policy and ineffective." [Sec. 2.1. Applicability]

Once approved, the declaration becomes the central instrument in all matters pertaining to the management and administration of the condominium association. The association has authority to levy assessments against unit-owners in event of losses to common areas of the development. It should be one of the principal documents referred to in matters of insurance placement, underwriting, or claims settlement, especially when there are disputes surrounding loss situations.

It will provide the parties involved with the guidance necessary to determine boundaries around ownership and responsibility, thereby minimizing disputes and confusion.

Section 4. Declaration – Contents of the Act delineates those boundaries.

Sec. 4. Declaration – Contents. The declaration shall set forth the following particulars:

(a) The legal description of the parcel.

(b) The legal description of each unit, which may consist of the identifying number or symbol of such unit as shown on the plat.

(c) The name of the condominium, which name shall include the word "Condominium" or be followed by the words "a Condominium".

(d) The name of the city and county or counties in which the condominium is located.

(e) The percentage of ownership interest in the common elements allocated to each unit. Such percentages shall be computed by taking as a basis the value of each unit in relation to the value of the property as a whole and having once been determined and set forth as herein provided, such percentages shall remain constant unless otherwise provided in this Act or thereafter changed by agreement of all unit-owners.

The declaration contains the legal description, which delineates the specific piece of real property of the condominium units as a whole and individually. Each unit has a specific legal description that identifies what part of real property the unit-owner owns. The percentage of ownership interest in the common elements is also defined. This is so that if the common elements are damaged and the association needs to make an assessment, each unit-owner can be fairly assessed for his ownership share of the common elements. As will be seen later in the review of insurance matters outlined in the act, this instrument, along with the association bylaws and rules, should be mandatory reference tools when dealing with the issue of condominium coverage.

Parcel

> (b) "Parcel" means the lot or lots, tract or tracts of land, described in the declaration, submitted to the provisions of this Act. [Sec. 2. Definitions]

This definition, among other things, helps in clarifying boundaries where there might be multi-layered, multi-phase condominium developments and where there might be potential for confusion about lot lines and possible liability exposures. Hand-in-hand with the definition of "parcel" in clarifying boundaries is the definition of "property."

Property

> (c) "Property" means all the land, property and space comprising the parcel, all improvements and structures erected, constructed or contained therein or thereon, including the building and all easements, rights and appurtenances belonging thereto, and all fixtures and equipment intended for the mutual use, benefit or enjoyment of the unit-owners, submitted to the provisions of this Act. [Sec. 2. Definitions]

This definition identifies the building itself and the common elements owned communally by the unit-owners. The parcel is the land the building is on, but the property is the actual tangible structure itself.

Unit

> (d) "Unit" means a part of the property designed and intended for any type of independent use. [Sec. 2. Definitions]

This definition draws the distinction between independent use of the unit-owner versus common use by all unit owners. This is significant since a unit owner needs to provide coverage for his unit only but be prepared for assessments for damage to common areas.

Common Elements

> (e) "Common Elements" means all portions of the property except the units, including limited common elements unless otherwise specified. [Sec. 2. Definitions]

This definition as with the others is of paramount importance in setting insurance requirements. As mentioned earlier, it is the understanding of the boundaries between the unit-owners property and the association property that facilitates understanding of coverage needs and establishing the details of coverage. Is the walkway directly outside of a unit the unit-owner's property and responsibility or the associations? When common areas are damaged, it is common for the unit-owners to be assessed equal shares of the damage that the association policy does not cover.

Unit-Owner

(g) "Unit-Owner" means the person or persons whose estates or interests, individually or collectively, aggregate fee simple absolute ownership of a unit, or, in the case of a leasehold condominium, the lessee or lessees of a unit whose leasehold ownership of the unit expires simultaneously with the lease described in item (x) of this Section. [Sec. 2. Definitions]

Fee simple absolute ownership means that the unit-owner in entitled to the full enjoyment of the property with limits set only by zoning laws, deeds, subdivision restrictions, or covenants. Unit-owners have fee simple rights to the individual units they purchase. The duration of the ownership is not limited and can be passed along to the owners' heirs. This defines the who is to be insured by a unit-owners policy. In addition to understanding who is to be insured, it is also important to understand the instruments that govern those insureds and to which they are subject.

Most property ownership in the United States is on a fee simple basis. A smaller percentage is leasehold ownership, where the tenant can use the land for a given number of years.

Condominium Instruments

(l) "Condominium Instruments" means all documents and authorized amendments thereto recorded pursuant to the provisions of the Act, including the declaration, bylaws and plat. [Sec. 2. Definitions]

The bylaws, which set out the rights and responsibilities of the unit-owners and the association, are also subject to the act. It is a very important document of reference in placing, underwriting, or settling claims for condominiums. It will assist in drawing the lines around the responsibility of unit-owners and condominium associations.

"Unit-Owner's Association" or Association

> (o) "Unit-Owner's Association" or "Association" means the association of all the unit-owners, acting pursuant to bylaws through its duly elected board of managers. [Sec. 2. Definitions]

The association is a valid entity under condominium acts. It is guided by bylaws laid out in the constitution of the association and registered under the terms of the condominium property act as contained in the developer's original declaration submission.

Developer

> (q) "Developer" means any person who submits property legally or equitably owned in fee simple by the developer, or leased to the developer under a lease described in item (x) of this Section, to the provisions of this Act, or any person who offers units legally or equitably owned in fee simple by the developer, or leased to the developer under a lease described in item (x) of this Section, for sale in the ordinary course of such person's business, including any successor or successors to such developers' entire interest in the property other than the purchaser of an individual unit. [Sec. 2. Definitions]

Here, too, the act clearly defines the role of the developer as well as the distinction between the developer and a purchaser of an individual unit. These distinctions are important as they could have liability implications for the stakeholders in a condominium complex. Additionally, understanding what constitutes unit ownership under the terms of the condominium declaration would make it easy to assign coverage for both the condominium association and the unit-owners. Note that item (x) of Sec 2 Definitions (referred to above) defines a "Leasehold Condominium" where part of a **lease** is owned rather than the land or property. Discussion of this complicated arrangement is beyond the scope of this text.

Also of note is the developer as owner or lessee. Depending on the developer's status vis-à-vis the condominium development, whether as owner or lessee, there could be insurance liability implications from both the developer's and lessor's perspective.

Remember that fee simple ownership means that the owner is entitled to full enjoyment of the property, limited only by zoning laws, deeds, or subdivision covenants or restrictions. The developer owns the units in fee simple until they are sold to individuals.

In assessing coverage it is important to understand any contractual relationships that exist and the insurance obligations that are owed the parties to the contracts.

It is possible that as insurance professionals untangle these contractual arrangements, they may discover that there are insurance obligations not only to the condominium association but also to the developer and/or lessor of the development property.

Limited Common Elements

> (s) "Limited Common Elements" means a portion of the common elements so designated in the declaration as being reserved for the use of a certain unit or units to the exclusion of other units, including but not limited to balconies, terraces, patios and parking spaces or facilities.

Limited common elements are generally elements shared between one or more units but that the rest of the community does not access, for example, a shared balcony or patio as noted above. Each state statute typically provides examples, but not all use the language "including but not limited to." Many are very precise. Again, the declarations of the association should align with the respective state statutes.

Building

> (t) "Building" means all structures, attached or unattached, containing one or more units. [Sec. 2. Definitions]

What constitutes "building" will be examined more in the insurance section of the act, but the importance of defining the boundaries advocated at the outset should be abundantly clear.

By dealing with the definitions under the Illinois condominium property act at length, one can see that all the instruments encountered in dealing with condominium insurance, whether they be bylaws, declaration, or other condominium instruments, have the force of law behind them. And nothing done in all phases of the insurance process should be either arbitrary or contrary to statute. If there is any doubt as to the validity or the efficacy of a coverage, bylaw, or declaration issue, simply look to the applicable state condominium property act to resolve the issue. It is the act that supersedes all matters including setting the boundaries around the critical structures of a condominium in order to clarify ownership. As Sec. 4.1. (a); (2), (3), (4), and (5) state, in defining the boundaries of the unit-owner:

> (2) To the extent that perimeter and partition walls, floors or ceilings are designated as the boundaries of the units or of any specified units, all decorating, wall and floor coverings, paneling, molding, tiles, wallpaper, paint, finished flooring and any other materials constituting any part of the finished surfaces thereof, shall be deemed a part of such units, while all other portions of such walls, floors or ceilings and all portions of perimeter doors and all portions of windows in perimeter walls shall be deemed part of the common elements.
>
> (3) If any chutes, flues, ducts, conduits, wires, bearing walls, bearing columns, or any other apparatus lies partially within and partially outside of the designated boundaries of a unit, any portions thereof serving only that unit shall be deemed a part of that unit, while any portions thereof serving more than one unit, or any portion of the common elements shall be deemed a part of the common elements.
>
> (4) Subject to the provisions of paragraph (3) of subsection (a), all space and other fixtures and improvements within the boundaries of a unit shall be deemed a part of that unit.
>
> (5) Any shutters, awnings, window boxes, doorsteps, porches, balconies, patios, perimeter doors, windows in perimeter walls, and any other apparatus designed to serve a single unit shall be deemed a limited common element appertaining to that unit exclusively.

Walls-in is commonly considered to be owner improvements, basic cabinets and flooring, and fixtures within a unit. It may also include everything from the studs in, or everything from the exterior framing inward excluding fixtures, depending.
Walls-out is often considered to be from the studs out, or everything outside of the unit owners owned space.
All-in includes interior wall surfaces, floors and ceilings but may or may not include improvements and appliances. Terms in use vary among states and insurers; what's important is what the association documents and state statutes require.

This section defines the "walls out" or "walls in" interpretation of what constitutes a unit. "Walls in" or "walls out" is not as straightforward as it seems; here some items are considered part of the unit if they serve only that unit but are association property if they serve multiple units. Each state has its own definition of what constitutes a unit, a common element, or a limited common element. While many are similar, there are differences, so it is important to refer to the definition provided in the act. If an adjuster has difficulty determining whether a loss belongs to the unit-owner's policy or the association's policy, this provides clarification. If the agent is unsure about which components make up the insurable value of a unit-owner's premises, this will help. This will also help the underwriter determine the exposures being assumed. See the Condominium Statutes by State chart located online.

The act clearly spells out what constitutes ownership, as well as when ownership takes place:

> Upon compliance with the provisions of Sections 3, 4, and 5 and upon recording of the declaration and plat the property shall become subject to the provisions of this Act, and all units shall thereupon be capable of ownership in fee simple or any lesser estate, and may thereafter be conveyed, leased, mortgaged or otherwise dealt with in the same manner as other real property, but subject, however, to the limitations imposed by this Act.
>
> Each unit-owner shall be entitled to the percentage of ownership in the common elements appertaining to such unit as computed and set forth in the declaration pursuant to subsection (e) of Section 4 hereof, and ownership of such unit and of the owner's corresponding percentage of ownership in the common elements shall not be separated, except as provided in this Act, nor, except by the recording of an amended declaration and amended plat approved in writing by all unit-owners, shall any unit, by deed, plat, judgment of a court or otherwise, be subdivided or in any other manner separated into tracts or parcels different from the whole unit as shown on the plat, except as provided in this Act. [Sec. 6. Recording – Effect].

This provision is important on several levels:

(a) It provides the timing of the transfer of ownership, which leads the claims adjuster to the proper policy for coverage.

(b) Knowledge of this provision gives the agent and underwriter an understanding of when to attach coverage to the property insured.

(c) This provision delineates the unit-owner's ownership portion of common elements. This determines the amount assessed to each owner in event of a loss to common property.

The act is an indispensable tool in handling condominium insurance coverage. The act also addresses insurance and required coverages.

Insurance

Section 12 of the Illinois Condominium Property Act clearly spells out the insurance requirements for that state, including types of coverage and minimum limits. So, too, do the acts for other states. Property and liability insurance, fidelity bond, and directors and officers coverages are required. The directors and officers coverage is required to include defense of nonmonetary actions, defense of breach of contract, and defense of decisions related to placement or adequacy of insurance, and include as insureds past, present and future board members while acting in their official capacity as members of the board.

Required Coverage

(a) Required coverage. No policy of insurance shall be issued or delivered to a condominium association, and no policy of insurance issued to a condominium association shall be renewed, unless the insurance coverage under the policy includes the following:

(1) Property insurance.

(i) on the common elements and the units, including the limited common elements and except as otherwise determined by the board of managers, the bare walls, floors, and ceilings of the unit,

(ii) providing coverage for special form causes of loss, and

(iii) providing coverage, at the time the insurance is purchased and at each renewal date, in a total amount of not less than the full insurable replacement cost of the insured property, less deductibles, but including coverage sufficient to rebuild the insured property in compliance with building code requirements subsequent to an insured loss, including: Coverage B, demolition costs; and Coverage C, increased cost of construction coverage. The combined total of Coverage B and Coverage C shall be no less than 10% of each insured building value, or $500,000, whichever is less. (765 ILCS 605/12) (from Ch. 30, par. 312) [Sec. 12. Insurance]

This section of the act clearly lays out the requirements for property insurance coverage for condominium associations. The use of the word "shall" in the act makes the coverage mandatory. It is not an option. The coverage mandated is a requirement both at the time coverage is written as new business as well as at renewal.

Every condominium association property policy issued in the state of Illinois must include coverage for:

- the common and limited common elements and the units;
- special form causes of loss;
- full replacement cost including demolition and increased construction costs due to building code requirements, as well as specified minimum limits.

Your state's act should also outline required insurance coverages. Many states also declare that if the unit-owner has his own coverage on the unit, that the association policy is primary and the unit policy is secondary in event of a loss.

Through this example though, you can see that the coverage to be afforded condominium associations is neither arbitrary, nor subject to the whims of insurers. Of course insurers could always broaden coverage, but they could never legally provide coverage that is less than that mandated under the appropriate act of a state.

And while the state has mandated coverage, it gives the board of managers leeway as respects coverage for common elements and units to determine how insurance is to apply. That is why in addition to consulting the act, you should also consult the declaration, bylaws and rules of the condominium in establishing coverage.

What does this mean? It means that after reviewing the state statutes and other documents, agents should have a very clear idea of the make-up of the coverage they should prescribe; that underwriters could approach association coverage with a clear understanding of the scope of coverage they assume and claims adjusters should have no doubt as to the boundaries surrounding key coverage elements.

General Liability

(2) General liability insurance. Commercial general liability insurance against claims and liabilities arising in connection with the ownership, existence, use, or management of the property in a minimum amount of $1,000,000, or a greater

> amount deemed sufficient in the judgment of the board, insuring the board, the association, the management agent, and their respective employees and agents and all persons acting as agents. The developer must be included as an additional insured in its capacity as a unit-owner, manager, board member, or officer. The unit-owners must be included as additional insured parties but only for claims and liabilities arising in connection with the ownership, existence, use, or management of the common elements. The insurance must cover claims of one or more insured parties against other insured parties. [Sec. 12. Insurance]

This section outlines the type of liability coverage to be afforded by the association. It establishes minimum limits but affords the association the leeway to increase those limits. It defines who is covered and the circumstances under which coverage would apply. That coverage includes the developer "in its capacity as a unit-owner, manager, board member, or officer." This is an important aspect of coverage to note because the developer's ownership, responsibility, and/or obligations under a condominium development could change depending on the phase of a given condominium development. For example, some acts specify that the developer relinquish ownership of a development to the association after a certain percentage or certain number of units are sold. In those circumstances the developer's liability exposure would cease at some point in the process. In understanding the content of a state's act, one can also understand where exposures begin and end.

Unit-owners are also included in coverage under this section but only with respect to common elements. Again, this helps draw the distinction between coverage as respects the individual units versus coverage relating to common elements.

This section also provides for separation of insureds and cross liability provision: where more than one named insured is present on the policy, it will respond as if each named insured had a separate policy. This allows one insured party to bring action against another. However, each distinct insured is not given a separate coverage limit.

Fidelity Bond and Directors and Officers Coverage

> (3) Fidelity bond; directors and officers coverage. (A) An association with 6 or more dwelling units must obtain and maintain a fidelity bond covering persons, including the managing agent and its employees who control or disburse funds of the association, for the maximum amount

> of coverage available to protect funds in the custody or control of the association, plus the association reserve fund. (B) All management companies that are responsible for the funds held or administered by the association must be covered by a fidelity bond for the maximum amount of coverage available to protect those funds. The association has standing to make a loss claim against the bond of the managing agent as a party covered under the bond. (C) For purposes of paragraphs (A) and (B), the fidelity bond must be in the full amount of association funds and reserves in the custody of the association or the management company. (D) The board of directors must obtain directors and officers liability coverage at a level deemed reasonable by the board, if not otherwise established by the declaration or bylaws. Directors and officers liability coverage must extend to all contracts and other actions taken by the board in their official capacity as directors and officers, but this coverage shall exclude actions for which the directors are not entitled to indemnification under the General Not For Profit Corporation Act of 1986 or the declaration and bylaws of the association. The coverage required by this subparagraph (D) shall include, but not be limited to, coverage of: defense of non-monetary actions; defense of breach of contract; and defense of decisions related to the placement or adequacy of insurance. The coverage required by this subparagraph (D) shall include as an insured: past, present, and future board members while acting in their capacity as members of the board of directors; the managing agent; and employees of the board of directors and the managing agent. [Sec. 12. Insurance]

Huge fidelity and officers and directors exposures exist in insuring condominium associations. Associations are responsible for, among other things, the collection, management, and disbursement of fees and other income. Mismanagement of these funds or their fraudulent use could easily bankrupt an association, causing it to collapse.

The right coverage is paramount. The act stipulates the people to be covered as well as the limit of coverage: "The maximum needed to protect funds in the custody or control of the association, plus the association reserve fund."

The act also mandates the coverage requirements for directors and officers, stipulating who is insured, as well as allowing the board the flexibility to set the appropriate level of coverage if such level is not otherwise established in the declaration or bylaws.

Contiguous Units and Improvements and Betterments

> (b) Contiguous units; improvements and betterments. The insurance maintained under subdivision (a)(1) must include the units, the limited common elements except as otherwise determined by the board of managers, and the common elements. The insurance need not cover improvements and betterments to the units installed by unit-owners, but if improvements and betterments are covered, any increased cost may be assessed by the association against the units affected. Common elements include fixtures located within the unfinished interior surfaces of the perimeter walls, floors, and ceilings of the individual units initially installed by the developer. Common elements exclude floor, wall, and ceiling coverings. "Improvements and betterments" means all decorating, fixtures, and furnishings installed or added to and located within the boundaries of the unit, including electrical fixtures, appliances, air conditioning and heating equipment, water heaters, or built-in cabinets installed by unit-owners, or any other additions, alterations, or upgrades installed or purchased by any unit owner. [Sec. 12. Insurance]

This subsection of the act continues to delineate the coverage boundaries. In it, insurance must include the units and the common elements. This is not true for all acts; that is why knowledge of specific states' acts is important, especially if a company operates in more than one state or serves clients in another state. One coverage size does not fit all. To make that assumption could lead to underinsurance or, in a worst-case scenario, no insurance.

Coverage may extend to unit improvements and betterments installed by the unit-owner. If improvements and betterments are to be covered, be sure that those values are included in the association's limit of coverage.

The act also states what things are included and excluded in the definition of "common elements," as well as what comprises "improvements and betterments." The juxtaposition of these definitions clarify which elements of the building would fall under the jurisdiction of the association and which would be the responsibility of unit-owners, leaving no doubt about where coverage lines are drawn.

Deductibles

> (c) Deductibles. The board of directors of the association may, in the case of a claim for damage to a unit or the

> common elements, (i) pay the deductible amount as a common expense, (ii) after notice and an opportunity for a hearing, assess the deductible amount against the owners who caused the damage or from whose units the damage or cause of loss originated, or (iii) require the unit-owners of the units affected to pay the deductible amount. [Sec. 12. Insurance]

The application of the deductible in condominium insurance is one of the most troublesome issues. The subject will be tackled in greater detail in the policy coverage and deductibles discussions.

This section of the act outlines the authority given to the board of directors of the association to apply deductibles within the organization in a loss situation. It is this internal authority and application that find expression in the external arena between insurance companies and condominium insureds when dealing with claims and the application of deductibles. Understanding the stipulations of the act vis-à-vis deductibles will make it easy to better understand the tug-of-war involving deductibles and will provide the tools to resolve some of that clash.

Other Coverages

> (d) Other coverages. The declaration may require the association to carry any other insurance, including workers compensation, employment practices, environmental hazards, and equipment breakdown, the board of directors considers appropriate to protect the association, the unit-owners, or officers, directors, or agents of the association. [Sec. 12. Insurance]

The power and importance of the declaration as a condominium instrument is evident in this section. It may require the association to carry any other insurance it deems necessary. So, although a coverage may not be specifically laid out in the act itself, the declaration could hold the key to any coverage required by the association because the act provides the mechanism for such coverage requirement.

Insured Parties; Waiver of Subrogation

> (e) Insured parties; waiver of subrogation. Insurance policies carried pursuant to subsections (a) and (b) must include each of the following provisions.
>
> (1) Each unit-owner and secured party is an insured person under the policy with respect to liability arising out of the unit-owner's interest in the common elements or membership in the association.

(2) The insurer waives its right to subrogation under the policy against any unit-owner of the condominium or members of the unit owner's household and against the association and members of the board of directors.

(3) The unit-owner waives his or her right to subrogation under the association policy against the association and the board of directors. [Sec. 12. Insurance]

Who is an insured and waiver of subrogation are critical insurance provisions. This subsection of the act makes clear how these two elements apply. Subrogation usually applies to recovery of a loss from a liable third party. Since the unit-owner is an insured under the act, the unit-owner is indeed a first party to the contract and not subject to subrogation provisions, hence the waiver. The same logic is true for the association and board of directors, so the unit-owner's right of subrogation against the association and the board of directors is waived.

Primary Insurance

(f) Primary insurance. If at the time of a loss under the policy there is other insurance in the name of a unit-owner covering the same property covered by the policy, the association's policy is primary insurance. [Sec. 12. Insurance]

The other insurance provision in condominium policies is backed by the wording in the act and draws an important line around how policies are to respond in the event of a loss.

Adjustment of Losses; Distribution of Proceeds

(g) Adjustment of losses; distribution of proceeds. Any loss covered by the property policy under subdivision (a) (1) must be adjusted by and with the association. The insurance proceeds for that loss must be payable to the association, or to an insurance trustee designated by the association for that purpose. The insurance trustee or the association must hold any insurance proceeds in trust for unit owners and secured parties as their interests may appear. The proceeds must be disbursed first for the repair or restoration of the damaged common elements, the bare walls, ceilings, and floors of the units, and then to any improvements and betterments the association may insure. Unit owners are not entitled to receive any portion of the proceeds unless there is a surplus of proceeds after the common

> elements and units have been completely repaired or restored or the association has been terminated as trustee. [Sec. 12. Insurance]

This subsection of the act spells out the process for covered property losses:

- Losses must be adjusted by and with the association.
- Proceeds must be made payable to the association or insurance trustee.
- Proceeds must be disbursed first for the repair or restoration of damaged common elements.
- Unit owners are entitled only to loss monies if there is a surplus after complete repair or replacement of the loss to the common elements and units, or the association has been terminated as trustee.

Mandatory Unit-Owner Coverage

> (h) Mandatory unit-owner coverage. The board of directors may, under the declaration and bylaws or by rule, require condominium unit owners to obtain insurance covering their personal liability and compensatory (but not consequential) damages to another unit caused by the negligence of the owner or his or her guests, residents, or invitees, or regardless of any negligence originating from the unit. The personal liability of a unit owner or association member must include the deductible of the owner whose unit was damaged, any damage not covered by insurance required by this subsection, as well as the decorating, painting, wall and floor coverings, trim, appliances, equipment, and other furnishings. [Sec. 12. Insurance]

If there is any question about the type of coverage a unit owner should carry, the scope of that coverage, or the unit owner's obligation, clarification is given in this subsection.

The deductible question also rears its head in this subsection with this statement: "The personal liability of a unit owner or association member must include the deductible of the owner whose unit was damaged," which clarifies how to structure coverage given an insured's obligation under the declaration, bylaws, or rules of the condominium association.

Certificates of Insurance

(i) Certificates of insurance. Contractors and vendors (except public utilities) doing business with a condominium association under contracts exceeding $10,000 per year must provide certificates of insurance naming the association, its board of directors, and its managing agent as additional insured parties. [Sec. 12. Insurance]

Insurers receive numerous requests for certificates of insurance. The nature of the requests they receive from condominium associations are often spelled out in the state's act as evidenced here. The association needs to be aware of this requirement to be sure to obtain the proper certificate of insurance. Being listed as additional insureds protects the association from claims against it from damage caused by the contractor. That said, agents and brokers will find insurers very reluctant to add or allow additional insureds to simply be added to a certificate of insurance. Certificates of insurance are not binding coverage. It's important that the policy itself conform to the requirement of the act.

Knowing this mandatory requirement also alerts the underwriter, agent, or adjuster to the existence of coverage available to an association under a vendor or contractor's policy.

Settlement of Claims

(k) Settlement of claims. Any insurer defending a liability claim against a condominium association must notify the association of the terms of the settlement no less than 10 days before settling the claim. The association may not veto the settlement unless otherwise provided by contract or statute. (Source: P.A. 92-518, eff. 6-1-02.) [Sec. 12. Insurance]

The obligation of an insurer defending a liability claim against a condominium association is clear. The association's response in such situations is also clear.

Summary

The purpose of the journey through the Illinois Condominium Property Act from definitions through to insurance provisions was to establish the importance of property acts in understanding condominium coverage and to clarify that all condominium insurance coverage is subject to the property act of each state.

The importance of the declaration, the bylaws, and other condominium association rules have been made clear. The force of statute stands behind those instruments and gives leeway to the condominium associations within the act to determine the obligations of condominium unit owners, as well as the scope of coverage they could assign both for the association itself and for unit owners.

Emphasis has been placed on the terms under the act that are most frequently encountered in insurance, beginning with the definitions under the act and ending with the insurance requirements of the act.

The boundaries of ownership and responsibility have been defined to sharpen understanding of where coverage begins and ends for the stakeholders in a condominium arrangement.

Having established those coverage boundaries, it is time to examine insurance coverage for both the condominium association and the condominium unit owner using the condominium property act as reference.

Endnote

1. Illinois Compiled Statutes. 765 ILCS 605/Condominium Property Act. pp 1-16.

Chapter 2

Policy Coverage and Condominium Property Acts

This chapter focuses on the coverage and limitation components that help to define boundaries around association coverage and unit-owners coverage.

Condominium Association Coverage Form

Beginning with Coverage A, the ISO Condominium Association Coverage Form, CP 00 17 10 12, meets the requirements of the condominium property act. With respect to property coverage, the act (765 ILCS 605/12) states the following:

> (a) Required coverage. No policy of insurance shall be issued or delivered to a condominium association, and no policy of insurance issued to a condominium association shall be renewed, unless the insurance coverage under the policy includes the following:
>
> (1) Property insurance. Property insurance (i) on the common elements and the units, including the limited common elements and except as otherwise determined by the board of managers, the bare walls, floors, and ceilings of the unit, (ii) providing coverage for special form causes of loss, and (iii) providing coverage, at the time the insurance is purchased and at each renewal date, in a total amount of not less than the full insurable replacement cost of the insured property, less deductibles, but including coverage sufficient to rebuild the insured property in compliance with building code requirements subsequent to an insured loss, including: Coverage B, demolition costs; and Coverage C, increased cost of construction coverage. The combined total of Coverage B and Coverage C shall be no less than 10% of each insured building value, or $500,000, whichever is less. [Sec. 12. Insurance]

Here is how the ISO form responds to this coverage requirement:

A. Coverage

We will pay for direct physical loss of or damage to Covered Property at the premises described in the Declarations caused by or resulting from any Covered Cause of Loss.

This section makes provision for losses resulting from "any covered cause of loss" by referencing the applicable causes of loss form in the declarations of the policy. In doing so, the form remains broad enough in its construction to allow for "special form causes of loss coverage" as required by the act. This is also known as an "open perils" form.

Covered Property

Covered Property, as used in this Coverage Part, means the type of property described in this section, A.1., and limited in A.2., Property Not Covered, if a Limit Of Insurance is shown in the Declarations for that type of property.

a. Building, meaning the building or structure described in the Declarations, including:

(1) Completed additions;

(2) Fixtures, outside of individual units, including outdoor fixtures;

(3) Permanently installed:

(a) Machinery; and

(b) Equipment;

(4) Personal property owned by you that is used to maintain or service the building or structure or its premises, including:

(a) Fire-extinguishing equipment;

(b) Outdoor furniture;

(c) Floor coverings; and

(d) Appliances used for refrigerating, ventilating, cooking, dishwashing or laundering that are not contained within individual units;

(5) If not covered by other insurance:

(a) Additions under construction, alterations and repairs to the building or structure;

(b) Materials, equipment, supplies, and temporary structures, on or within 100 feet of the

> described premises, used for making additions, alterations or repairs to the building or structure;

The covered property in the coverage form meets the requirements under the act in defining what is included and what is excluded in coverage.

Under A. Coverage, a. Building (2), it is careful to include fixtures "outside of individual units" or under subsection (d) to include personal property "not contained within individual units."

Within these coverage qualifications, the form clearly sets the boundaries of coverage, making the distinction between what should be covered under the association's policy and what should be covered under the unit owner's policy.

Even as it draws these lines of demarcation, the form is careful not to contravene any sections of the act that allow coverage for both units and common elements by clearly stating that coverage would apply to the following:

> (6) Any of the following types of property contained within a unit, regardless of ownership, if your Condominium Association Agreement requires you to insure it:
>
> (a) Fixtures, improvements and alterations that are a part of the building or structure; and
>
> (b) Appliances, such as those used for refrigerating, ventilating, cooking, dishwashing, laundering, security or housekeeping.
>
> But Building does not include personal property owned by, used by or in the care, custody or control of a unit-owner except for personal property listed in Paragraph A.1.a.(6) above.

Through definition and limitation, the association form leaves no doubt as to what it intends to cover as well as the scope of coverage, all within the requirements of the act.

Increased Cost of Construction

The act requires insurance to be carried:

> in a total amount of not less than the full insurable replacement cost of the insured property, less deductibles, but including coverage sufficient to rebuild the insured property in compliance with building code

> requirements subsequent to an insured loss, including: Coverage B, demolition costs; and Coverage C, increased cost of construction coverage. The combined total of Coverage B and Coverage C shall be no less than 10% of each insured building value, or $500,000, whichever is less. [Sec. 12. Insurance (a) Required Coverage (iii)]

The association form meets this requirement under section A 4.e:

A 4 e. Increased Cost Of Construction

(1) This Additional Coverage applies only to buildings to which the Replacement Cost Optional Coverage applies.

(2) In the event of damage by a Covered Cause of Loss to a building that is Covered Property, we will pay the increased costs incurred to comply with the minimum standards of an ordinance or law in the course of repair, rebuilding or replacement of damaged parts of that property, subject to the limitations stated in e.(3) through e.(9) of this Additional Coverage.

(3) The ordinance or law referred to in e.(2) of this Additional Coverage is an ordinance or law that regulates the construction or repair of buildings or establishes zoning or land use requirements at the described premises and is in force at the time of loss.

(4) Under this Additional Coverage, we will not pay any costs due to an ordinance or law that:

(a) You were required to comply with before the loss, even when the building was undamaged; and

(b) You failed to comply with.

(5) Under this Additional Coverage, we will not pay for:

(a) The enforcement of or compliance with any ordinance or law which requires demolition, repair, replacement, reconstruction, remodeling or remediation of property due to contamination by "pollutants" or due to the presence, growth, proliferation, spread or any activity of "fungus", wet or dry rot or bacteria; or

(b) Any costs associated with the enforcement of or compliance with an ordinance or law which requires any insured or others to test for, monitor, clean up, remove, contain, treat, detoxify or neutralize, or in any way respond to, or assess

> the effects of "pollutants", "fungus", wet or dry rot or bacteria.

Even as it meets the requirements of the act, the coverage form is careful not to afford coverage broader than is required by the act. It accomplishes this by excluding increased costs relating to pollution and fungi.

Deductible

The deductible in the association form operates as any policy deductible.

> D. Deductible
>
> In any one occurrence of loss or damage (hereinafter referred to as loss), we will first reduce the amount of loss if required by the Coinsurance Condition or the Agreed Value Optional Coverage. If the adjusted amount of loss is less than or equal to the Deductible, we will not pay for that loss. If the adjusted amount of loss exceeds the Deductible, we will then subtract the Deductible from the adjusted amount of loss and will pay the resulting amount or the Limit of Insurance, whichever is less.
>
> When the occurrence involves loss to more than one item of Covered Property and separate Limits of Insurance apply, the losses will not be combined in determining application of the Deductible. But the Deductible will be applied only once per occurrence.

The deductible clause in this form is how the deductible works for the association itself. However, the act dictates how the association spreads the deductible among the unit owners. The act states:

> (c) Deductibles. The board of directors of the association may, in the case of a claim for damage to a unit or the common elements, (i) pay the deductible amount as a common expense, (ii) after notice and an opportunity for a hearing, assess the deductible amount against the owners who caused the damage or from whose units the damage or cause of loss originated, or (iii) require the unit owners of the units affected to pay the deductible amount. [Sec. 12. Insurance]

The act states how the deductible from the association insurance policy may be applied to the unit owners depending on the nature of the loss. Losses to common elements can be assessed to all owners. If particular owners caused the damage, the deductible can be assessed to them, or losses to specific units may be assessed only to the affected unit owners. The unit-owners policy describes how the individual unit-owner's policy responds when the owner has been assessed by the association.

Loss Payment

The act states the following regarding loss payment:

> (g) Adjustment of losses; distribution of proceeds. Any loss covered by the property policy under subdivision (a)(1) must be adjusted by and with the association. The insurance proceeds for that loss must be payable to the association, or to an insurance trustee designated by the association for that purpose. The insurance trustee or the association must hold any insurance proceeds in trust for unit owners and secured parties as their interests may appear. The proceeds must be disbursed first for the repair or restoration of the damaged common elements, the bare walls, ceilings, and floors of the units, and then to any improvements and betterments the association may insure. Unit owners are not entitled to receive any portion of the proceeds unless there is a surplus of proceeds after the common elements and units have been completely repaired or restored or the association has been terminated as trustee. [Sec. 12. Insurance]

The coverage form complies with this requirement:

> If you name an insurance trustee, we will adjust losses with you, but we will pay the insurance trustee. If we pay the trustee, the payments will satisfy your claims against us. [E 4 g. Loss Payment]

Once the insurer has discharged its responsibility to the association as respects type and amount of coverage, its obligations end. Although the act outlines how the association is to handle the claims payment as well as the priority of payment, the insurer has no such obligation, but it may opt to disburse payments in accordance with the association's wishes as part of the claims settlement process.

Unit-Owners Insurance

The act makes provision for the association's policy to be primary:

> (f) Primary insurance. If at the time of a loss under the policy there is other insurance in the name of a unit owner covering

> the same property covered by the policy, the association's policy is primary insurance. [Sec. 12. Insurance]

The coverage form wording under E 6. Unit-owner's Insurance is crafted to be in harmony with the act. It states:

E 6. Unit-owner's Insurance

> A unit-owner may have other insurance covering the same property as this insurance. This insurance is intended to be primary and not to contribute with such other insurance.

Waiver of Subrogation

In keeping with the requirement of the act, the coverage form includes a waiver against unit owners:

E 9. Waiver Of Rights Of Recovery

> We waive our rights to recover payment from any unit-owner of the condominium that is shown in the Declarations.

The key property coverages under CP 00 17 10 12 are juxtaposed with the key property insurance requirements of the condominium property act of the state of Illinois. The purpose of this approach is to show the context for condominium association coverage to reinforce the fact that condominium association coverage is mandated by law:

> No policy of insurance shall be issued or delivered to a condominium association, and no policy of insurance issued to a condominium association shall be renewed, unless the insurance coverage under the policy includes...[the coverage mandated by the condominium property act]. [Sec. 12. Insurance (a) Required Coverage]

Again, each state will have its own statutory requirements.

Homeowners 6 – Unit-Owners Form

This is the coverage form that individual (personal) condominium owners would use (HO 00 06 03 22). In Chapter 3 we will drill down with a more specific analysis of this form. In Chapter 4, we discuss the details of the commercial unit-owners form (CP 00 18 10 12), as well as the commercial condominium association form discussed above (CP 00 17 10 12). SECTION I - PROPERTY COVERAGES A.

Coverage A – Dwelling

1. We cover:

a. The alterations, appliances, fixtures and improvements which are part of the building contained within the "residence premises";

b. Items of real property which pertain exclusively to the "residence premises";

c. Property which is your insurance responsibility under a corporation or association of property owners agreement; or

d. Structures owned solely by you, other than the "residence premises", at the location of the "residence premises".

Any fixtures and fittings or improvements and betterments attached to the building belong to the unit owner and are subject to unit-owners coverage. The policy is careful to limit the items subject to coverage so as not to overstep the boundaries that exist between what is subject to unit-owners coverage versus what is subject to association policy coverage. Even as it makes this distinction, the policy is mindful that such limitation may put the wording in conflict with the act or association rules, and as a result contains the provision to accommodate association rules and the act, by referring to "property which is your insurance responsibility under a corporation or association of property owners agreement."

One of the critical things to remember when establishing coverages, determining exposures, or settling losses is to examine the policy wording in conjunction with the declarations, bylaws, and the act. Within the condominium instruments and the act lie the truth regarding scope and parameters of coverage. So they should be the documents consulted when coverage is being established.

Ultimately, the act is the final authority of coverage. It will always clarify the unit and coverage boundaries in detail, making sure to subject all condominium instruments to it. This is demonstrated in subsections (a)–(b) of Section 4.1 of the Illinois Act:

(a) Except to the extent otherwise provided by the declaration or other condominium instruments:

(1) The terms defined in Section 2 of this Act shall be deemed to have the meaning specified therein unless the context otherwise requires.

(2) To the extent that perimeter and partition walls, floors or ceilings are designated as the boundaries of the units or of any specified units, all decorating, wall and floor coverings, paneling, molding, tiles, wallpaper, paint, finished flooring

and any other materials constituting any part of the finished surfaces thereof, shall be deemed a part of such units, while all other portions of such walls, floors or ceilings and all portions of perimeter doors and all portions of windows in perimeter walls shall be deemed part of the common elements.

(3) If any chutes, flues, ducts, conduits, wires, bearing walls, bearing columns, or any other apparatus lies partially within and partially outside of the designated boundaries of a unit, any portions thereof serving only that unit shall be deemed a part of that unit, while any portions thereof serving more than one unit or any portion of the common elements shall be deemed a part of the common elements.

(4) Subject to the provisions of paragraph (3) of subsection (a), all space and other fixtures and improvements within the boundaries of a unit shall be deemed a part of that unit.

(5) Any shutters, awnings, window boxes, doorsteps, porches, balconies, patios, perimeter doors, windows in perimeter walls, and any other apparatus designed to serve a single unit shall be deemed a limited common element appertaining to that unit exclusively.

(6) All provisions of the declaration, bylaws and other condominium instruments are severable.

(b) Except to the extent otherwise provided by the declaration or by other condominium instruments recorded prior to the effective date of this amendatory Act of 1984, in the event of a conflict between the provisions of the declaration and the bylaws or other condominium instruments, the declaration prevails except to the extent the declaration is inconsistent with this Act. [Sec. 4.1. Construction, Interpretation and Validity of Condominium Instruments]

Through an understanding of the importance of the act in insurance coverage as well as the relationship among the policy, the act, and the condominium instruments, it is much easier to both develop and apply insurance coverage. The act provides clear definitions of the unit, common elements, and limited common elements, which are critical to determining coverage and useful for resolving confusion that could arise during claim settlement.

When set in this context, Coverage A of the Condominium Association Form and Coverage A – Dwelling of the Unit-Owners Form dovetail in covering the respective insureds. The lines where coverage begins and ends are made clear in each form. For example, where ISO HO 00 06 includes personal property, ISO CP 00 17 excludes it. The checks and balances in both forms leave no doubt as to their intent. Where lines are perceived to be unclear in either form, reference to the act, declarations, and bylaws would clarify any differences.

SECTION I – CONDITIONS B.

Deductible

Unless otherwise noted in this policy, the following deductible provision applies:

With respect to any one loss:

1. Subject to the applicable limit of liability, we will pay only that part of the total of all loss payable that exceeds the deductible amount shown in the Declarations.
2. If two or more deductibles under this policy apply to the loss, the highest deductible amount will apply.

As with CP 00 17, the HO 00 06 deductible clause is very specific as to how it would respond: only loss amount that exceeds the deductible is payable. This is the unit owner's deductible. It makes no mention of an association's authority under the act or under covenants of an association as respects deductible assessments. As it is written, the operation of the deductible is very clear and straightforward.

SECTION I – PROPERTY COVERAGES D. Additional Coverages 6.

Loss Assessment

6. Loss Assessment

   a. We will pay up to $2,000 for your share of loss assessment charged during the policy period against you, as owner or tenant of the "residence premises", by a corporation or association of property owners. The assessment must be made as a result of direct loss to property, owned by all members collectively, of the type that would be covered by this policy if owned by you, caused by a Peril Insured Against under Coverage A, other than:

      (1) Earthquake; or

      (2) Land shock waves or tremors before, during or after a volcanic eruption.

The limit of $2,000 is the most we will pay with respect to any one loss, regardless of the number of assessments. We will only apply one deductible, per unit, to the total amount of any one loss to the property described above, regardless of the number of assessments.

b. We do not cover assessments charged against you or a corporation or association of property owners by any governmental body.

c. Paragraph Q. Policy Period under Section I – Conditions does not apply to this coverage.

This coverage is additional insurance.

The condominium act and instruments give the condominium association authority to assess unit owners for many things including deductibles and unpaid fees. Yet not every assessment is covered under an insurance policy, and Section 6. Loss Assessment makes this clear. The assessment coverage under HO 00 06 responds to direct loss to commonly owned property. Assessments for general property maintance, such as roof replacement, would not be covered. Additionally, Additional Coverage D. Loss Assessment covers the unit owner's share of liability losses assessed by the association. In each case the limit of coverage is $2,000.

Additional Coverages 9

Ordinance or Law

9. Ordinance Or Law

a. You may use up to 10% of the limit of liability that applies to Coverage A for the increased costs you incur due to the enforcement of any ordinance or law which requires or regulates:

(1) The construction, demolition, remodeling, renovation or repair of that part of property covered under Coverage A damaged by a Peril Insured Against;

(2) The demolition and reconstruction of the undamaged part of property covered under Coverage A, when that property must be totally demolished because of damage by a Peril Insured Against to another part of that property covered under Coverage A; or

(3) The remodeling, removal or replacement of the portion of the undamaged part of property covered under Coverage A necessary to complete the remodeling,

repair or replacement of that part of the property covered under Coverage A damaged by a Peril Insured Against.

b. You may use all or part of this ordinance or law coverage to pay for the increased costs you incur to remove debris resulting from the construction, demolition, remodeling, renovation, repair or replacement of property as stated in a. above.

c. We do not cover:

(1) The loss in value to any property covered under Coverage A due to the requirements of any ordinance or law; or

(2) The costs to comply with any ordinance or law which requires any "insured" or others, to test for, monitor, clean up, remove, contain, treat, detoxify or neutralize, or in any way respond to, or assess the effects of, pollutants in or on any property covered under Coverage A.

Pollutants means any solid, liquid, gaseous or thermal irritant or contaminant, including smoke, vapor, soot, fumes, acids, alkalis, chemicals and waste. Waste includes materials to be recycled, reconditioned or reclaimed

Demolition is mentioned in the HO unit owners form, but not in the association form. This appears to be due to the fact that the HO Unit Owners Form was updated by ISO in 2022, but not the Condo Association Form.

This section of HO 00 06 dovetails with the increased cost of construction under CP 00 17. It ensures that coverage involving the same building elements are afforded the same coverage opportunity, and in doing so, complies with the act.

SECTION 1 – CONDITIONS D.

Loss Settlement

D. Loss Settlement

Covered property losses are settled as follows:

1. Personal property and grave markers, including mausoleums, at actual cash value at the time of loss but not more than the amount required to repair or replace.

2. Coverage A – Dwelling:

   a. If the damage is repaired or replaced within a reasonable time, at the actual cost to repair or replace;

   b. If the damage is not repaired or replaced within a reasonable time, at actual cash value but not more than the amount required to repair or replace.

   In this provision, the terms "repaired" or "replaced" do not include the increased costs incurred to comply with the enforcement of any ordinance or law, except to the extent that coverage for these increased costs is provided in D.9. Ordinance Or Law under Section I – Property Coverages.

This coverage section of the HO 00 06 details how claims are to be settled for the unit owner's portions of the unit itself. Endorsements exist that can modify the settlement to replacement cost instead of actual cash value.

Summary

The operative word when dealing with ISO CP 00 17, ISO HO 00 06, and the condominium property act is "balance." The policy forms seek to strike a balance between the coverages so they dovetail with one another and do not overlap. And where the coverage lines appear to be blurred, the act becomes the final authority.

If the intent of the policy forms and the coverage they provide are so clear cut, why are there disagreements in claims settlement proceedings, particularly where insurers for the unit owner and association are different?

Why are there not only amount, but also deductible and loss assessment issues in settling claims?

Many of the problems arise from interpretation of how policy conditions and provisions are applied; but some of it begins on the day insureds apply for condominium insurance and their expectation and understanding of what they are getting.

Chapter 3

ISO Condominium Form: Homeowners 6 – Unit-Owners From

A cross between a rental and a dwelling policy, the individual unit-owners form is specific to the needs of the condominium owner. This is the dwelling of an individual and is used for general living quarters. Sometimes they may be a secondary residence at a vacation locale.

In 2022, ISO updated its Condominium Unit-Owners form (HO 00 06 03 22) from the previous version which was available since 2011 (HO 00 06 05 11). As we explore this coverage form, we will point out the differences between the two editions. It's important to note that since the 2022 revisions include both broadenings AND restrictions of coverage, the liberalization clause in the 2011 condominium unit-owners condominium policy does not apply with regard to the updated 2022 form. Consequently, no 2011 policyholder is affected by the 2022 changes unless or until their older policy is replaced or renewed with the 2022 version.

The 2022 version of the form introduced a major formatting change. ISO insurance policy forms have historically used a double column format. The 2022 version has a single column format. This was done to help make the form easier to read on a computer screen.

The form is broken into two sections, Section I and Section II. Section I deals with the property issues, while Section II deals with liability. Section I is broken down as follows:

- Definitions
- Section I PROPERTY COVERAGES
- Section I PERILS INSURED AGAINST
- Section I EXCLUSIONS
- Section I CONDITIONS

Section II is broken down separately, as follows:

- Section II LIABILITY COVERAGES
- Section II EXCLUSIONS
- Section II ADDITONAL COVERAGES
- Section II CONDITIONS

The last part of the policy is about conditions that apply to both sections I and II together. There are some specific conditions that apply to property losses alone and others that apply to liability losses alone, but some apply to all coverages. Hence the separation of conditions for each type of coverage and a third section for overall conditions.

Definitions

As with any policy, "you" and "your" refer to the "named insured" and resident spouse, and "we", "us", and "our" refer to the company providing the insurance. Note that the spouse must be a resident of the household to be considered an insured; while standard in personal property coverages, many overlook this critical detail. Those in committed relationships who aren't married still need to add an endorsement to be sure the other person is receiving all the coverage they need. The HO 04 58, Other Members of Your Household allows an insured to schedule an individual onto the policy and provide property and liability coverage for them as if they were a resident relative. The insured is required to notify the company within thirty days if the living arrangements change.

Aircraft, Hovercraft, Motor Vehicle, and Watercraft Liability

Because aircraft, hovercraft, motor vehicles and watercraft are all vehicles of some sort, liability for them is defined. They are best insured under policies specifically designed to provide such coverage, and they are defined here so that exclusions that appear later are clear to the insured.

In the 2011 form, this definition is extremely broad, and liability coverage for a motor vehicle in most cases is excluded due to this broad definition. In the 2022 version, the definition is narrowed to only involve the maintenance, occupancy, operation, use, loading, or unloading of a motor vehicle by an insured.

Similar to the 2011 form the 2022 form defines "motor vehicle liability" as:

a. Liability for "bodily injury" or "property damage" arising out of the:

  (1) Ownership of such vehicle or craft by an "insured";

  (2) Maintenance, occupancy, operation, use, loading or unloading of:

    (a) An aircraft, hovercraft or watercraft by any person; or

    (b) A motor vehicle by an "insured";

  (3) Entrustment of such vehicle or craft by an "insured" to any person;

  (4) Failure to supervise or negligent supervision of any person involving such vehicle or craft by an "insured"; or

  (5) Vicarious liability, whether or not imposed by law, for the actions of a child or minor involving such vehicle or craft.

It varies slightly from the 2011 form, which phrased section (2) differently but the meaning did not change.

This allows potential coverage where an insured homeowner might be responsible for a guest's liquor-related auto loss involving the guest's own automobile (this is also referred to as "host liquor liability.") Maintenance, occupancy, use, loading, unloading, and operation of a vehicle are all considered part of "motor vehicle liability" as well as vicarious liability, entrustment of a vehicle to another person, and failure to supervise or negligent supervision. Exclusions for liability will be discussed later.

The separate types of vehicles are then defined; aircraft are those craft designed for flight except for model or hobby aircraft not used or designed to carry people or cargo. Drones present a unique issue here; while not designed to carry people some can carry cargo, and is a drone carrying a camera considered to be carrying cargo? They could be considered an aircraft or could fall into the hobby category, depending. The potential liability of the use of drones is huge, and whether or not regulations will be imposed on owners is yet to be seen.

The HO 34 02 Model or Hobby Aircraft Liability Exclusion endorsement was designed to modify the definition of aircraft so that unmanned aircraft, whether or not hobby or model, are part of the definition. This then makes unmanned aircraft, or drones, part of the aircraft exclusion when the endorsement is added to the policy.

Hovercraft are self-propelled ground vehicles and includes flare craft and air cushion vehicles. Watercraft are craft principally designed to be propelled on water by wind, engine power or electric motor, and motor vehicles have a separate definition to be discussed later. In the 2022 update, the definition of watercraft was extended to except model or hobby watercraft not used or designed to carry people or cargo. With the new form, radio-controlled model yachts and similar watercraft will fall outside the watercraft liability exclusion. The reason motor vehicles have a separate definition is because they are much more prevalent than aircraft, hovercraft and watercraft, and covers a broad range of vehicles. The liability for all three combined is significantly less than the liability present for motor vehicles.

Bodily Injury and Business

"Bodily injury" has the standard definition; bodily harm, sickness or disease including required care, loss of services or death. As always, there is no mention of mental distress on anguish. Such things are difficult if not impossible to quantify, and therefore are not considered bodily injury.

"Business" is a trade, profession or occupation engaged in on a full-time, part-time or temporary basis. Activities for which the insured is compensated by no more than $5,000 (increased from the $2,000 given in the 2011 form) in a twelve-month period is not considered business. Likewise volunteer activities—home day care on a reciprocal basis with others, with no financial compensation, and day care of relatives of an insured—are not considered businesses either. Grandma can watch the grandkids, or a neighbor can watch the neighbor kids in exchange for similar services at another time and business has not been conducted. This is significant since business in generally excluded from liability coverages.

"Home-sharing host activities" have been added both as a definition to the policy and as part of the definition of "business". With the growth of companies like Airbnb and Vrbo which allow homeowners to rent out rooms or their homes for extra income, such activity needed to be addressed in the policy.

Also newly added is the leasing of mineral rights of an "insured location". The leasing of such rights by a homeowner to another party to extract natural gas, or oil from underneath the ground is generally characterized as a business use of the property, so this was added in the 2022 edition of the policy.

Cannabis

The 2022 update to the condo unit-owners form now includes a definition for "cannabis." The property section of the 2011 condo unit-owners from contained no provisions that address controlled substances. However, the liability section contained a controlled substances exclusion that applied to controlled substances which included marijuana. Because an increasing number of states have passed laws that make the possession, growth, and use of cannabis legal within the state for medical and/or recreational purposes, it has become necessary to address these exposures more specifically.

The first step involves adding to the 2022 policy a lengthy definition of cannabis, which means any good or product that contains or consists of tetrahydrocannabinol (THC) (whether natural or synthetic). THC is the main psychoactive compound in marijuana that produces intoxication. It also includes any plant of the genus Cannabis L, or any part thereof, or any compound, by-product, extract, or derivative of such plant. This definition includes but is not limited to marijuana.

Employee

"Employee" is straightforward and is someone employed by or leased to an insured by a labor leasing firm whose duties are other than "residence employee". This employee is more of an actual employee for a business instead of a housekeeper or gardener who tends the insured's property or dwelling.

Home-sharing Host Activities

As discussed under the "business" definition, home-sharing has become popular and many people are renting out their premises. Thus definitions of "home-sharing host activities", "home-sharing network platform" and "home-sharing occupant" have been added to the policy in the 2022 update.

Home-sharing host activities are defined as the rental or holding for rental, or mutual exchange of services, of the "residence premises" in whole or part by an insured to a "home-sharing occupant" through the use of the "home-sharing network platform". Included in the definition of host activities is any other related property or services made available for use during the rental or exchange of services of the premises except those provided by another party.

For example, and insured rents his condo out via Airbnb. Along with the use of the condo the insured provides the occupant with the pass to the swimming pool and information on accessing the clubhouse.

Home-sharing Network Platform

The network platform is defined as an online-enabled application, digital site or network that is used for facilitating for some form of compensation or exchange of services, the rental of a dwelling or other structure in whole or part, and allows the agreement and compensation for same to transact through the platform.

Home-sharing Occupant

The "home-sharing occupant" is defined as a person other than the "insured" who has entered into an agreement through the platform for rental of the premises, and includes guests of the occupant who arranged for the rental.

Insured

"Insured" is not only the insured as listed in the beginning of the policy, but relatives and others under the age of twenty-one who are in the care of an insured or resident relative. Students are also insureds as long as they are full-time students and were members of the household before going away to school, as long as they are under 24 years of age or under 21 and under the care of the insured or a relative.

There are some specific parameters that apply to Section II, liability coverages. Regarding animals or watercraft, any person or organization legally responsible for the animals or watercraft which are owned by the "insured", liability does not apply to people or organizations having custody of the animals or watercraft in the course of any "business" or without consent of the owner. For example, the insured asks a neighbor teenager to watch the dog for a week while he is on vacation. The teen is not in the course of a business but is liable for the animal while it is in his custody; the insured's liability coverage would apply. The doggie hotel is not covered since it is in the business of boarding dogs; the marina is not covered since it is in the business of housing boats, and the dognapper is not covered since he did not have permission to take custody of the dog.

Regarding "motor vehicles" under the liability coverage, the definition of "insured" applies as do persons engaged in the insured's employment, and other people using the vehicle on the "insured location" with the insured's permission. How actual coverage applies will be discussed later; this simply who is defined as an "insured" within the liability section regarding "motor vehicles".

Insured Location, Motor Vehicle, Occurrence, Property Damage

These are the standard definitions as found in the HO 00 03. "Insured location" includes the residence premises, other premises used by the insured as a residence and shown in the declarations, premises used in connection with the residence premises, temporary locations where the insured is residing, vacant land owned or rented to the insured, land on which a dwelling is being built, cemetery plots or burial vaults, and premises occasionally rented to an insured for other than business purposes. A premises used in connection with the residence premises can be a location rented by the insured for an event such as a wedding, graduation or anniversary party. The condominium is too small to accommodate the invitees, so the insured rents a hall or restaurant. This is being used in connection with the "insured location". Temporary locations could be hotel rooms or homes of friends or relatives when the insured is visiting; it is a temporary location where the insured is residing.

"Motor vehicle" is a self-propelled land or amphibious vehicle or capable of being self-propelled, as well as trailers or semitrailers carried on, towed by or hitched for towing by a "motor vehicle". Bicycles and scooters with motors have become increasingly common, especially in some urban areas. Some are fully self-propelled, while others—bicycles in particular—use electric motors that assist in pedaling. As a result, ISO extended the definition of "motor vehicle" to include vehicles that are capable of being self-propelled. There are policies designed for "motor vehicles", but they are defined here so that what limited coverage exists on the condominium policy can be explained. This is a broad definition; not only automobiles, but four-wheelers, ATVs, golf carts, go carts, and even children's motorized toy cars could be considered motor vehicles.

"Occurrence" is what triggers liability coverage; it is an accident, including continued or repeated exposure to the same harmful conditions which result in "bodily injury" or "property damage". For example, an insured uses pesticide that drifts onto the neighbor's property and poisons his prize-winning azaleas. That is repeated exposure to a harmful condition. "Property damage" is then defined as physical injury to, destruction of or loss of use of tangible property.

Residence Employee and Residence Premises

Known definitions are again used here. "Residence employees" are those employees of the insured whose duties are related to the maintenance or use of the "residence premises" including household duties. They could be direct employees or employees of a labor leasing firm who are leased to the insured. However, temporary substitutes for permanent "residence employees" on leave or to help meet seasonal or short-term needs are not considered "residence employees". "Residence premises" is the unit in which the insured resides as shown in the declarations.

Section I – Property Coverages; Coverage A Dwelling

This section delineates the sections of the unit that are covered as well as personal and other property. Coverage A-Dwelling is key, since this shows what coverage the insured has for the property owned. If the association policy requires coverage for property not listed here, then the insured has a gap, and needs to find coverage for those sections. What is covered as part of the dwelling is alterations, appliances, fixtures and improvements that are part of the building within the "residence premises". So fixtures, such as sinks, toilets, tubs, and other built in features are covered, as are alterations and improvements. These could be the addition of wall-to-wall carpet, installation of bookcases, entertainment systems, chandeliers, hardwood floors, or other such items. Appliances such as stoves, refrigerators, furnaces, and hot water heaters are also covered. Also included are items of real property which pertain exclusively to the "residence premises" – driveways or gardens, for example.

Property that is the responsibility of the insured under the association agreement is covered, as are structures owned solely by the insured at the "residence premises" but other than the "residence premises" such as a garage, storage unit, patio or balcony. So the policy provides broad coverage and avoids gaps by providing coverage that the insured is required to have per the association agreement. This keeps the carrier from having to specify with each different insured whether or not the pipes, electrical wiring and other features that could be outside the walls are covered or not, especially as state statutes vary.

Not covered is land (including land on which the "residence premises" is located), structures rented or held for rental to someone not a tenant of the dwelling unless used as a private garage, structures from which business is conducted or used to store business property. An exception to the storage of business property is if the property is owned solely by the insured or tenant, and does not include any gaseous or liquid fuel unless in a tank permanently attached to a vehicle or craft parked in the structure. So an insured or tenant can store woodworking equipment or office equipment, but not gallons of fuel. Because other structures are included in coverage A, there is no coverage B in the condominium policy.

Coverage C – Personal Property

The coverage C section is standard and follows the coverage C section of the HO 00 03. Personal property is covered while anywhere in the world, and at the insured's request property of others is covered if it was on the part of property occupied by an "insured" or property of a guest or "residence employee" while in any residence occupied by the "insured".

Coverage for property at other residences is limited to 10 percent of the limit for coverage C or $1,500 whichever is greater (the 2011 form only provided $1,000). This is for property usually located at the insured's residence. If property has been moved from the residence because it is being remodeled, renovated or repaired, and the unit is not fit to live in or store property, or is in a newly acquired property for thirty days from the time the insured began to move, the limit does not apply. The carrier would rather have the insured protect his property by moving it from further loss, than leave it at the residence exposed to potential loss. For example, the insured sustains a fire and removing the furniture allows the repairs to be completed quickly without having to work around furniture in the way. If the insured is moving to a new residence, he has thirty days in which to get settled into the new dwelling and move the coverage to that new home.

> It's important to note that the unit must be unfit to live or store property in AND the property is under renovation, repair or remodeling. This generally occurs where there has been a loss to the property.

Property in storage facilities has the same limits as property at other residences, and similar exceptions for when the dwelling has been damaged and is under repair or if property is usually in an insured's residence other than the "residence premises". This would be property at a second home. Again, the limit of 10% or $1,500 applies, and again the $1,500 is an increase over the earlier $1,000 in the 2011 policy form.

Special limits exist in all personal dwelling policies. These limits restrict coverage for certain types of items including specialty or particularly valuable items; valuable items should be scheduled by endorsement or placed on specific policies designed to provide the proper coverage. Note that in the 2022 updated of condo unit-owners form, many sub-limits were increased as noted below.

\$300 (increased from \$200	Money, bank notes, bullion, gold other than goldware, silver other than silverware, platinum other than platinum ware, coins, medals, scrip, stored value cards or smart cards.
\$2,000 (increased from \$1,500)	Securities, accounts, deeds, evidence of debt, letters of credit, notes other than bank notes, manuscripts, personal records, passports, tickets and stamps. Applies regardless of medium on which they exist.
\$2,000 (increased from \$1,500)	Watercraft including trailers, furnishings, equipment and outboard engines or motors.
\$2,000 (increased from \$1,500)	Trailers or semitrailers not used with watercraft of all types.
\$2,000 (increased from \$1,500)	Loss by theft of jewelry, watches, furs, precious and semiprecious stones.
\$3,000 (increased from \$2,500)	Theft of firearms or related equipment.
\$3,000 (this was increased from \$2,500)	Theft of silverware, silver-plated ware, goldware, gold-plated ware, platinumware, platinum-plated ware and pewterware, including flatware, hollowware, tea sets, trays, and trophies.
\$3,000 (this was increased from \$2,500)	On property on the "residence premises" used primarily for business.
\$1,500	On property away from the "residence premises" used primarily for business purposes, but this does not apply to tapes, antennas, wires, records or other media used with electronic equipment that reproduces, receives or transmits audio, visual or data signals and in or upon a motor vehicle.

$2,000 (increased from $1,500)	On portable electronic equipment that reproduces, receives or transmits audio, visual or data signals, is designed to be operated by more than one power source, one of which is a motor vehicle's electrical system and is in or upon a motor vehicle.
$300 (increased from $250)	On antennas, tapes, wires, records, disks or other media that are used with electronic equipment that reproduces, receives or transmits audio, visual or data signals that is in or upon a motor vehicle.
$2,000 (this was added to 2022 form)	On model or hobby aircraft not used or designed to carry people or cargo.

Coverage C – Property Not Covered

This section lists property that is not covered. A variety of items are included in this section. First are articles separately insured elsewhere; the policy does not want to duplicate coverage that already exists elsewhere, regardless of the limit of the other policy.

Animals, birds and fish are not covered. Creating a value for a living creature is virtually impossible; many people consider their pets family, even if it was a rescue from a shelter. Show dogs or cats may have value for breeding champion animals but again, attaching value to emotional attachment is virtually impossible.

Motor vehicles are excluded for obvious reasons; they belong on an auto policy, as do their equipment and parts except for certain exceptions. Portable equipment that reproduces, receives or transmits audio, visual or data signals and can be operated from the vehicle's power or another power source is excepted. A change has been made in the 2022 form to exclude a "motor vehicle's" equipment and parts that are in or upon the "motor vehicle". In the earlier form, the equipment and parts were excluded completely, and not just when there were in or upon the vehicle.

Also, vehicles not required to be registered on public roads that are used to service a residence or are designated to assist the handicapped are also excepted, similar to the homeowners policy. These vehicles are generally golf carts, atvs, and other smaller vehicles with limited power used for very specific purposes. As would be expected, aircraft and hovercraft are excluded, except for hobby aircraft not designed to carry cargo or persons.

Certain types of property are also excluded; property of a "home-sharing occupant," property of any other person occupying the "residence premises" as a result of "home-sharing activities," property of roomers, boarders, other tenants, unless related to an insured; property in a space while rented or primarily held for rental to a "home-sharing occupant," or property in an apartment regularly rented or held for rental to others by an "insured", property used primarily for "home-sharing host activities," property rented or held for rental off the "residence premises" are all excluded. The insured has no interest in property of tenants, they should have their own coverage. Property of the insureds that is in a rented space is particularly susceptible to theft or damage by renters who aren't conscientious about property of others. Therefore such property is excluded from coverage since the exposure to loss is greater. As explained at the beginning of this Chapter the 2022 update added references to "home-sharing" that did not exist in the 2011 version due to the proliferation of sharing services such as Airbnb, Vrbo, etc. Until the 2022 update, this language had to be added by mandatory endorsements.

Business data, including data stored in books of account, drawings or other paper records, or computers or related equipment are excluded, although the cost of blank recording or storage media and prerecorded computer programs available on the retail market are covered. These items are relatively generic and not specialized; if the insured is running a business, those records and the data they are stored on should be covered by a business policy.

In the 2011 form, there was some incidental coverage for credit card, electronic fund transfer cards or access devices used solely to transfer, withdraw or deposit funds. In the current 2022 form, this type of property is excluded (it can be added back by endorsement if needed.) The thinking was that this coverage is really unnecessary since financial institutions typically absorb these types of losses. Water or steam is also excluded.

Additional excluded property added in the 2022 update includes virtual currency of any kind, by whatever name known, whether actual or fictitious including, but not limited to, digital currency, crypto currency or any other type of electronic currency.

The last type of property not covered under section C deals with "cannabis" and other potentially controlled substances. Controlled substance, other than "cannabis," follows the Federal Food and Drug Law at 21 U.S.C.A. Sections 811 and 812. Controlled substances and cannabis are excluded from coverage, regardless of whether you are in a state where "cannabis" is legalized. However, an exception is given for prescription drugs obtained following the lawful orders of a licensed health care professional or goods or products containing or derived from hemp, including but not limited to seeds, food, clothing, lotions, oils, extracts, building materials or paper. That said, the hemp derived property is excluded if such goods or products are prohibited under an applicable state or local statute, regulation or ordinance in the state where such goods or products are located.

Coverage D – Loss of Use

There are four sections under the loss of use coverage; additional living expenses, fair rental value, civil authority prohibits use, and loss or expense not covered. The additional living, fair rental, and civil authority coverages do not terminate if the policy expires before the repairs or designated coverage period expire.

Like the homeowners form, additional living expense provides coverage for increased expenses the insured incurs when the residence premises is unfit to live in. The expenses must be in order for the insured to maintain his normal standard of living, not improve it. For example, the insured pays $1500 mortgage, $300 utilities, and $400 per month on food. The condominium is damaged and not fit to live in; the insured moves into a rental dwelling for $1200 per month, with utilities of $250. His food expense remains the same, as does his mortgage; his utility payments are reduced on the condominium to $150 since no one is living there. The additional living expense coverage will give the insured $1200 for the rental and $100 for utilities. The insured had a decrease in his regular utilities, so the extra above normal expenses is really $100. The $150 plus $250 is $400, only $100 above what the insured is used to paying for utilities. Had the insured's utilities remained the same at the condominium, then the additional living expense would have paid him the $250 for the utilities at the rental property. Payment is for the shortest time to repair the dwelling or for the insured to permanently relocate elsewhere.

The 2011 form specified that only the named insured—and not insured family members—were eligible to receive reimbursement for additional living expenses. Consequently, if the named insured were to die because of the loss, resident family members might lack this coverage. The 2022 form revises this provision so that such family members (relatives and other persons under the age of 21 and in your care or the care of a resident of your household who is a relative) are now specifically provided this coverage as well. Coverage in the new form applies to expenses incurred by covered residents of the named insured's household to enable the household to maintain its normal standard of living.

Note that coverage is for relatives of the insured, but relative is not a defined term. When a term is not defined in a policy courts turn to a standard desk reference – Merriam-Webster online defines relative as: a person connected with another by blood or affinity. Affinity is defined as: relationship by marriage. Therefore, no matter how much someone considers their domestic partner to be a family member, technically they are not covered.

Fair rental value applies when part of the residence premises is rented or held for rental by the insured. The fair rental value is paid to the insured less expenses that do not continue, such as utilities in the earlier example. Payment is for the shortest time to repair or replace the premises. However, the 2022 form was updated to specify that rental value arising out of or in connection with "home-sharing host activities" is not covered.

Civil authorities may prohibit use of a property due to direct damage to a neighboring property; wildfires in the western United States are a prime example. If a neighboring premises catches fire and the local authorities restrict access in order to keep people safe and allow authorities easier access to damaged properties or properties in danger, coverage is provided for up to two weeks for additional living expense or fair rental value.

The last section under loss of use is loss or expense not covered. Not covered is the loss or expense due to cancellation of a lease or agreement. For example, the insured rents part of the property and due to the damage and length of time to restore the property, the tenant cancels the lease and moves elsewhere. The loss of that lease is not covered.

Additional Coverages

There are ten additional coverages added to the policy that apply to particular types of losses or property. There were eleven in the 2011 policy, but the coverage for credit card, electronic fund transfer and related losses has been removed. Because most banks and financial institutions assume or forgive losses due to unauthorized use, the coverage has been removed from the form. Coverage may be added by endorsement if desired, HO 04 53 Credit Card, Electronic Fund Transfer Card or Access Device, Forgery and Counterfeit Money Coverage.

The first is debris removal. Coverage is available for the insured's reasonable expense incurred to remove covered property if damaged by a peril insured against, or the removal of ash, dust, or particles from a volcanic eruption that has caused direct loss to a building or property contained in a building. So the removal of a deck or flooring damaged by fire is covered.

For volcanic damage, the ash or dust must cause the loss itself; the insured's attempts to remove ash from the windows that scratches the windows is not covered; the ash did not scratch the windows, the insured's poor technique in cleaning caused the loss. A common type of this loss is when the weight of ash or dust on a roof causes the roof to collapse and fall into the dwelling. The cost of removal is added into the total of coverage that applies to the damaged property; if the limit is exceeded, and additional 5 percent of that limit is available for debris removal. There is also coverage up to $3000 (this was increased in 2022 from $1,000) for the removal of trees felled by windstorm, hail, weight of ice, snow or sleet, or a neighbor's tree felled by a coverage C peril, as long as the trees damage a covered structure. So if the tree falls on the deck or garage and damages those structures, there is coverage. If the tree just falls in the yard, there is no coverage for removal of the tree. No more than $1500 (increased in 2022 from $500) is paid for removal for any one tree, and $3,000 (increased in 2022 from $1,000) is the maximum regardless of number of trees involved in any one loss. This coverage is additional insurance; use of this coverage does not subtract from the coverage limit of property under coverages A or C.

The policy provides coverage for reasonable repairs the insured makes on a temporary basis in order to protect covered property from further damage if it has been damaged by a peril insured against. Repairs to other damaged property are covered too as long as the property was damaged from a peril insured against and is covered under the policy. However, this coverage does not increase the limit of liability that applies to the covered property or relieve the insured of any of his duties listed under the conditions section. This is for immediate, emergency measures or repairs the insured must make to prevent further damage. For example, boarding up a window to prevent water from damaging the interior contents, or putting a tarp on a hole in the roof. These aren't repairs so much as preventative measures to protect further damage; they are covered.

Trees, shrubs, plants and lawns are subject to specific named causes of loss. Fire or lightning, explosion, riot or civil commotion, aircraft, vehicles not owned or operated by a resident of the resident premises, vandalism or malicious mischief, or theft are the covered perils. Up to 10 percent of coverage C limits can be applied, although no more than $1500 (increased in 2022 from $500) will be paid for any one tree, shrub or plant. This coverage is additional coverage. Property grown for business use is not covered. In 2022, the form was updated to specify that "cannabis" is not covered regardless of whether it is grown for business purposes or not.

In more remote areas there may be no municipal fire department to protect property. In such cases the insured may have a contract with the fire department to pay certain charges. The policy provides up to $500 for such charges when they are called to save or protect property from a covered peril. This does not apply if the insured is in an area with a municipal or city limits protection area. This is additional insurance with no deductible.

Property that has been removed from the home because the home is in danger is covered for thirty days for damage from any loss. This is unique since the damage could be from anything, including flood or other hazards that generally are not covered under this policy.

Loss assessment coverage is particularly important for condominium owners. Because of the ownership of only the unit and its associated property, damages to the common property, that is owned by the association, is shared among members of the association or unit-owners. For example, if a number of roofs are damaged in a hail storm and the association has a large deductible, it may assess each unit owner a share of that deductible. The policy provides up to $2,000 (increased in 2022 from $1,000) for assessments charged against the unit owner by a corporation or association of property owners. The assessment must be due to direct loss to property owned by all members collectively, such as the swimming pool or clubhouse, of the type that would be covered by this policy if owned by the unit owner and caused by a peril insured against other than an earthquake or land shock waves before, during or after a volcanic eruption.

The most that is paid per loss is $2,000 (increased in 2022 from $1,000) regardless of the number of assessments. An association could assess members more than once for the same loss, for example if more damages were found once repairs were begun. Assessments charged against the association by a governmental body are not covered under this coverage. Those governmental assessments tend to be related to failure to adhere to regulations, and not a result of property damage from a loss.

With a large loss, the assessment could reasonably be more than $2,000. In order to provide the insured coverage, the Supplemental Loss Assessment Coverage Endorsement HO 04 35 can be added to the form. This allows the insured to schedule a specific amount of loss assessment coverage. Not only can the insured schedule an increase in loss assessment coverage, but he can also schedule other locations as well, with their own assessment coverage. This is additional insurance, over and above the other coverage limits.

Collapse is a unique coverage. It applies only to an abrupt collapse, and not just sagging, bulging, leaning, or acting like it could collapse. The property must collapse completely or cave in with the result that the building or part of the building cannot be occupied for its intended use.

Falling into a heap of rubble is a common description. Collapse coverage does not apply to parts of a building or buildings in danger of falling down or caving in; parts of a building that are standing, even if separated from the building itself; buildings that are standing but show signs of cracking, bulging, sagging, bending, leaning, settling shrinking or expanding. These are indicators that the insured needs to maintain the property to prevent a collapse.

In order for collapse to be covered, there must be direct physical damage involving collapse of a building or part of a building caused by a coverage C peril, decay that is hidden from view as long as the insured was unaware of it, insect or vermin damage hidden from view that the insured was unaware of, weight of contents, people, equipment or animals, weight of rain collecting on a roof, or use of defective material or methods during construction, renovation, remodeling as long as the loss occurred during the construction period. Losses to awnings, fences, patios, decks, pavements, pools, underground pipes, flues, drains, cesspools, septic tanks, foundations, piers, retaining walls, bulkheads, wharves or docks are not covered unless caused by the collapse of a building or part of a building. Collapse coverage does not increase the limit of liability that applies to damaged property.

The next additional coverage is for glass or safety glazing material. Coverages is for breakage of glass or safety glazing material that is part of a storm door, storm window or building under coverage A, including when caused directly by earth movement, and including property damaged solely by pieces, fragments or splinters of broken safety glass or glazing material which was part of a building or storm door or window. Other damage by fragments, pieces or splinters is not covered, is not covered if the building containing the unit has been vacant for sixty consecutive days before the loss except when caused by earth movement. Glass and safety glazing is one of the few places where coverage is provided due to earth movement. Further on in the policy earth movement is excluded for the rest of the covered property. Like other additional coverages, this does not increase the limit of insurance for the damaged property; any payment is taken out of the existing limit.

Ordinance or law is a very important coverage, especially if the insured has purchased an older unit. Up to 10 percent of the coverage A limit is available for the costs incurred by the insured when an ordinance or law enforces, requires or regulates the construction, renovation, remodeling, demolition of damaged property, or undamaged parts of property that must be demolished, remodeled or removed due to the damage to another part of covered property, or increased cost to remove debris due to an ordinance or law. For example, an insured's unit is forty years old. The insured had remodeled the unit, removing walls and adding a hi-tech entertainment/gaming center and room with specialty heat lamps and humidity controls for his collection of exotic lizards. The county codes regulating wiring and construction have changed since the unit was built and remodeled, and under the association policy the insured is responsible for insuring the wiring and plumbing for his unit. The insured has a fire that damages the entertainment center, and in order to repair the entertainment center in compliance with county ordinances part of the lizard room must be replaced as well since the entertainment center is on an adjoining wall. This would be covered. This is additional insurance, and can be increased by the addition of endorsement HO 04 77 Ordinance or Law Increased Amount of Coverage. This allows the insured to increase the total percentage amount of coverage A that can be used for ordinance or law related issues. Not included in this coverage is anything related to pollution or pollutants, including costs to monitor, assess, clean up, treat, detoxify or in any way respond to the effects of pollutants in or on any property covered under coverage A. The policy then provides the standard definition of pollutant including solids, liquids, gaseous substances or contaminate including smoke, acids, alkalis, chemicals and waste.

Grave markers are the last of the additional coverages. Up to $5,000 in coverage is allowed for damage to grave markers, including mausoleums, away from the residence premises and damaged by a peril insured against. Grave markers are unique property; they are not exactly personal property since they are not mobile, but they are not like buildings or other structures that could be considered part of the residence premises or insured location. This coverage is included in the limits that apply to covered property.

Perils Insured Against

Because the condominium owner is not responsible for the entire structure, and may only be responsible for part of the structure and his contents, the policy is on a named perils basis. The named perils are the standard coverage C named perils. Fire or lightning, explosion, riot or civil commotion have no restrictions or explanatory language, so they are taken at face value. Windstorm or hail includes loss to watercraft and its equipment as long as it is inside a fully enclosed building when damaged; property left outside is going to be subject to weather hazards and damage can be expected. Other property inside a building is not covered by snow, sleet, sand or dust unless the elements have first caused an opening in a roof or wall through which the snow, rain, sand, sleet or dust can enter. If the insured leaves the windows open and a thunderstorm comes up and soaks the inside of the dwelling, there is no coverage.

Aircraft and Vehicles

Aircraft explains that included in aircraft is self-propelled missiles or spacecraft, and the vehicles peril does not include damage to a fence, driveway or walk caused by a vehicle owned or operated by a resident of the insured premises. If the insured carelessly drives into a fence after an evening of celebrating, that loss is not covered. The insured or any other resident of the premises should know where the fences, driveways and walks are on the property. However, if a visiting friend drives through the bay windows, that damage is covered since the insured was not driving the vehicles.

Smoke

While smoke is pretty self-explanatory, there is some clarifying language here. Coverage is for sudden and accidental damage, and includes the emission or puffback of smoke, soot, fumes or vapors from a boiler, furnace or related equipment. It is not unheard of in the fall for some types of heating equipment to send smoke or soot throughout the house. However, the long term accumulation of smoke residue from wood stoves, fireplaces, furnaces or even candles is not covered. That type of residue or smoke is neither sudden nor accidental. Also excluded is loss from agricultural smudging or industrial operations.

Vandalism and Malicious Mischief

Vandalism and malicious mischief are covered causes of loss, but only as long as the building containing the unit has not been vacant for more than sixty consecutive days before the loss, and the loss does not arise out of or results from "home-sharing host activities." (the home-sharing exclusionary language was added in 2022). Vacant property is often attractive to vandals. Likewise, ensuing losses from intentional acts of vandalism or malicious mischief are not covered if the building containing the property was vacant for those sixty days before the loss.

Property under construction is not considered vacant. Vacant is often confused with unoccupied. When the insured is away at his vacation home for the summer, and leaves his unit full of furnishings and other property while he is gone, the property is unoccupied, not vacant. Vacant is when the property is without content or occupant. For example the insured moves out all furniture to paint and wallpaper the unit and it takes longer than planned; the property is then vacant, and if it stays that way for more than sixty days, vandals spray painting the inside is not covered. When a property is under construction, people are around working on the property and it is not left unattended for long periods of time. It is the leaving a property unattended for long periods of time that attracts individuals prone to committing vandalism or acts of mischief. Because theft is treated separately, a few words about vandalism and malicious mischief. This is destruction/ defacement purely for its own sake; the individual is not breaking in to steal something, but is painting letters on the walls, breaking windows, and causing deliberate damage just for the sake of doing it or making racial, political or generally mean statements against the insured.

Theft

The theft peril includes attempted theft and loss of property from a known place where it is likely that the property was stolen. For example, the insured parks his bicycle outside his garage nightly, and gets up one morning and it is missing. It is likely that the bicycle was stolen, although there is no forced entry of a premises or anything that can be fingerprinted to prove it; the fact that the bicycle is missing from its usual spot is enough. Not covered however is theft caused by an insured; the insured cannot claim his property was stolen by himself or a resident relative and get paid for it. It is not uncommon for resident relatives to, on occasion, steal property from each other.

Property that is used in or to a premises under construction is not covered for theft as it is often left open at the worksite; such property is not covered until the premises is finished and occupied. Theft of trailers, semitrailers, campers, watercraft and their furnishings and equipment, including outboard engines and motors are not covered if stolen while away from the residence premises. Property that is in the part of a residence rented to another person is also not covered; the insured is basically leaving that property in the custody of a stranger. Property left at another premises owned, rented or occupied by an insured is not covered unless the insured is temporarily living there. For example, the insured has a vacation property at the beach. When the insured is not there, the possessions left in that property are not covered for theft. However when the insured is living there during the summer, the property is covered for loss by theft. The same applies for students away at school; as long as the student has been at the dwelling anytime during the ninety days immediately before the loss, there is coverage for theft.

Falling Objects

Damage by falling objects is not covered unless the object has first damaged the roof or outside wall of the residence, and damage to the object itself is not included. If a lead crystal vase falls off the mantle damaging the coffee table before it shatters on the floor, there is no coverage for the table nor the vase. However, if a meteorite comes through the wall, knocks the vase into the coffee table, then there is coverage for damage to the vase and the table.

Weight of Ice, Snow or Sleet

Weight of ice, snow or sleet is covered if it damages either the building or contents within the building. Notice that weight of rain is not covered; ice, snow and sleet are all frozen or partially frozen; rain is a different, although related, substance. The pooling of water on a flat roof that damages the unit is not covered, while the accumulation of snow on the roof that damages the unit is covered. Not covered is loss to awnings, fences, patios, pavements, swimming pools, foundations, retaining walls, bulkheads, piers, wharves or docks.

Accidental Discharge or Overflow of Water or Steam

Plumbing leaks happen, and coverage is provided for the accidental discharge or overflow of water or steam from within plumbing, heating, air conditioning, automatic fire sprinkler systems or household appliances. Should such a leak occur the cost to tear out and replace part of a building owned solely by the insured in order to repair the system from which the water leaked is covered. For example, if a pipe springs a leak behind the insured's tub, the cost to tear out the wall to access and repair that pipe is covered, but the cost of repair of the pipe itself is not. This applies only if the leak causes actual damage to a building owned solely by the insured at the "residence premises".

Coverage does not apply if the property has been vacant for more than 60 consecutive days before the loss, to the system from which the water discharged, caused by freezing except as provided in the freezing peril, caused by discharge away from the building where the "residence premises" is located or caused by mold, fungus, or wet rot unless hidden within the walls, ceilings or floors of the unit.

Sudden and Accidental Tearing Apart, Cracking, Burning

Sudden and accidental tearing apart, cracking, burning or bulging of a steam or hot water system or heater, air conditioning or automatic fire protective sprinkler system is covered. Note that the loss must be sudden and accidental; the simple wear-out and failure of any of these objects is not covered. Loss caused by freezing is not covered either unless as is specified by the freezing peril.

Freezing

The freezing peril applies as long as the insured has maintained heat in the building or shut off the water supply and drained all systems and appliances of water. An exception, of course, is if a sprinkler system exists; then the heat must be left on so the sprinkler system can remain functional. The policy does not indicate what temperature the dwelling must be left at in order to maintain heat in order to prevent freezing. Unfortunately there are cases where insureds set the heat at 35 or 45 degrees in order to save on energy costs, only to have the pipe freeze and damage the property, and have the carrier deny the claim. Building experts seem to agree that 55 degrees is the minimum temperature in order to keep pipes from freezing in a dwelling. While the form does not define plumbing systems or appliances, it does make note that not included in plumbing systems or appliance is sump, sump pumps, related equipment, roof drains, gutters, downspouts or similar fixtures or equipment. Sump pumps run only when there's an excess of water in the basement, and are not used daily as are household appliances and plumbing. The same is true of downspouts and similar equipment designed to move excess water away from the dwelling.

Sudden and Accidental Damage from Artificially Generated Electrical Current

While there is coverage for sudden and accidental damage from artificially generated electrical current, it is not much. The reason is that coverage is excluded for loss to tubes, transistors, circuits or electronic components that are part of appliances, fixtures, computers, home entertainment units, and other electronic apparatus. Once these components have been excluded, what is left is pretty much casings, knobs, switches, and other nonelectrical components.

Volcanic Eruption

Volcanic eruption is another covered peril with only the exception for earthquake, land shock waves or tremors. Loss from a volcano is covered, earthquakes are not. The most common loss from a volcano involves ash, fire and lava. Earth tremors may occur and although related to the volcano, are still excluded as earth movement.

EXCLUSIONS

This section identifies what specifically is excluded from coverage. First there is anticoncurrent causation language, which states that the loss is excluded regardless of any other cause or event contributing concurrently or in any sequence to the loss. This is often seen regarding hurricane and flood damage. If a hurricane hits an area and the property is damaged by wind and flood waters, the flood waters are excluded. However, if the wind tears off the roof and rain enters the dwelling that is different than flood waters damaging the walls from the outside in. Something that is encountered here in this section is a caveat for several excluded items that fire, explosion or theft resulting from the excluded peril are covered. So, the anticoncurrent clause is removed from some excluded causes for certain basic perils. The exclusions must be read closely so that it is completely understood what is and what is not excluded.

Ordinance or Law

Ordinance or law is excluded except for the limited amount of coverage provided for under additional coverages. Aside from that, any ordinance that requires or regulates the construction, remodeling, repair or renovation of property, including debris removal, is excluded. If the insured's house burns local building codes may require the insured to update wiring or plumbing. Coverage for ordinance or law can be increased by endorsement, so if the insured wants to increase the limited coverage he can. Also excluded, and what is not covered in the additional coverage, is requirements which result in a loss of value to property; for example the removal of trees because of codes, or the addition of retaining walls or other supporting structures can affect property values, and a change in property value is not direct damage to property.

As always requirements to test for, monitor, clean up, remove, contain, treat, detoxify or otherwise assess for or treat pollutants is excluded. Pollutants always require special handling, and the average homeowner does not have pollution exposure issues. The exclusion for ordinance applies even if no damage has been done to the property. For example, the insured decides to remodel the den, and comes to find out that the wiring is out of compliance and must be brought up to code. This is not a loss; this is simply maintenance issues the insured must handle, so while it is caused by an ordinance, it is not related to a loss and there is no coverage. This is also not something the association will handle for all unit-owners; the aging of wiring and the changing of county codes is something that just happens overtime, and property owners just have to deal with it as the issue arises.

Earth Movement

Earth movement is always excluded, whether caused by natural or other causes. So, if the county is blasting nearby and this causes the insured's ground to shift and damage the foundation and the building, there is no coverage. The exclusion specifically excludes earth movement and defines it as earthquake, including land shock waves before, during or after a volcano, landslide, mudflow or mudslide, subsidence or sinkhole, or any other movement including rising, sinking or shifting. As you can see the cause of the movement can be from various sources; water from heavy rains may cause mudflows or mudslides, underground water may cause subsidence or sinkholes, and tectonic movement causes earthquakes. Likewise, anything else that could cause the earth to shift or move is excluded. An exception is made for subsequent losses caused by fire, explosion or theft. Therefore, if an earthquake causes the gas lines to rupture and this sets the house on fire, damage from that fire is covered, even though it is a concurrent loss.

Water

Water is the next exclusion, and it is extensive. Flood, surface water, waves, tidal waves, tsunamis, tides, tidal water, overflow of any body of water or spray from any of these, whether or not driven by wind, including storm surge, are excluded. Surface water is water that meanders along the surface of the ground in no particular pattern. Water than has overflown from a river or stream can be considered surface water once it is outside its bounds. Heavy rains may cause certain areas to collect water that can then run into ground level premises. Also excluded is water which backs up through sewers or drains, overflows from sumps, sump pumps or related equipment, water below the surface of the ground including that which exerts pressure on or seeps, leaks or flows through a building, patio, driveway, walk, foundation, pool or other structure.

Backup and overflow are two different things; a backup is when water reverses direction and flows backwards; for example a child flushes a rubber ducky down the toilet, the water backs up and reverses and flows onto the floor. An overflow is when water exceeds its container; someone leaves the tub running and water exceeds the tub's capacity and flows onto the floor. Water below the surface of the ground is often caused by heavy rains that saturate the ground; then the water can exert pressure on underground structures or flow into basements, swimming pools, or other structures. However not just the water is excluded; the policy makes it clear that waterborne material is excluded as well. Moving water is very strong and exerts a significant amount of pressure on anything it encounters; therefore it is very likely to accumulate branches and other debris as it moves across the ground, and sewer backups may contain waste products as well. These objects in the water are also excluded. Water r that escapes, overflow or discharges for any reason from a dam, levee, seawall or any other boundary or containment system is excluded. This was added after Hurricane Katrina and the problems from the levees breaking and causing damage. As with the earth movement exclusion, there is an exception for resulting fire, explosion of theft resulting from any of the excluded water losses.

Power Failure

Power failure is excluded if the failure takes place off the residence premises. This is when the power company's transformer on the corner down the street fails, or some other event happens to power company equipment. However, if the failure results in a covered loss on the insured premises, that ensuing loss is covered. If a vehicle hits the transformer causing a power failure in the unit, and that causes a fire, that resultant fire is covered.

Neglect

Insurance coverage is designed to compensate the insured for accidents and sudden losses. In event of a loss, the insured is expected to take steps to prevent the loss from becoming worse; put a tarp over the roof, gather up property from an area that is now open to prevent loss from theft, and other such measures. Neglect to take such steps is excluded. If the insured is not willing to take care of her own property, the carrier is not going to compensate her for such negligence.

War

War is something that cannot be covered; it is not something for which actuarially sound rates can be set, and damage is devastating. Not only war but warlike acts are excluded, as is undeclared war, civil war, insurrection, rebellion, revolution, or destruction, or seizure or use for a military purpose. If the government seizes the condo in order to set up operations from there, there is no coverage. Discharge of a nuclear weapon, even if it is accidental, is always seen as a warlike act.

Nuclear Hazard

While the discharge of a nuclear weapon is excluded under war, nuclear hazard has its own separate exclusion. This exclusion is for nuclear reaction, radiation, or radioactive contamination, however caused, and any loss will not be considered loss by fire, explosion or smoke whether or not included as perils insured against. However, direct loss by fire resulting from the nuclear hazard is covered. If Peter Parker is exposing spiders to radioactive materials and the unit becomes radioactive there is no coverage. If however during the radioactive experiments a fire starts, there is coverage for the fire.

Intentional Loss

Intentional loss is an insured's deliberate damaging of property; this is excluded, whether the insured actually commits the damaging act or conspires with someone else, for example hiring someone to burn the building so the insured gets the insurance money. A clause here eliminates coverage for what's known as innocent coinsureds; a spouse who knows nothing about the plot to burn the house also gets no insurance proceeds, even though he had no part in the planning of or committing of the destructive act.

Governmental Acts

Similar to part of the war exclusion, governmental acts or acts by a public authority ordering the destruction, confiscation or seizure of property covered in coverage A or C are not covered. An exception is for such acts taken at the time of a fire to prevent the spread of fire as long as the loss would be covered under the policy. With severe wildfires properties may be burned as a firebreak in order to prevent further spread of the fire; in such situations coverage applies.

CONDITIONS

The conditions section of any policy explains what is agreed to by both parties; what is required in event of a loss, how losses and disputes are handled, how suits are handled and other such details.

Insurable Interest

The first condition is that even if more than one person has an insurable interest in the property that the carrier is not liable in any one loss to more than an insured's interest in the property or more that the applicable limit of liability. If an insured has two mortgages on the property that total more than the unit it worth, then the most that will be paid if the unit is totaled is the limit of the policy; the insured will have to make arrangements for any outstanding debt he has with whatever bank is involved.

Deductible

Losses are not paid until the amount of the loss exceeds the deductible; the deductible is the insured's responsibility. Some additional coverages are subject to the deductible as well; if two or more deductibles apply to the same loss, then only the larger of the two deductibles is taken. The insured is not subjected to having to pay two deductibles for one loss.

Duties After Loss

There are several duties after a loss for the insured. These duties help the carrier determine what happened in the loss and the value of any damaged property. The duties also help mitigate the loss by requiring the insured to protect any damaged property from further loss. The carrier can deny coverage if the insured refuses to perform these duties and such refusal is prejudicial to the carrier. Duties must be performed by the insured, an insured seeking coverage, or a representative of either. Insureds sometimes hire public adjusters or attorneys to handle their claim.

The first duty is to promptly inform the carrier or the agent of the loss; promptly is not defined, so what a reasonable person would consider to be promptly is the standard to be used. The police are to be notified in case of theft; the police may be able to recover the stolen goods. The insured is to protect the property from further damage, and if repairs are needed the insured is to make reasonable and necessary repairs to protect the property and keep an accurate record of repair expenses. Note that the repairs required are to protect the property, not the final repairs needed. This would be boarding up windows or putting a tarp over a hole in the wall, not replacing the window and the wall. The carrier needs to see the damage. The insured must also prepare an inventory of damaged personal property showing the quantity, description, actual cash value and amount of loss. Any bills, receipts, and related documents that justify the figures must be attached. The carrier wants to see documentation as there are those who invent destroyed property in order to claim a larger loss.

The insured is to cooperate with the carrier in the investigation, and as often as the carrier reasonably requires show the damaged property, provide records and documents as requested and allow copies to be made, and submit to an examination under oath without another insured being present and sign the same. This helps the carrier quantify the loss and also ensure that no fraud is being committed.

A signed, sworn proof of loss is required within sixty days of the carrier's request for one. The proof of loss is to contain the time and causes of loss, interest of all insureds and all liens on the property, other insurance available, changes in title or occupancy during the policy period, specifications of damaged buildings and repair estimates, inventory of personal property as described earlier, receipts for additional living expenses and records that support fair rental value loss, and evidence or affidavits that support claims under credit card, electronic fund transfer losses, forgery and counterfeit money.

Loss Settlement

Loss settlement is the next section of conditions. It defines how losses are to be settled. Losses under coverage A that are repaired or replaced within a reasonable time are settled at actual cash value. Losses that are not repaired or replaced within a reasonable time are settled at actual cash value, but not more than the amount needed to repair or replace the property. These repairs or replacements do not include any ordinance or law coverage.

Personal property including grave markers and mausoleums are also settled at actual case value but no more than the actual cost to repair or replace the property. This can be changed by using endorsement HO 04 90, Personal Property Replacement Cost Loss Settlement. This allows all but certain listed types of property to be covered on a replacement cost basis. Losses to pairs or sets are slightly different because of the nature of the property. When part of a set is damaged, it may be impossible to replace it with a matching item. The carrier has two options; to repair or replace any part in order to restore the pair or set to its value before the loss, or to pay the difference between the actual cash value of the property before and after a loss. This could result in payment for the entire set, if the missing part is critical to the value of the pair or set as a whole.

Appraisal

Appraisal is used when the insured and insurer fail to agree on the amount of the loss; either party may request an appraisal of the loss. Note that the appraisal function is to determine amount of loss, not coverage. An appraisal will determine whether the cost to repair the roof is $8,000 or $15,000, but will not determine whether or not there is coverage for personal property due to a stampeding herd of buffalo. Once a written request has been made from the other party, each party has 20 days to choose a competent and impartial appraiser to review the claim. The appraisers will select an umpire. If an umpire cannot be agreed on within 15 days, either party may request that a judge of a court of record in the state choose the umpire. The appraisers will separately set the amount of loss; if they agree on the amount that amount will be the amount of the loss. If the appraisers disagree, they will submit their differences to the umpire. Any agreement by two of the three parties will set the amount of the loss. , If the umpire and the insured's appraiser agree on the amount of loss that is the amount the insured is due. Likewise, if the umpire and the carrier's appraiser agree, that will be the amount due the insured. Each party is to pay its own appraiser and bear the other expenses of the appraisal process and the umpire equally.

Other Insurance

The possibility exists that the property could be covered under more than one insurance policy. In situations where there is other coverage but not in the name of a corporation or association of property owners, the carrier pays only the proportion of the loss that the limit of liability bears to the total amount covering the loss. For example, the insured's policy on the unit is $100,000, and another policy exists for $50,000. A loss of $40,000 occurs. The insured's carrier covers 66 percent of the total limit of coverage. Therefore, the insured's carrier will cover 66 percent of the loss, or $26,400. The other policy will cover the remainder.

If there is a service agreement other than one in the name of an association or corporation of property owners, then this policy is excess over that policy. When the other policy or service agreement is in the name of an association or corporation of property owners, then this policy is excess over that coverage, whether or not the association has collected that coverage amount. If the loss is not covered under such association agreement or service policy due to a deductible, then this policy provides coverage on a primary basis. For clarification a service agreement is defined as a service plan, property restoration plan, home warranty or other similar service warranty agreement, even if it is characterized as insurance.

Suit Against Us and Our Option

Suit can be filed only after the insured has adhered to all the terms of the policy, and suit must be filed within two years of the date of loss. The carrier has the option to repair or replace any part of damaged property with like kind and quality if they provide the insured with written notice within thirty days of receipt of the signed, sworn proof of loss. If the carrier does not give this written notice, then the loss settlement provisions of the policy apply.

Loss Payment and Abandonment

Losses are settled with the insured unless another person is named in the policy or is legally entitled to receive payment. Loss is payable sixty days after the carrier receives the proof of loss and either the carrier and insured reach an agreement, there is a final entry of judgment, or there is a filing of an appraisal award with the carrier. The carrier is not required to accept any property abandoned by an insured; if an insured abandons damaged parts of the unit it will not fall to the carrier to clean up the parts; it will go back to the insured.

Mortgage Clause

When there is a mortgagee on the policy, payment is made to both the insured and the mortgagee as their interests appear. If there is more than one mortgagee, payment is in the order of precedence of the mortgages. Denial of a claim does not deny the mortgagee payment, as long as the mortgagee has taken steps to notify the carrier of change in occupancy, ownership or change in risk of which the mortgagee is aware, paid any premium due if the insured has failed to make payment, and submitted a signed, sworn statement of loss within sixty days of receiving notice from the carrier of the insured's failure to do so. The suit and loss payment sections apply to a mortgagee as well. For example, the insured moves out of the unit and abandons the mortgage. The mortgagee discovers this, notifies the carrier of the abandonment and pays the premium. If the building suffers a loss such as a fire, the mortgagee will get paid once completing the notice of loss procedures.

If the carrier cancels or nonrenews the policy, the mortgagee will be notified at least ten days before the date the cancellation or nonrenewal takes effect. When the carrier pays the mortgagee to the exclusion of payment to the insured, the carrier is subrogated to the rights granted to the mortgagee, or the carrier may pay the whole principal and interest and will receive a full assignment and transfer of the mortgage and all securities held as collateral to the debt. Subrogation does not impair the right of the mortgagee to recover the full amount of the mortgagee's claim.

No Benefit to Bailee

The "no benefit to bailee" clause states that no coverage is provided for any person or organization storing or moving property for a fee regardless of any other policy provisions. For example, the insured has stored her furs for the summer at the furriers. The furrier has a fire which damages the furs. Since the furs were in the custody of the furrier at the time of loss, the furrier's policy should provide coverage for the loss, not this policy, even though fire is a covered peril for personal property.

Nuclear Hazard Clause

The nuclear hazard clause was discussed earlier with war and discharge of a nuclear weapon. To reiterate, the clause removes coverage for nuclear reaction, radiation, or radioactive contamination, however caused, and any loss will not be considered loss by fire, explosion or smoke whether or not included as perils insured against. Direct loss by fire resulting from the nuclear hazard is covered.

Recovered Property

When property that the carrier has paid out a loss for has been recovered, for example a theft, the insured has the option of keeping the property and returning the claim payment or keeping the payment and letting the carrier have the recovered property. If the claim for the property was part of a larger loss, the loss payment is adjusted based on what the insured had received for the covered property that was recovered.

Volcano, Policy Period, Fraud, Loss Payable

The final conditions for section I are self-explanatory; volcanic eruption period simply states what time frame is considered to be one eruption, and that is all discharges within seventy-two hours. The policy applies only to claims made during this policy, not before or after. No coverage is provided if it is discovered that the insured intentionally concealed or misrepresented any fact or circumstance, engaged in fraudulent conduct or made false statements relating to this insurance. This includes statements made on the application or in the filing of a claim, whether it be details of the loss or claims of damaged property. If a loss payee is shown on the policy for certain insured personal property, such as expensive jewelry, the definition of insured is changed to include that loss payee with respect to that property. The loss payee will be notified of any cancellation or nonrenewal of the policy.

Section II – Liability Coverages

Section II provides the insured with liability coverages; personal liability and medical payments to others. Personal liability coverage is for "bodily injury" or "property damage" to others that the insured is legally liable for that is due to an "occurrence". The defined terms are important and were discussed earlier. Remember that bodily injury does not include mental anguish or distress. Also, the carrier provides a defense at the carrier's expense even if the suit is groundless, false or fraudulent; counsel is at the choice of the carrier, and the carrier has the right to settle or defend any claim or suit as it sees fit. You may sometimes hear that an insurer's "duty to defend it broader than its duty to indemnify." This is where that statement comes from. It also may be less expensive to settle a claim or suit, even if there is no wrongdoing on the part of the insured. However, the duty to defend ends when the limit has been exhausted.

Medical payments coverage provides payment for necessary medical expenses that occur within three years from the date of an accident causing bodily injury. Included in medical expenses are reasonable charges for medical, surgical, x-ray, dental, ambulance, hospital, professional nursing, prosthetic devices and funeral expenses. This does not apply to insureds or regular residents of the household other than residence employees. Coverage applies to others on the premises with the insured's permission, off an insured location if the injury arises out of a condition on the location or the ways adjoining it (for example a walkway), is caused by the activities of the insured, or a residence employee of the insured while in the course of employment, or by an animal owned by or in the care of an insured (for example the insured's pet or a neighbor's pet if the insured is walking the dog).

EXCLUSIONS

The next section is exclusions and begins with motor vehicle exclusions. Motor vehicles are excluded with certain exceptions. Exceptions are if the vehicle is in dead storage, is used solely to service a residence, or is designed to assist the handicapped and at the time of loss is being used to assist the handicapped or is parked on an insured location. Also, if the vehicle is designed for use off public roads and is not owned by an insured, or owned by an insured and the occurrence takes place at certain locations there is coverage. The locations are the residence premises, part of other premises, other structures and grounds used by the insured as a residence and listed on the declarations or acquired during the policy period, part of a premises not owned by an insured and where the insured is temporarily residing, vacant land other than farm land owned or rented to an insured, and any part of a premises occasionally rented to an insured for other than business use.

Vehicles designed as a toy for children under the age of seven and powered by one or more batteries and not built or modified to exceed five miles per hour on level ground are covered. Motorized golf carts owned by an insured, designed to carry up to four people, not built or modified to exceed twenty-five miles per hour and at the time of the occurrence are on a golfing facility to play golf or other recreational activity, travel to or from where golf carts are parked or stored, or crossing public roads at the golf facility, or are on a private residential community under the auspices of a property owners association are covered as well. These are the same exceptions found in the homeowners policy.

Watercraft

In general liability for watercraft is excluded. The chart below represents ISO's attempt to simplify this somewhat confusing exclusion with some new language they introduced in their 2022 form update. Coverage is granted through exceptions to the exclusion noted below.

	With Auxiliary Power	**Without Auxiliary Power**	**25 hp or less**	**More than 25 hp**
Sailing Vessel	Less than 26 ft. overall length	Less than 26 ft. overall length		
	26 ft. or more not owned by insured	26 ft. or more not owned by insured		
Nonsailing Vessel **Powered by one or more engines or motors, including those that power water jet pump**			X	Not owned by insured
Nonsailing Vessel **Powered by one or more engines or motors, including those that power water jet pump**				Outboard engines or motors owned by insured: • who acquired such motors during the policy period or • declared at inception or • intent to insure within 45 days of acquisition

Aircraft and hovercraft liability are easy as there are no exceptions; they are simply excluded from the policy with no exceptions.

COVERAGE E AND F LIABILITY AND MEDICAL PAYMENTS

Expected or Intended Injury

The next section is exclusions for both personal liability and medical payments coverage outside of vehicle exclusions. Expected or intended injury is not covered; even if the injury was intended for someone else and a bystander was injured instead, injury was intended, so the act is not accidental. Also, if the resultant injury or damage is different than what was expected, some type of injury or damage was still expected. The only exception is for the use of reasonable force to protect persons or property. Coverage applies if the insured intentionally injures someone in an attempt to protect people or property from harm.

Business

Injury or property damage from business conducted from an insured location, or engaged in by an insured whether or not the business is owned, operated, or employs an insured is not covered. Excluded are acts or omissions including those that involve services or duties rendered, promised, owed or implied to be provided because of the nature of the business. The purpose of the policy is to protect the insured from his individual liability; any liability generated from business activities belongs on a business liability policy.

There are some exceptions (other than "home-sharing host activities"); if the insured occasionally rents or holds for rental an insured location as a residence, or as an office, school, studio or private garage, there is coverage. Also excepted are endeavors of an insured under the age of twenty-one years of age involved in a part-time or occasional self-employed business with no employees; this allows the younger members of the family to have their dog-sitting, baby-sitting, lawn-mowing services without having to worry about insurance. The rendering or failure to render professional services is excluded; this ties in with the business exclusion, since professional services would involve actions of medical personnel, accountants, attorneys, and other such professions.

Insured's Premises Not an Insured Location

In order for liability coverage to apply to injury or damage arising out of a premises owned by, rented to, or rented to others by an insured the property in question must be part of an insured location. If it is not, coverage is excluded. An insured location is discussed in the definitions, and includes the residence premises, temporary residences, vacant land, cemetery plots, premises occasionally rented to an insured for other than business use, and other areas.

War

War cannot be covered by insurance; excluded with war is civil war, insurrection, rebellion, revolution, warlike acts by military personnel, or destruction or use for a military purpose. Nuclear weapons are always considered an act of war even if they are accidentally discharged.

Communicable Diseases and Molestation

Communicable diseases are not covered, nor are injury or property damage as a result of sexual molestation, corporal punishment or mental or physical abuse. Most of these are intentional acts; transmission of communicable diseases may not be intentional, but it is still not covered by insurance.

Controlled Substances

The use, sale, manufacture, delivery, transfer or possession of controlled substances that results in injury or damage to people or property of others is excluded. Controlled substances are defined by the Federal Food and Drug Law at 21 U.S.C.A. Sections 811 and 812, or any cannabis regardless of whether such cannabis is considered a Controlled Substance. Controlled substances include but are not limited to cocaine, LSD, marijuana, and all narcotics. Cannabis (marijuana) falls into an interesting category since it is now legal in many states either for medicinal or recreational purposes. Nevertheless, it is still federally a controlled substance, so there is only coverage for medical, and not recreational, cannabis , even though it is legal in some areas. The 2022 revision makes this clear by specifically stating that cannabis is not covered whether it is considered a controlled substance or not.

For example, if the insured is making methamphetamine in his condo the residue seeps into the next condo or the condo catches fire and burns the condo next door, there is no coverage. An exception exists for the legitimate use of prescription drugs by a person following the directions of a licensed health care professional. If the insured has an adverse reaction to a prescribed drug and he pounds holes in the walls through to the adjoining condo, that damage would be covered.

Motorcraft, Aircraft, Watercraft, Hovercraft Exception

The exclusions for motorcraft, aircraft, watercraft, and hovercraft liability and for insured's premises not an insured location do not apply to injury to a residence employee arising out of the employee's employment by an insured. A residence employee is a separate category of individual, and as they are working for the insured the listed exclusions do not apply while the employee is on duty. Therefore, if the residence employee is with the insured at a location that is not an insured location and the employee is injured while performing his gardening duties, that injury would be covered.

COVERAGE E LIABILITY EXCLUSIONS

Loss Assessment

The next section of exclusions applies to coverage E, Personal Liability section only. Other than what is covered under additional coverages, loss assessments charged against the insured as a member of an association, community, or corporation of property owners is excluded. However liability does apply if a contract or agreement existed and relates directly to the ownership, maintenance or use of an insured location, or where the liability of others is assumed by the insured prior to an occurrence unless excluded elsewhere in the policy.

Property Owned by the Insured

Property owned by the insured is covered under section I, and is not covered here for direct damage or expenses to repair, replace, or maintain such property to prevent injury to people or damage to property of others; these things are general maintenance items. Likewise, damage to property rented to, occupied by, used by or in the care of an insured is not covered unless the damage is caused by fire, smoke or explosion.

Workers Compensation

Some states require residence employees to be provided with workers compensation benefits; in such situations there is no coverage from this policy if such benefits are voluntarily or are required to be provided by an insured under any workers compensation, nonoccupational disease, or occupational disease law.

Nuclear Energy

If the insured is covered under any sort of nuclear energy liability policy issued by the Nuclear Energy Liability Insurance Association, Mutual

Atomic Energy Liability Underwriters, Nuclear Insurance Association of Canada or any of their successors, or would be covered except that the policy limits have been exhausted; bodily injury or property damage to others is excluded.

Bodily Injury to an Insured

Bodily injury to the insured is excluded, and the exclusion applies to any claim made or suit brought against the insured to repay or share damages with another person who may be obligated to pay damages because of injury to an insured. This is not a health insurance policy for the insured, so injury to the insured is excluded, even if another insured could possibly be held responsible for the injury; for example, two brothers got into a fist fight and injured each other.

Coverage F Medical Payments Exclusions

The next section is exclusions that apply only to coverage F, Medical Payments to Others. Injury to a residence employee is not covered if the injury occurs off the insured location and does not arise out of the course of the employee's employment by the insured. These are accidents that could happen to anyone in general, and the insured is not responsible since it is not employment related. For example, if the employee is doing his Christmas shopping and falls on the ice getting out of the car and injures his hip, there is no coverage. Similar to the exclusion under coverage E, those eligible to receive coverage due to any workers compensation, nonoccupational disability, or occupational disease law are not covered.

Nuclear Radiation, Reaction, Contamination

Injury from any nuclear radiation, reaction, or contamination, whether controlled or uncontrolled or however caused is excluded. Nuclear material is so hazardous that even if a qualified insured is working with such material, it is excluded from the policy. A scientist experimenting in the garage has no coverage for any nuclear experiments that may injure others.

Injuries to Others While Living With Insured

Injuries to a home-sharing occupant or any person other than residence employees regularly residing on any part of an insured location are not covered. There are specific coverages for residence employees, but other residents, either relatives or tenants, are not provided with any coverage. Medical payments to others is truly geared to those outside the household who are accidently injured in some way.

Section II – Liability Additional Coverages

Section II has its own set of additional coverages. Claim expenses, expenses the insured incurs, and costs taxed against the insured, premiums on bonds although the insurer does not need to apply for or furnish the bond, expenses incurred by an insured at the insurer's request including loss of earnings up to $250 per day, and interest on the entire judgment which accrues after entry of the judgment and before payment can be made are all paid by the insurer. These expenses are in addition to the limit of liability; they do not reduce the coverage amount available to the insured.

First Aid and Damage to Property of Others

First aid expenses the insured incurs for injury to others are covered; first aid to an insured is not covered, just aid to others. The injury must be covered under the policy.

Damage to property of others is often called "good neighbor" coverage. It is coverage for things that just happen regardless of legal liability, for example an insured's tree falls onto a neighbor's car, or a child's baseball breaks a window. Coverage is for up to $5,000 (the 2022 updated increased this limit from $1,000) per occurrence for damage to property of others caused by an insured. Excluded is damage covered under section I, damage caused intentionally by an insured thirteen or older, damage to property owned by an insured, or damage to property owned by or rented to a tenant of an insured living in the household.

Also not covered is damage arising out of a business engaged in by an insured or an act or omission in connection with a premises owned, rented or controlled by an insured, other than the "insured location". Remember "insured location" refers to specific properties listed in the definitions. Damage caused by the ownership, maintenance, occupancy, operation, use, loading or unloading of vehicles, aircraft, hovercraft or watercraft is excluded except for vehicles designed for recreational use off public roads, not owned by an insured, and at the time of loss was not required by law or regulation to have been registered for it to be used on public roads or property.

Loss Assessment

Loss assessment is also an additional coverage under section II. Up to $2,000 (the 2022 update increased this limit from $1,000) is available if the insured is assessed as owner or tenant by a corporation or association of property owners. The assessment must be the result of injury or damage not excluded from Section II, and the assessment is due to liability for an act of a director, officer or trustee in their official capacity provided the person is elected by the association and serves without any income for the exercise of such duties. This is for decisions or actions of members of the association, and not property damage. The most that is paid out is $2,000 regardless of the number of assessments, and repeated or continuous exposure to the same general harmful condition is considered one accident. Likewise, and act involving more than one director, officer or trustee is considered to be a single act. Assessments generated by a governmental body are not covered.

Section II – CONDITIONS

Limits and Severability

Because of the nature of the coverage, there are some specific conditions that apply to the liability coverages of the policy. Obviously no more than the limits of the policy will be paid out, regardless of the number of insureds, claims made or persons injured. All injury or damage from one accident or a continuous exposure to harmful conditions is considered to be one accident. Coverage applies separately to each insured, however this does not increase the limit of liability for any one occurrence. If two insureds are walking two dogs and each dog attacks a different neighbor on the walk, with each insured losing control of the dog that they were walking, each insured has coverage for the injuries caused to the neighbor injured by the respective insured's dog.

Duties after "Occurrence"

The duties after an occurrence are very similar to the section I duties after a loss; differences are because this deals with injuries or damage to property of others instead of damage to property of the insured. The carrier requires written notice as soon as possible with the time, place, circumstances of the loss, names and addresses of claimants and witnesses, cooperation from the insured in any investigation and assistance in making settlement, forward any notice, demand or summons the insured receives, and other such activity to assist the insurer in handling the loss to completion. If the damaged property is in the insured's control a sworn statement of loss is required within sixty days. Insured's shall not voluntarily make any payments except for immediate first aid at the time of injury. Otherwise, it could be construed as admission of liability.

Duties of an Injured Person

Claimants also have some duties to fulfill with regard to Coverage F – Medical Payment to Others. They are to give the insurer written proof of claim, under oath if necessary, as soon as practicable and authorize the carrier to obtain medical reports and records. The injured party will submit to an examination by a doctor of the insurer's choice if required as often and as reasonably as required. Multiple visits may be necessary over the course of recovery to ensure proper healing and treatment for the injury.

Payments and Other Conditions

Payments for medical payments do not admit liability of an insured or the insurer. Suits cannot be filed until all duties have been fulfilled, similar to Section I conditions. Any bankruptcy of an insured does not affect the insurer's responsibility to make payments or settle claims under this policy. This policy is excess over other insurance except for that written specifically to cover as excess over this policy. Coverage applies only during the specified policy period. Coverage is not provided for insured's who intentionally conceal or misrepresent any material fact or circumstance, engage in fraudulent conduct, or make false statements regarding this insurance.

SECTIONS I AND II CONDITIONS

Sections I and II have separate conditions due to the different nature of the coverages provided; Section I is providing coverage for the insured's own property, while section II is providing coverage for issues involving the insured's liability for injury to others or damage to their property. There are conditions that apply to the policy as a whole, and this section deals with those conditions.

Liberalization and Waiver of Provisions

The first condition is the liberalization clause; insurers change policy language and coverages from time to time, and this provides that any changes that broaden coverage without an increase in premium are automatically applied to this policy sixty days prior to or as of the date it occurs. Changes that include both a broadening and restriction in coverage are handled separately, either through a subsequent edition of the policy or an amendatory endorsement. As noted at the beginning of this Chapter, liberalization does not include changes made in the 2022 update if an insured is still covered under the prior 2011 edition.

If an insured wants to waive or change a policy provision, it must be in writing from the company in order to be valid. The insurer is not going to allow the insured to simply change the policy as he sees fit.

Cancellation and Nonrenewal

There are a number of cancellation provisions. The insured may cancel the policy in writing with a date of cancellation or may return the policy to the insurer. The insurer may cancel the policy but only for certain circumstances; the insurer is to give the insured notice a specified number of days in advance.

For nonpayment of premium, the insurer may cancel the policy with ten days' notice before the cancellation takes effect. If the policy has been in effect for less than sixty days and is not a renewal, then the insurer may cancel for any reason with ten days' notice. However, once the policy has been in effect for sixty days or more, or any time the policy is up for renewal, the insurer may cancel due to a material misrepresentation of fact that had the insurer known about it would not have issued the policy; or if the risk has changed substantially since the inception of the policy; under both situations notice must be thirty days before the cancellation takes effect. The same applies if the policy has been in force for more than one year; cancellation can occur at the anniversary date with thirty days' notice. Premium is refunded on a pro rata basis.

Nonrenewal works the same way, and thirty-day notice is required before the expiration of the policy. It is important to note that cancellation and non-renewal statutes vary widely from state to state. The provisions described here are generic and may not conform with state law. This issue is solved at policy issuance by adding a required amendatory endorsement which specifies the cancellation and nonrenewal laws applicable to the state where the insurance is procured.

Assignment, Subrogation and Death

The insured cannot assign the policy benefits to another party without written consent by the insurer. The insurer could be adopting a riskier insured than it wants to take on. While an insured may before a loss waive in writing all rights of recovery against another party, if the rights are not waived, the insurer may require an assignment of such rights of recovery for a loss to the extent of the payout made by the insurer. If the carrier requests such an assignment the insured must sign and deliver all related paperwork to the insurer and cooperate with them. Subrogation does not apply to Coverage F Medical Payments to Others or Damage to Property of Others.

The last policy condition concerns the death of the insured named in the declarations or the spouse, as long as the spouse is a resident of the household. The legal representative of the deceased will be covered by the policy but only with regard to the property and premises covered under the policy at the time of death. Insured's are considered to be residents of the household at the time of death but only while a resident at the residence premises, or the person having proper temporary custody of the property until appointment of a legal representative.

Summary

This concludes a review of the ISO HO 00 06 Unit Owners policy. While similar to the homeowners' policy there are some distinct differences that must be paid attention to. This policy must be reviewed in combination with the Association policy to ensure that there are no coverage gaps. That is what makes unit owners policies unique; the necessity to merge them with another policy in order to be sure the insured is properly covered for what he is responsible for insuring.

Chapter 4

ISO Condominium Association Form and Commercial Unit-Owners Coverage Form

The condominium concept has evolved into many different forms. The commercial condominium is one such form. With the condominium concept a success in the dwelling arena, it was not long before it was adapted to the world of commerce.

This chapter reviews the coverage afforded in the Condominium Association Coverage Form – CP 00 17 10 12. The chapter also examines the Commercial Unit-Owners Coverage Form – CP 00 18 10 12 against CP 00 17 10 12, in the following nine key areas:

- Covered Property—Building
- Covered Property—Business Personal Property
- Covered Property—Personal Property of Others
- Property Not Covered
- Additional Coverages
- Coverage Extensions
- Loss Conditions
- Additional Condition
- Definitions

The relationship between CP 00 17 and HO 00 06 is not very different from the relationship between CP 00 17 and CP 00 18.

CP 00 17 and CP 00 18 aim to do the same thing as CP 00 17 and HO 00 06, namely, to balance and detail boundaries, scope of coverage, and coverage responsibility, all within the context of the act. Therefore, the handling of condominium coverage requirements for commercial unit-owners is very similar to that of coverage for personal unit-owners.

CONDOMINIUM ASSOCIATION COVERAGE FORM, CP 00 17 10 12

This form is designed to cover buildings and structures that are jointly owned by all members of the condominium association. The first paragraph of the preamble cautions that various provisions in the policy restrict coverage and that the entire policy should be read carefully to determine rights and duties as well as what is and is not covered under the policy.

The second paragraph explains that "you" and "your" refer to the named insured shown in the declarations and that "we," "us," and "our" refer to the company providing the insurance.

The final paragraph of the preamble advises that other words and phrases that appear in quotation marks have special meaning, which are defined later in the policy. ISO denotes defined terms through quotations. You may see other proprietary forms due this using *italics* or **bold** font.

Coverage

Under the coverage section the insurer agrees to pay for direct physical loss of or damage to covered property at the premises described in the declarations as long as loss or damage is a result of a covered cause of loss.

The three key points in the coverage section are as follows:

- Payment is for direct physical loss or damage—indirect loss is not covered.
- The covered property must be at the location described in the declarations—if the covered property is not at the described location, no coverage applies.
- Loss must be from a covered cause of loss.

Covered Property—Building

Property covered under this section must be as described in this section A. 1., Covered Property and limited in section A.2., Property Not Covered provided a limit of insurance is shown in the Declarations for this type of property.

The section is designed to provide the boundaries around what is covered and what is not covered by the policy. To this end, a covered building includes the following:

- Completed additions
- Fixtures outside of individual units, including outdoor fixtures
- Permanently installed machinery and equipment
- Personal property like fire-extinguishing equipment, outdoor furniture, floor coverings, and appliances used for refrigerating, ventilating, cooking, dishwashing, or laundering. This type of property must be owned by the association, be used to maintain or service the building, and not be contained within individual units
- Additions under construction and alterations and repairs to the building or structure, if not covered by other insurance
- Materials, equipment, supplies, and temporary structures, on or within 100 feet of the described premises, used for making additions, alterations, or repairs to the building or structure, if not covered by other insurance
- Any of the following types of property contained within a unit regardless of ownership if the condominium association agreement requires the association to insure it:
    - Fixtures, improvements, and alterations that are part of the building or structure
    - Appliances such as those used for refrigerating, ventilating, cooking, dishwashing, laundering, security, or housekeeping.

A covered building does not include personal property owned by, used by, or in the care, custody, or control of a unit-owner.

The clarity of the boundaries delineating coverage provided by the policy is unmistakable from these descriptions.

Covered Property—Your Business Personal Property

The policy provides coverage for business personal property located in or upon the building or structure described in the declarations, in the open, or in a vehicle within 100 feet of the described premises. Such property consists of the following:

- Personal property owned by the association or owned indivisibly by all unit-owners.
- The association's interest in labor, materials, or services furnished or arranged by the association on personal property of others.
- Leased personal property for which the association has a contractual responsibility to insure unless otherwise provided for under the personal property of others section.

The policy also makes it clear that the association's business personal property does not include personal property owned only by a unit-owner, illustrating another boundary drawn.

Covered Property—Personal Property of Others

Personal property of others in the care, custody, or control of the association is afforded if located in or on the building or structure described in the declarations or in the open (or in a vehicle) within 100 feet of the described premises.

> It is important to note that personal property of others is not the individual unit owners property in the units. That is still the responsibility of the unit owner to insure. This coverage is for personal property of owners that is in the care, custody or control of the association. Property in the clubhouse for the community Christmas party, for example that the association allowed the unit owners to store there temporarily.

Payment for any covered loss, however, will only be for the owner of the property.

Property Not Covered

The excluded property under this section is typical of most multiperil or open perils policies. The exclusions are designed to limit exposure to certain types of property that are better covered under more specialized types of policies. Property not covered includes the following:

a. Accounts, bills, currency, food stamps or other evidences of debt, money, notes or securities. Lottery tickets held for sale are not securities;

These items are excluded because they can be better underwritten and covered under crime and inland marine policies.

b. Animals, unless owned by others and boarded by you;

c. Automobiles held for sale;

Automobiles held for sale would be more appropriately covered under some form of an automobile policy.

d. Bridges, roadways, walks, patios or other paved surfaces;

This type of property is more suitably insured under inland marine forms.

e. Contraband or property in the course of illegal transportation or trade;

The insurance contract is a contract enforceable by law and is subject to the law; therefore, it does not support any illegal activity or illegal commerce.

f. The cost of excavations, grading, backfilling or filling;

g. Foundations of buildings, structures, machinery or boilers if their foundations are below:

(1) The lowest basement floor; or

(2) The surface of the ground if there is no basement;

h. Land (including land on which the property is located), water, growing crops, or lawns (other than lawns that are part of a vegetated roof);

The 2012 revision to the form added the exception for lawns that are part of a vegetated roof, which are treated as a covered part of the building.

i. Personal property while airborne or waterborne;

Coverage for this property is better provided under an inland marine form.

j. Bulkheads, pilings, piers, wharves or docks;

Coverage for this property is better provided under a marine policy.

k. Property that is covered under this or any other policy in which it is more specifically described, except for the excess of the amount due (whether you can collect on it or not) from that other insurance;

l. Retaining walls that are not part of a building;

m. Underground pipes, flues or drains;

n. Electronic data, except as provided under the Additional Coverage, Electronic Data. Electronic data means information, facts or computer programs stored as or on, created or used on, or transmitted to or from computer software (including systems and applications software), on hard or floppy disks, CD-ROMs, tapes, drives, cells, data processing devices or any other repositories of computer software which are used with electronically controlled equipment. The term computer programs, referred to in the foregoing description of electronic data, means a set of related electronic instructions which direct the operations and functions of a computer or device connected to it, which enable the computer or device to receive, process, store, retrieve or send data. This paragraph, n., does not apply to electronic data which is integrated in and operates or controls the building's elevator, lighting, heating, ventilation, air conditioning or security system;

The wide-ranging definition of "electronic data" under this subsection speaks to the need for much better coverage for such items as is found under a specialized policy. Note that due to the age of this form, some terms (floppy disks) are not likely applicable given today's technology.

> Forms aren't changed unless there are significant changes in policy language or new coverages or perils that need to be addressed. It's not uncommon for endorsements to be used to make minor changes, so that changes to the actual form can be delayed until there are enough changes that warrant changing the forms and making filings with the state insurance departments.

The 2012 revision of the form removed electronic data that is integrated in or operates or controls the building's elevator, lighting, heating, ventilation, air conditioning, or security system from the property not covered section. Particularly in more modern condominium associations, this integration is very common.

o. The cost to replace or restore the information on valuable papers and records, including those which exist as electronic data. Valuable papers and records include but are not limited to proprietary information, books of account, deeds, manuscripts, abstracts, drawings and card index systems. Refer to the Coverage Extension for Valuable Papers And Records (Other Than Electronic Data) for limited coverage for valuable papers and records other than those which exist as electronic data;

The scope of the definition contained in this subsection is broad and extensive to exclude as many items as possible that could be considered valuable papers. The net result is to encourage the insured to seek coverage on a more specialized form.

p. Vehicles or self-propelled machines (including aircraft or watercraft) that

(1) Are licensed for use on public roads; or

(2) Are operated principally away from the described premises

This paragraph does not apply to:

(a) Vehicles or self-propelled machines or autos you manufacture or warehouse;

(b) Vehicles or self-propelled machines, other than autos, you hold for sale;

(c) Rowboats or canoes out of water at the described premises; or

(d) Trailers, but only to the extent provided for in the Coverage Extension for Non-owned Detached Trailers;

q. The following property while outside of buildings:

(1) Grain, hay, straw, or other crops; or

(2) Fences, radio or television antennas (including satellite dishes) and their lead-in wiring, masts or towers, trees, shrubs, or plants (other than trees, shrubs or plants which are "stock" or are part of a vegetated roof), all except as provided in the Coverage Extensions

Better coverage for these items would be provided under farm and inland marine policies.

Covered Causes of Loss

This section makes reference to the declarations as the place to find the applicable causes of loss form.

A policy written under the simplified language commercial property program of Insurance Services Office must incorporate one of three alternative causes of loss forms: basic, CP 10 10 10 12; broad, CP 10 20 10 12; or special, CP 10 30 10 12. The forms are differentiated by the scope of covered perils (referred to in the forms as causes of loss rather than perils) each provides. Basic and Broad are named perils forms. Special is an open perils form. There is also an endorsement available, form CP 10 40 10 12, which provides earthquake coverage for insureds who choose to add it to their policies. A number of optional endorsements are also available to modify the terms of the policy.

Basic Form CP 10 10 10 12

The basic form includes the following eleven causes of loss that are insured under the policy: fire, lightning, explosion, windstorm or hail, smoke, aircraft or vehicles, riot or civil commotion, vandalism, sprinkler leakage, sinkhole collapse, and volcanic action.

The term "fire" is not defined in any way. The courts have long interpreted the standard fire policy as covering only hostile fire, which is a fire that is out of bounds and threating life or property. For example, a fire within a furnace or stove fire box is considered friendly, and loss arising from it has typically not been held to be covered. Another example is personal property burned in a trash fire, which would not typically be considered covered for the fire damage to it. However, when the fire escapes its normal boundaries—such as when flames jump from a campfire to a forest or buildings—it is transformed into a hostile fire and resulting damage to covered property typically is covered.

Although "explosion" also is not defined, the coverage for damage caused by explosion is narrowed through two exclusions: neither explosion arising from the operation of pressure relief devices nor rupture due to expansion of the contents of any structure or its contents caused by water are covered.

> Included in the explosion peril is the explosion of gases or fuel within the furnace of any fired vessel, or within the flues or passages through which the combustion gases pass.

The windstorm or hail basic cause of loss does not encompass coverage for damage caused by frost or cold weather, or ice, snow, or sleet, even if driven by wind. Hail is considered distinct from ice in general. The exterior of a building or structure must be damaged by wind or hail before coverage is provided for damage to the building interior or its interior property by rain, snow, sand, or dust that enters the building or structure.

Smoke damage from agricultural smudging or industrial operations is not covered, although sudden and accidental damage to covered property by smoke is covered.

In addition to physical contact with an aircraft or vehicle, including a spacecraft or self-propelled missile, the aircraft cause of loss applies specifically to objects falling from aircraft and to objects thrown up by a vehicle. Damage by vehicles owned by the named insured or by vehicles operated in the course of the named insured's business is excluded.

Acts of striking employees occupying the described premises are covered under the riot or civil commotion cause of loss, as is looting at the time and place of a riot or civil commotion.

Vandalism includes willful and malicious damage to or destruction of the insured property. Building damage caused by the break-in or exit of burglars is covered, but other loss caused by or resulting from theft is excluded. For example, vandals break into a property and spray paint graffiti on the walls and otherwise damage the property. They also steal the copper pipes from the property. The damage caused by the breaking in of the vandals and the graffiti on the walls is covered, but the theft of the copper pipes is not since that is not vandalism, that is theft. Theft is not a covered peril.

Sprinkler leakage coverage is for leakage or discharge from an automatic sprinkler system. Automatic Sprinkler System is specifically defined and includes any automatic fire-protective or extinguishing system, including the following:

- Sprinklers and discharge nozzles
- Ducts, pipes, valves and fittings
- Tanks, including component parts and supports, and
- Pumps and private fire protection mains

If supplied from an automatic fire-protective system, the following are included:

- Non-automatic fire-protective systems and
- Hydrants, standpipes and outlets

Sinkhole collapse applies to the sudden sinking or collapse of land caused by the underground erosion of limestone or dolomite by water. The cost of filling the sinkhole itself is not covered. The form clarifies that sinkhole collapse coverage does not include those instances where the ground sinks or collapses into manmade cavities in the earth. This exposure is more appropriately the subject of mine subsidence coverage.

Volcanic action covers damage from the above-ground effects of a volcanic eruption—airborne blast and shock waves, ash, dust, particulate matter, and lava flow. It does not include, as detailed in the earth movement exclusion, the removal cost of volcanic ash or dust that has not physically damaged insured property, nor the seismic effects of a volcanic eruption. This covered peril also states that all volcanic eruptions within a 168-hour will constitute a single occurrence.

Broad Form CP 10 20 10 12

The broad form includes the same eleven as the basic, plus three additional causes of loss: falling objects; weight of snow, ice, or sleet; and water damage.

Loss or damage caused by falling objects to personal property in the open is not covered. There also is an exception to the falling objects cause of loss that precludes coverage for personal property within a structure or the interior of the structure itself unless the roof or an outside wall is first damaged by a falling object. Under this exception, there would be no coverage for damage to personal property located within a manufacturing plant if, for example, a piece of steel being lifted by a crane were dropped and crushed the personal property. In that instance, even though the piece of steel can be considered a falling object, the steel did not pierce a hole in the roof or an outside wall on its way down.

The weight of snow, ice, or sleet peril includes an exception for loss of or damage to personal property outside of buildings or structures that is caused by the weight of snow, ice, or sleet, and, with the 2012 form, loss or damage to lawns, trees, shrubs, or plants that are part of a vegetated roof. Property that is outside of the building or on the roof is naturally subject to the weather. Property that could be damaged by the weather should be stored inside.

Coverage under the water damage cause of loss applies to accidental discharge or leakage of water or steam when a system or appliance containing water or steam breaks or cracks. Water damage coverage does not encompass leakage or discharge from an automatic sprinkler system, which is the subject of coverage under a separate cause of loss. Water damage also does not include discharge or leakage from a sump and its related equipment, roof drains, gutters, downspouts, or similar fixtures and equipment. Also excluded is the cost to repair any defect that caused the loss or damage.

Damage from repeated leakage or seepage of water or the presence of condensation or humidity, moisture or vapor that occurs over a period of 14 days or more is excluded. The form does not specify that the damage must be sudden and accidental, but a leak that runs for over 14 days is a maintenance issue, and not something contemplated by the policy. Forms vary on the language regarding repeated leakage or seepage; the ISO form specifies 14 days, but many forms do not.

Freezing is also excluded unless the insured maintained heat in the building or drained the equipment and shut off the water if the heat is not maintained. While not specified in the policy, the heat should be left at 55 degrees or higher to avoid a loss.

Included as a covered part of water damage losses is the cost of tearing out and replacing part of the building or structure to repair damage to the system or appliance.

A general water exclusion is found elsewhere in the form; it excludes all other types of loss or damage caused by the items listed within it. The cause of loss for water damage must be read in conjunction with that exclusion.

Special Form CP 10 30 10 17

The special form is the broadest causes of loss form. It covers all causes of loss except those that are excluded or limited. This type of form is often referred to as "open perils." In rare instance, you may see or hear reference to an "all risk" form. The industry moved away from that reference many years ago since it sets up an expectation than "all" losses are covered. As is clearly specified in the Special Form, all losses are not covered, and the Special or Open Perils form should never be referred to as "all risk." In addition, with a Special Form, the legal burden is on the **insurer** to prove a loss is excluded. With named peril forms, the legal burden shifts to the **insured** to argue that a loss was caused by a covered peril.

Exclusions

There are eight exclusions comprising subsection B.1. of each of the three causes of loss forms. These exclusions operate to eliminate coverage as specified, regardless of other concurrent causes that contribute to the loss. The eight exclusions are ordinance or law; earth movement; governmental action; nuclear hazard; utility services; war and military action; water; and fungus, wet rot, dry rot, and bacteria.

Losses arising out of the enforcement of building laws or ordinances, including those that may require the demolition of damaged structures, are not covered.

All forms of earth movement, other than sinkhole collapse, which is specifically covered as a basic or broad cause of loss, are excluded from coverage. Ensuing fire or explosion damage is covered. The 2012 edition of the form added tremors and aftershocks as part of the term "earthquake." Also, language was added to the exclusion to make it clear that earth movement is excluded whether caused by acts of nature or otherwise. Also ruled out by the earth movement exclusion is loss caused by volcanic eruption, explosion, or effusion. Exempt from this part of the exclusion (and therefore covered) is ensuing fire damage and loss attributable to volcanic action—the above-ground effects of volcanic eruption—an insured cause of loss under the basic and broad forms.

Seizure or destruction of covered property as an act of governmental authority is not covered, except for destruction of property ordered to prevent the more general spread of fire when the fire itself would be a covered cause of loss.

The nuclear hazard exclusion eliminates coverage of loss by nuclear reaction, radiation, or radioactive contamination regardless of the cause. Ensuing fire loss is covered.

The failure of power, communication, water, or other utility service supplied to the described premises, however caused, is excluded if the failure originates away from the described premises or originates at the described premises, but only if the failure involves equipment used to supply the utility service to the described premises from a source away from the described premises. For example, a tree falls on the transformer down the street, causing a power outage at the insured's building. Failure includes lack of sufficient capacity and reduction in supply. Losses caused by surge—if the surge would not have occurred but for the power failure—are also excluded. However, if the failure or surge of power results in a covered cause of loss, there is coverage for damage from that cause. If the power surge causes a fire at the insured premises, then the fire is covered, even if the proximate cause is the excluded power surge.

The war and military action exclusion applies to three related causes of loss: war (including undeclared or civil war); warlike action by any governmental military force; and acts of insurrection, rebellion, revolution, or usurped power.

> War and related aggressive actions are always excluded. Such losses are generally catastrophic and cannot be predicted or rated for.

The water exclusion includes flood, surface water, waves (including tidal wave and tsunami), tides, tidal water, overflow of any body of water, or spray from any of these, all whether or not driven by wind (including storm surge); mudslide or mudflow; water that backs up or overflows or is otherwise discharged from a sewer, drain, sump, sump pump, or related equipment; water under the ground surface pressing on, or flowing or seeping through foundations, walls, floors, paved surfaces, basements—whether paved or not—doors, windows, or other openings; waterborne material carried or otherwise moved by any of the water—other than mudslide or mudflow—or material carried or otherwise moved by mudslide or mudflow. This is a particularly noteworthy exclusion since floods/water damage are among Earth's most common–and most destructive–natural hazards. No other kind of natural disaster in America has caused more death and destruction than floods. There are few places on Earth where flooding is not a concern. Developing a reasonable and accurate rate for flood damage is one of the large problems in providing flood coverage. Another is getting people to understand their flood risk and getting them to buy the coverage that exists.

The water exclusion applies whether caused by an act of nature or otherwise caused. If a dam ruptures and that water damages the premises, coverage is still excluded. But if fire, explosion, or sprinkler leakage results, that loss or damage is covered.

"Fungus" is defined as "any type or form of fungus, including mold or mildew, and any mycotoxins, spores, scents or by-products produced or released by fungi." There are two exceptions to the exclusion. There is coverage if the fungus, rot, or bacteria results from fire or lightning and to the extent that coverage is provided under the additional coverage for fungus, wet rot, dry rot, and bacteria.

The forms also contain exclusions not subject to the concurrent causation language, starting at B.2. The basic form contains exclusions for artificially generated electrical, magnetic, or electromagnetic energy damages, disturbances, disruptions, and interferences; rupture or bursting of water pipes; leakage or discharge of steam or water from an appliance; explosion of steam boilers, steam pipes, steam engines, or steam turbines; mechanical breakdown; and the insured's neglect to use reasonable means to protect property from further damage. The broad and special forms contain these exclusions, except for the rupture or bursting of pipes and leakage or discharge of steam or water from an appliance, which are covered on the broad form. The remainder of the special form exclusions are discussed in the next section. Steam boilers can (and should) be covered under a separate Machinery & Equipment Policy (sometimes referred to as "Boiler and Machinery").

The forms exclude "artificially generated electrical, magnetic, or electromagnetic energy that damages, disturbs, disrupts or otherwise interferes" with electrical and electronic wires, systems, and devices, appliances, systems, or networks that use cellular or satellite technology. These types of electrical damage are typically insured on equipment breakdown coverage forms. If fire results, there is coverage for the loss or damage cause by that fire.

Rupture or bursting of pipes is excluded unless caused by a covered cause of loss. Water pipes do not include automatic sprinkler systems.

If a leakage or discharge from a system containing water or steam results from a covered cause of loss, it is not excluded. Otherwise, it is not covered. Such appliances do not include automatic sprinkler systems.

If explosion of steam boilers, steam pipes, steam engines, or steam turbines results in fire or combustion explosion, that is covered.

Mechanical breakdown includes rupture or bursting caused by centrifugal force. If the mechanical breakdown results in a covered cause of loss, that is covered.

Even if damage by a cause of loss (such as artificially generated electrical current) is excluded, insureds must protect the property from further damage. So, for example, if artificially generated electrical current causes damage to electrical equipment, the insured must try to prevent that from developing into a fire by disconnecting the equipment from the electrical source.

In addition to the exclusions discussed under the basic and broad forms, the special form contains many other exclusions, including delay, loss of use, and loss of market; smoke, vapor, or gas from agricultural smudging or industrial operations; wear and tear; rust or other corrosion, decay, deterioration, hidden or latent defect or any quality in a property that causes it to damage or destroy itself; smog; settling, cracking, shrinking, or expansion; and nesting or infestation, or discharge or release of waste products or secretions, by insects, birds, rodents, or other animals.

Certain causes of loss are excluded for personal property: dampness or dryness of atmosphere, changes in or extremes in temperature, and marring or scratching.

If any of these excluded causes of loss results in a "specified cause of loss" (a defined term in the policy) or building glass breakage, that loss or damage is covered. This is sometimes referred to as an ensuing loss give-back. Specified causes of loss are fire; lightning; explosion; windstorm or hail; smoke; aircraft or vehicles; riot or civil commotion; vandalism; leakage from fire extinguishing equipment; sinkhole collapse; volcanic action; falling objects; weight of snow, ice, or sleet; and water damage (G. Definitions).

The special form also excludes continuous or repeated seepage or leakage of water, or the presence or condensation of humidity, moisture, or vapor. These must occur over a period of fourteen or more days.

Loss or damage caused by water, other liquids, powder, or molten material that leaks from a plumbing, heating, air conditioning, or other equipment is excluded if caused by freezing. Fire protective systems are not included, and the exclusion does not apply if the insured does his best to maintain heat in the building or drains the equipment and shuts off the supply if heat is not maintained.

The special form contains an exclusion for dishonest or criminal acts committed by the named insured, partners, employees, directors, trustees, or authorized representatives of the named insured, or anyone to whom the named insured entrusts covered property, which was revised in 2012 to distinguish among partners, employees, and others who have a role in the insured's business and those to whom property was entrusted, such as bailees and tenants.

A related exclusion rules out coverage for voluntary parting losses. It applies to loss of property with which the named insured has been induced to part voluntarily by any fraudulent scheme, trick, device, or false pretense. You may sometimes see or hear this referred to as "theft by trickery."

Also applicable to personal property is an exclusion for loss or damage caused by rain, snow, ice, or sleet if such property is left in the open. Losses are preventable by not leaving such property outside exposed to the weather; an insured is expected to take reasonable care of his property. Collapse is excluded, unless the collapse results in a Covered Cause of Loss at the described premises. There are also two other exceptions to the exclusion for collapse. The exclusion does not apply to the coverage provided by the form's additional coverage for collapse (discussed in the next section), and it does not apply if the collapse is caused by any of the specified causes of loss, the breakage of building glass, the weight of rain that collected on a roof, or the weight of people or personal property.

Discharge, dispersal, seepage, migration, release, or escape of pollutants is excluded unless caused by a specified cause of loss. Resulting specified causes of loss are also covered. Damage to glass caused by chemicals applied to the glass is not part of this exclusion.

Neglect of an insured to use all reasonable means to save and preserve property from further damage at and after the time of loss it excluded. Insureds are expected to take care of property after a loss and do what they can to prevent further damage.

The following causes of loss are excluded, but if they result in a covered cause of loss, that loss is covered: weather conditions that contribute in any way to excluded causes of loss; acts or decisions, including the failure to act or decide; faulty, inadequate, or defective planning, zoning, development, surveying, siting, design, specifications, workmanship, repair, construction, renovation, remodeling, grading, compaction, materials used in repair, construction, renovation or remolding, or maintenance of part or all of any property on or off the described premises.

There are three special exclusions that apply only to the specified coverage forms; they are exclusions for Business Income and Extra Expense, Leasehold Interest, and Legal Liability.

The exclusion for Business Income and Extra Expense states that coverage is not provided for loss caused by damage or destruction to "finished stock" or the time to reproduce said stock. This does not apply to extra expense coverage. Also excluded is loss caused by damage to radio or television antennas, their lead-in wiring or mast towers; any increase of loss caused by or resulting from delay in rebuilding, repairing or replacing property or resuming operations, or the suspension, lapse or cancellation of any lease. If that suspension, lapse or cancellation is the direct result of the "suspension" of "operations" then any loss that affects the business income during the "period of restoration" will be covered in accordance with the optional coverage.

Extra Expense caused by or resulting from the suspension, lapse or cancellation of a license, lease or contract beyond the "period of restoration" is excluded. Likewise any other consequential losses are excluded as well.

The exclusion that applies to the Leasehold Interest Coverage form excludes coverage for losses caused by cancellation, suspension, or lapse of any lease or other consequential losses. The Ordinance or Law coverage provided in B.1.a. does not apply to the Leasehold Interest Coverage form.

Certain exclusions do not apply under the Legal Liability Coverage form; those exclusions are the ordinance or law, governmental action, nuclear hazard, utility services, and war and military action. Two exclusions are added, one for contractual liability that states there is no coverage for defense of any claim or suit for damages the insured is legally liable to pay based solely on assumption of liability in a signed contract or agreement. The exclusion does not apply to contracts where the insured assumed liability for building damage from an actual or attempted burglary or robbery as long as the contract was executed before the attempted robbery and the building is covered under the policy form.

The second exclusion is for nuclear hazard; no defense will be provided for any claim or suit, and damages for losses, expenses or any obligations as a result of nuclear reaction, radiation, radioactive contamination, however caused will not be covered.

There is one last additional exclusion. Loss or damage to merchandise, goods, or other products caused by or resulting from an error or omission by any person or entity in any stage of development, production, or use of the product is excluded. If the error or omission results in a covered cause of loss, that is covered

Additional Coverages on the Causes of Loss Forms

Collapse is covered under broad and special forms CP 10 20 and CP 10 30 not as a cause of loss but as an additional coverage. The term "abrupt" is frequently used to reinforce that coverage applies only to collapses that are abrupt in nature. A building or any part of it that is in imminent danger of collapsing does not qualify as a collapse for purposes of this additional coverage. The forms also require that the building or part of the building must be uninhabitable because of the abrupt collapse in order to qualify for coverage. For example, two walls of a building are bowing inward, cracking and sagging. Such a situation does not qualify as collapse, even though collapse seems imminent. The walls must have abruptly caved in or collapsed abruptly in order to qualify for this additional coverage.

An annual aggregate amount of $15,000 is available for fungus, wet rot, dry rot, and bacteria that results from a "specified cause of loss" except fire, lightning, or flood (if flood insurance is purchased). However, the $15,000 is a lifetime limit for mold caused by the same event. The exception for such damage arising from "specified causes of loss" or flood is provided so that the additional coverage dovetails with the parallel exclusion. The 2012 edition of the form added that the additional coverage does not apply to lawns, trees, shrubs, or plants that are part of a vegetated roof. Also, the coverage provided under this Limited Coverage does not increase the applicable Limit of Insurance on any Covered Property.

Limitations on the Causes of Loss Forms

The basic and broad forms add a series of limitations to the policy in three sections. The first section applies limitations to the policy and all endorsements. Coverage for losses involving certain perils or certain kinds of property is further modified under the special form by a set of limitations. These limitations must be read in conjunction with the form's exclusions to fully comprehend how the broad coverage this form provides is tempered.

The special form states that loss or damage to steam boilers, steam pipes, steam engines, or steam turbines caused by any condition or event inside such equipment is excluded except for loss or damage caused by or resulting from an explosion of gas or fuels within the furnace or any fired vessel or within the flues or passages that the gases of combustion pass. Loss or damage to hot water boilers and other water heating equipment is excluded, but an exception is made for explosion.

Loss or damage to the interior of any building or structure or to personal property in buildings or structures is excluded if caused by rain, snow, sleet, ice, sand, or dust unless the building or structure first sustains damage by a covered cause of loss to its roof or walls that allows these substances in or results from thawing of snow, sleet, or ice on the building or structure.

Theft of building materials and supplies not attached as part of the building or structure is excluded unless held for sale by the insured (unless insured under builders risk coverage).

There is no coverage for missing property where the only evidence of loss or damage is a shortage disclosed when taking inventory or if there is no physical evidence to show what happened to the property.

Loss or damage to property that has been transferred to a person or place outside the described premises on the basis of unauthorized instructions is not covered.

Loss or damage to the trees, lawns, shrubs, or plants that make up a vegetated roof are not covered for the following causes of loss: dampness or dryness of atmosphere or of soil supporting the vegetation; changes in or extremes in temperature; disease; frost or hail; or rain, snow, ice, or sleet.

Certain categories of property are covered under the special form only if the cause of loss is the "specified causes of loss" or building glass breakage. These categories are animals if killed or their destruction made necessary by the effect of breakage of building glass or one of the specified causes of loss; fragile articles other than glass or containers of property held for sale; and builders' machinery, tools, and equipment owned by or entrusted to the named insured and away from the insured premises, unless the property is located on or within 100 feet of the described premises, unless insured under the Builders Risk Coverage Form.

The next set of limitations on the special form places maximum dollar amounts on theft coverage for enumerated types of property. The special form, unlike the basic and broad forms, covers theft losses unless theft has been specifically excluded by endorsement. For this reason, form CP 10 30 applies these internal limits to property that may be considered particularly attractive to thieves: $2,500 on furs, including fur and fur-trimmed garments; $2,500 on jewelry, watches, precious metals, and similar property other than worth less than $100 per item; $2,500 on patterns, dies, molds, and forms; and $250 on stamps, tickets (including lottery tickets held for sale), and letters of credit. The question of whether "stamps" includes philatelic items or collections is not addressed. Each of these categories of property may be more specifically insured under one of several commercial inland marine forms. The loss of other types of property—such as business furnishings, manufacturing or building materials, and electronic equipment—is covered per policy limits for theft unless specifically limited or excluded by endorsement.

The final set of limitations on the special form involves damage to systems or appliances from which liquid, powder, or molten material escapes. There is no coverage for damage to the appliance or system unless it involves fire extinguishing equipment and special circumstances. The special form thus conforms to the basic and broad forms, which provide coverage for sprinkler leakage as a basic cause of loss. On those forms, the sprinkler system will be repaired under the same circumstances as in the special form—if the sprinkler discharges its fire protection substance or if the loss is directly caused by freezing.

Special Form Additional Coverage Extensions

The special form offers coverage extensions to the insured dealing with property in transit, liquid damage, and glass.

The property in transit coverage applies to covered personal property and is limited to certain causes of loss and to a maximum of $5,000. If the insured wants an open perils type coverage for property in transit, an inland marine form needs to be purchased. Damage must be from fire, lightning, explosion, windstorm, hail, riot, civil commotion, vandalism; vehicle collision upset or overturn, but collision does not mean contact with roadbed; theft of an entire bale, case or package if the vehicle is broken into by forced entry.

As for the liquid damage coverage extension, the form offers to pay the cost to tear out and replace any part of the building or structure that is needed in order to repair the damage to the system or appliance from which the liquid escaped. So, if the damaged appliance is behind a wall in the covered building, this clause removes the uncertainty as to whether the insurer will pay to have the wall torn out when it is necessary to do so in order to get at the appliance and fix it. This extension is tied to covered water/liquid damage. The extension must be read in conjunction with the water damage exclusion and the definition of "water damage."

The glass coverage extension notes that the insurer will pay for boarding up openings if repair or replacement of damaged glass is delayed. This is meant to lessen the threat that the interior of the covered building and property in the building will be damaged or lost. Also covered is the cost to remove or replace obstructions when repairing glass that is part of a building. Window displays are not included as part of removing obstacles.

The amounts paid under both the liquid damage extension and the glass extension are within the limits of insurance. The amount for the property in transit extension is in addition to the limits of insurance.

Now that we have reviewed the separate causes of loss forms, we return to the condominium association coverage form. We pick up with a discussion on additional coverages.

Additional Coverages

Debris Removal

Debris removal is a perennial challenge in loss settlement. Where damage or destruction has occurred to the extent that it generates debris, the debris must be removed before construction or reconstruction can begin. The challenge for the insured is how to assess the cost of such debris removal at the beginning of the policy when the future costs of debris removal are unknown. Since the allocated amount of debris removal comes from the amount of insurance shown for the insured property, the insured has the added challenge of making sure that the limit of insurance covers the replacement cost of the property including costs for debris removal.

The insurance company also has a challenge: how to ensure that the coverage offered is limited to the clearing away of debris from damaged or destroyed property, without having its coverage intent interpreted to include pollutants. The policy is therefore crafted to take care of these concerns and challenges.

The policy states:

> (1) Subject to Paragraphs (2), (3) and (4), we will pay your expense to remove debris of Covered Property and other debris that is on the described premises, when such debris is caused by or results from a Covered Cause of Loss that occurs during the policy period. The expenses will be paid only if they are reported to us in writing within 180 days of the date of direct physical loss or damage.

In the 2012 form revision, the coverage for debris removal was expanded to include removal of debris of property of others. With this expanded coverage, ISO also created a more explicit list of items that are not covered by the debris removal additional coverage.

> (2) Debris Removal does not apply to costs to:
>
> (a) Remove debris of property of yours that is not insured under this policy, or property in your possession that is not Covered Property;
>
> (b) Remove any property that is Property Not Covered, including property addressed under the Outdoor Property Coverage Extension;
>
> (c) Remove property of others of a type that would not be Covered Property under this Coverage Form;
>
> (d) Remove deposits of mud or earth from the grounds of the described premises;
>
> (e) Extract "pollutants" from land or water; or
>
> (f) Remove, restore or replace polluted land or water.

The policy is not meant to cover debris of property that would not be covered, either the insured's or property of others. It is also clear that the policy is not meant to be a pollution policy.

As previously stated, the insured faces challenges in establishing a high enough insurance limit to take care of both debris removal and construction or reconstruction. In the subsection that follows, the form states how it will handle such payments:

> (3) Subject to the exceptions in Paragraph (4), the following provisions apply:
>
> (a) The most we will pay for the total of direct physical loss or damage plus debris removal expense is the Limit of Insurance applicable to the Covered Property that has sustained loss or damage.
>
> (b) Subject to (a) above, the amount we will pay for debris removal expense is limited to 25% of the sum of the deductible plus the amount that we pay for direct physical loss or damage to the Covered Property that has sustained loss or damage. However, if no Covered Property has sustained direct physical loss or damage, the most we will pay for removal of debris of other property (if such removal is covered under this Additional Coverage) is $5,000 at each location.

The most the insurer will pay for direct physical loss or damage plus debris removal is the limit of insurance applicable to the covered property. However, the 2012 revision, while adding coverage for the removal of debris of the property of others, also stated that—even if no covered property has sustained direct physical loss or damage—the policy will pay $5,000 at each location for removal of debris of other property.

The amount the insurer will pay for debris removal expense is 25 percent of the sum of the deductible plus the amount paid for direct physical loss or damage.

The need for adequate limits of insurance to take care of loss settlement under this coverage is critical. In recognition of the challenge of setting adequate limits and the potential limit deficit upon the occurrence of a loss, the policy builds in a buffer that would help the insured by affording an additional $25,000 of coverage if one or both of the following circumstances apply:

> (4) (a) The total of the actual debris removal expense plus the amount we pay for direct physical loss or damage exceeds the limit of insurance on the covered property that has sustained loss or damage.
>
> (b) The actual debris removal expense exceeds 25% of the sum of the deductible plus the amount that we pay for direct physical loss or damage to the covered property that has sustained loss or damage.

If either one or both of these circumstances apply, the insurer's maximum liability for direct physical loss or damage and debris removal expense will be the limit of insurance on the covered property, plus $25,000. That buffer could prove helpful to many insureds.

Preservation of Property

If it is necessary for the insured to move covered property to protect it from direct loss or damage by a covered cause of loss, the policy makes provisions for coverage. It will protect the covered property while it is being moved or while temporarily stored at another location. Coverage is provided for a maximum thirty days after the property is first moved.

This coverage provision rewards the insured for taking such action that has the potential to limit the insurer's liability since the absence of such action on the part of the insured could result in a higher loss payment by the insurer. It's important to note that any physical damage or loss is covered; not just from the covered perils, but any loss. Therefore, if an excluded peril damages the property while it has been removed for safekeeping, there is coverage.

Fire Department Service Charge

If the insured is required to pay fire department charges, either by contract or agreement prior to loss, or as a result of local ordinance, the policy will pay $1,000 for service at each described premises, unless a higher amount is shown in the declarations.

The 2012 form revision added that the limit is the most that will be paid, regardless of the number of responding fire departments or units or the number of types of services performed.

No deductible applies to this additional coverage.

Pollutant Clean-Up and Removal

Under the debris removal additional coverage, the policy excludes pollution in order to clearly define what is considered debris as well as debris removal expense. Here, pollution coverage is afforded the insured, subject to the following conditions:

- The expense must be for the extraction of pollutants from land or water from the described premises.

- A covered cause of loss must cause the pollutants to discharge, disperse, seep, migrate, release, or escape.

- The covered cause of loss must occur during the policy period.

- The expenses will be paid if they are reported in writing within 180 days of the date on which the covered cause of loss occurs.

- While the policy will pay for testing that is performed in the course of extracting the pollutants from land or water, expenses for testing, monitoring, or assessing the existence, concentration, or effects of pollutants will not be covered.

The policy will pay an aggregate of $10,000 during each separate twelve-month period of the policy.

The pollution expense exclusion under the debris removal additional coverage and its inclusion here, albeit in a modest amount, helps the insurer strike a balance between the coverage it is willing to offer and the extent of that coverage.

Increased Cost of Construction

In order for this additional coverage to apply, the replacement cost option must be purchased. Coverage will apply to the increased cost to repair, rebuild, or replace damaged parts of the insured property if ordinance or law creates such additional cost. The form promises to pay only the minimum standards of an ordinance or law.

The ordinance or law must regulate the construction or repair of buildings or establish zoning or land use requirements at the described premises. It must also be in force at the time of loss.

There is, however, no coverage for costs related to an ordinance or law that the insured was required to comply with before the loss, even when the building was undamaged and the insured failed to comply with said ordinance.

Under this additional coverage, no costs associated with the enforcement of or compliance with any ordinance or law that requires demolition, repair, replacement, reconstruction, remodeling, or remediation of property by pollutants, or due to the presence, growth, proliferation, spread, or any activity of fungus, wet or dry rot, or bacteria are covered. Nor is there coverage for costs that require the insured or others to test for, monitor, clean up, remove, contain, treat, detoxify or neutralize, or in any way respond to, or assess the effects of pollutants, fungus, wet or dry rot, or bacteria.

The extent and scope of the exclusions shows that the policy is not intending to cover pollution.

The maximum limit of coverage available under this additional coverage is $10,000 or 5 percent of the limit of insurance applicable to that building, whichever is less. If the building is part of a blanket limit of coverage, then the amount payable is the lesser of $10,000 or 5 percent of the value of the damaged building at the time of loss multiplied by the applicable coverage percentage. The amount payable under this this Additional Coverage is additional insurance.

The additional coverage reflects some conditions that are typical of any replacement cost endorsement, such as:

- Payment will not be made until the repairs or replacement have actually been made.

- There will be no payment unless repairs or replacement are made as soon as reasonably possible after the loss or damage, not to exceed two years. A written extension may be permitted by the insurer.

- The insured has the option to repair or replace the building at the same premises or at another premises. If the insured elects to rebuild at another premises, the increased cost paid will be that which would apply at the described premises.

- If the ordinance or law requires relocation to another premises, the maximum payable for the increased cost will be the increased cost at the new premises.

If there is conflict between this coverage and the ordinance or law exclusion, then this additional coverage is not subject to the exclusion.

This is the only section that covers increased costs due to ordinance or law. It emphasizes this by referencing the loss payment, valuation, and replacement cost optional coverage wording, which exclude increased cost coverage due to ordinances or laws. Additionally, any limitation regarding increased cost of construction due to ordinance or law coverage wording does not apply to this additional coverage.

Electronic Data

This additional coverage provides limited electronic data coverage. It restricts coverage in a way that limits the insurer's exposure. If the insured has a sizeable exposure, it would find more suitable coverage under a form such as an electronic data processing policy.

This additional coverage section will pay the cost to replace or restore electronic data that has been destroyed or corrupted by a covered cause of loss. If electronic data is not replaced, the loss will be valued at the cost to replace the media on which the electronic data was stored, with blank media of substantially identical type.

The form contains variations on how coverage would apply under your business personal property, depending on which causes of loss form is used or is endorsed to add a covered cause of loss. These checks and balances within coverage application coupled with the $2,500 aggregate limit speak to the insurer's desire to control exposures related to this additional coverage.

Because the 2012 form revision added an exception for electronic data that is integrated in and operates or controls the building's elevator, lighting, heating, ventilation air conditioning, or security systems, those items are not included in this additional coverage.

Coverage Extensions

The form contains coverage extensions that apply to property located in or on the described building or in the open or in a vehicle within 100 feet of the described premises. The extensions apply if a coinsurance percentage of 80 percent or more is shown in the declarations.

Newly Acquired Or Constructed Property

(1) Buildings

You may extend the insurance that applies to Building to apply to:

(a) Your new buildings while being built on the described premises; and

(b) Buildings you acquire at locations, other than the described premises, intended for:

(i) Similar use as the building described in the Declarations; or

(ii) Use as a warehouse.

The most we will pay for loss or damage under this Extension is $250,000 at each building.

The insured may acquire new buildings or buy new buildings in the course of everyday commerce. The insured may not always remember to advise its agent or request coverage for the new buildings or new acquisitions. This coverage extension affords the insured peace of mind by providing protection.

Key to the extension, in addition to the coinsurance requirement, is that the buildings must be for similar use as described in the declarations or used as a warehouse. It is the insurer's way of protecting the exposures it wishes to assume. By incorporating these two conditions, it is ensuring that it will be dealing with known exposures similar to the ones already being covered.

(2) Your Business Personal Property

(a) If this policy covers Your Business Personal Property, you may extend that insurance to apply to:

(i) Business personal property, including such property that you newly acquire, at any location you acquire other than at fairs, trade shows or exhibitions; or

(ii) Business personal property, including such property that you newly acquire, located at your newly constructed or acquired buildings at the location described in the Declarations.

The most we will pay for loss or damage under this Extension is $100,000 at each building

(b) This Extension does not apply to:

(i) Personal property of others that is temporarily in your possession in the course of installing or performing work on such property; or

(ii) Personal property of others that is temporarily in your possession in the course of your manufacturing or wholesaling activities.

Again, checks and balances are applied to limit an insurer's exposure, evidenced by exclusions at fairs, trade shows, or exhibitions to exclusions relating to personal property of others.

In addition to the coverage scope limitations, the policy adds a time limit on when coverage will apply, namely

- When the policy expires
- Thirty days after the property is acquired or construction has begun
- Values are reported to the insurer

Insurers do not want to be responsible for too many unknown exposures. As a result, limitations are put in place to ensure that any unknown exposures are limited. And even as they extend coverage to facilitate the insured carrying on business as effortlessly as possible, they ensure that they receive a charge for the exposures they assume as follows:

> We will charge you additional premium for values reported from the date you acquire the property or begin construction of that part of the building that would qualify as covered property.

Personal Effects and Property of Others

It is common practice for employees to have personal property on the premises of their place of employment; from extra clothes to cell phones. The policy recognizes this reality and affords coverage under the policy, to a limit of $2,500.

It also stipulates that payment for losses under this subsection would be directly to the owner of the property. This both simplifies the payment process and ensures that payment is received by the owner of the property.

Valuable Papers and Records (Other Than Electronic Data)

Coverage is extended to cover the cost to replace or restore the lost information on valuable papers and records for which duplicates do not exist. This last statement reflects the reason for the limited coverage applicable under this section. If the limits are high, insurers would usually require duplicates of valuable papers be stored at a site other than the described location. Given the low limit of coverage provided here ($2,500), the insurer is willing to forego the duplicate requirement. Again, this is a way of controlling exposure to loss. If more specialized coverage is required, the insured would be wise to obtain coverage on an inland marine valuable papers and records form.

The policy also responds in ways applicable to the type of causes of loss form that applies to the policy, whether that is the special form or the broad form.

Property Off-Premises

In keeping with the intent of reflecting the realities of current-day businesses, the policy responds to off-premises coverage as follows:

d. Property Off-premises

(1) You may extend the insurance provided by this Coverage Form to apply to your Covered Property while it is away from the described premises, if it is:

(a) Temporarily at a location you do not own, lease or operate;

(b) In storage at a location you lease, provided the lease was executed after the beginning of the current policy term; or

(c) At any fair, trade show or exhibition.

(2) This Extension does not apply to property:

(a) In or on a vehicle; or

(b) In the care, custody or control of your salespersons, unless the property is in such care, custody or control at a fair, trade show or exhibition.

(3) The most we will pay for loss or damage under this Extension is $10,000.

The extension is crafted in part to ensure that the exposures being covered are in a location temporarily or did not exist when the policy was put in place. The exclusion to the extension is for property that is difficult to cover and for which the policy was not designed. The exclusion is for property in or on vehicles or in the possession of salespersons unless at a fair or trade show.

Outdoor Property

Coverage is extended to outdoor property like fences, radio and television antennas (including satellite dishes), trees, shrubs, and plants, including debris removal expense for losses caused by fire, lightning, explosion, riot or civil commotion, or aircraft. Trees, shrubs, or plants that are stock—as well as those that are part of a vegetated roof—are not included as part of this extension.

Scope of coverage is limited by both the named causes of loss and by the $1,000 limit, with a maximum of $250 for any one tree. The coverage includes the expense of removing debris of trees, shrubs, or plants that are the property of others.

Non-owned Detached Trailers

Coverage for non-owned trailers applies if:

- The trailer is used in the insured's business.
- The trailer is in the insured's care, custody, or control at the premises described in the declarations.
- The insured has a contractual responsibility to pay for loss or damage to the trailer.

The policy will not respond while the trailer is attached to any motor vehicle or motorized conveyance, whether or not the conveyance is in motion. Nor will it respond during hitching or unhitching or when a trailer becomes accidentally unhitched from a motor vehicle.

The crafting of this section attempts to define what is truly automobile coverage and what is coverage under this policy so as not to pick up any automobile exposures.

The coverage is excess coverage and is limited to $5,000. A higher limit can be purchased as on option and shown in the Declarations.

Business Personal Property Temporarily in Portable Storage Units

In the 2012 form revision, ISO added this coverage extension to address property that is beyond the reach of the business personal property coverage grant of personal property in the open or in a vehicle within 100 feet of the described premises.

This extension provides coverage for up to ninety days for business personal property that is temporarily stored in a portable storage unit within 100 feet of the described premises. A detached trailer is considered a portable storage unit under this coverage. Even if the property has not been in the storage unit for ninety days, if the unit has been on the premises more than ninety days, coverage does not apply to its contents.

No matter how many storage units are located within 100 feet of the described premises, the limit is $10,000. This is additional insurance and higher limits are available.

Exclusions and Limitations

Exclusions and limitations are contained in the applicable causes of loss form.

Limits of Insurance

The maximum amount payable for loss or damage in any one occurrence is the applicable limit shown in the declarations. The most that will be paid for loss or damage to outdoor signs, whether the sign is attached to a building, is $2,500 per sign in any one occurrence.

Additionally, under the following coverages, the limits are separate from the limit of insurance:

- Fire Department Service Charge
- Pollutant Clean-up And Removal
- Increased Cost Of Construction
- Electronic Data

Also, payments made under the preservation of property additional coverage will not increase the applicable limit of insurance.

Deductible

The deductible is applied on an occurrence basis. If an occurrence involves loss to more than one item of Covered Property, and separate limits apply, the losses will not be combined and the deductible will be applied only once per occurrence. In any one occurrence, the amount of the loss is first reduced if required by the coinsurance condition or the agreed value optional coverage. If the adjusted amount of loss is less than or equal to the deductible, the loss will not be paid.

If the adjusted amount of the loss exceeds the deductible, then the insurer will subtract the deductible from the adjusted amount of the loss and pay the remaining amount of loss or limit of insurance, whichever is less.

Loss Conditions

Abandonment: the insured cannot abandon the damaged or destroyed property to the insurer. Control of the property will be maintained by the insured until a determination about settlement and disposition of the property is made by the insurer.

Appraisal: where there is disagreement about the value of the property or the amount of loss, either party (the insured or the insurer) may make written demand for an appraisal of the loss.

In this event, each party selects a competent and impartial appraiser. The two appraisers select an umpire. If the two appraisers cannot agree on an umpire, a judge of a court having jurisdiction may be requested to select one.

The appraisers separately state the value of the property and amount of loss. If they fail to agree, they must submit their differences to the umpire. A decision agreed to by any two is binding.

Each party pays its chosen appraiser and bears the other expenses of the appraisal and the umpire equally.

Even if there is an appraisal, the insurer still retains its right to deny the claim.

This process is a fair and equitable approach to dispute resolution under the policy.

The insured must fulfill eight requirements in order to collect following a loss:

3. Duties In The Event Of Loss Or Damage

    a. You must see that the following are done in the event of loss or damage to Covered Property:

        (1) Notify the police if a law may have been broken.

        (2) Give us prompt notice of the loss or damage. Include a description of the property involved.

        (3) As soon as possible, give us a description of how, when and where the loss or damage occurred.

(4) Take all reasonable steps to protect the covered property from further damage, and keep a record of your expenses necessary to protect the covered property, for consideration in the settlement of the claim. This will not increase the Limit of Insurance. However, we will not pay for any subsequent loss or damage resulting from a cause of loss that is not a Covered Cause of Loss. Also, if feasible, set the damaged property aside and in the best possible order for examination.

(5) At our request, give us complete inventories of the damaged and undamaged property. Include quantities, costs, values and amount of loss claimed.

(6) As often as may be reasonably required, permit us to inspect the property proving the loss or damage and examine your books and records.

Also, permit us to take samples of damaged and undamaged property for inspection, testing and analysis, and permit us to make copies from your books and records.

(7) Send us a signed, sworn proof of loss containing the information we request to investigate the claim. You must do this within 60 days after our request. We will supply you with the necessary forms.

(8) Cooperate with us in the investigation or settlement of the claim.

The duties required of the insured are designed to do many things, such as:

- guard against fraudulent claims by requiring the insured to report possible illegal activity to the police.
- facilitate prompt settlement—the sooner the insurer knows about the loss, the sooner it will be able to handle it.
- validate that the property damaged or destroyed is indeed the insured property and that the damage or destruction was caused by a covered cause of loss.
- fulfill its responsibility to preserve insured property.
- ensure proper valuation of property lost or destroyed.
- allow for proof of loss or damage through examination of books and records.

- attest to the all conditions surrounding the loss through the submission of a signed proof of loss submitted to the insurer within sixty days of the insurer's request to furnish said proof of loss.

The insurer may also examine any insured under oath about any matter relating to the insurance claim. In the event of an examination, the insured's answers must be signed.

Such ironclad loss requirements ensure that the utmost good faith principle underlying the insurance agreement is underpinned by a rigorous process.

4. Loss Payment

   a. In the event of loss or damage covered by this Coverage Form, at our option, we will either:

      (1) Pay the value of lost or damaged property;

      (2) Pay the cost of repairing or replacing the lost or damaged property, subject to b. below;

      (3) Take all or any part of the property at an agreed or appraised value; or

      (4) Repair, rebuild or replace the property with other property of like kind and quality, subject to b. below.

Where the insurer has elected to repair, rebuild, or replace damaged or destroyed property, such cost would not include the increased cost attributable to the enforcement of or compliance with any ordinance or law. If the insured requires such coverage, that coverage could be purchased using CP 04 05 – Ordinance or Law Coverage.

The insurer will give the insured notice of its intentions within thirty days following receipt of a sworn proof of loss from the insured.

The insurer will pay no more than the insured's financial interest in the covered property. This reinforces the principle of indemnity that is central to the coverage provided. Additionally, it minimizes any occasion for fraud.

This subsection reinforces the coverage extension made under the personal property of others subsection, which extends coverage to property of others in the care, custody, or control of the insured. Here, the insurer emphasizes that payment for loss will be only to the owner of the property, a sentiment that is reiterated in the current subsection:

   e. We may adjust losses with the owners of lost or damaged property if other than you. If we pay the owners, such

> payments will satisfy your claims against us for the owners' property. We will not pay the owners more than their financial interest in the Covered Property.

The insurer exercises its option to settle directly with the owners of the property for their financial interest only, thereby satisfying any claim by the insured against the company for such loss.

At its option, the insurer elects to defend any suit brought against the insured by third parties whose property has been damaged or destroyed. If the insurer elects to defend the insured, it will bear the cost of such suits.

The insurer confirms its commitment to pay covered losses within thirty days of the insured filing a sworn proof of loss and complying with all terms under this coverage part. Additionally, the payment will be made if agreement is reached with the insured on the amount of the loss or if an appraisal award has been made.

In keeping with the act, if an insurance trustee is named, the insurer will adjust the loss with the insured but will pay the insurance trustee. Upon making such payment, all claims against the insurer will have been satisfied.

The policy addresses the situation where the insured shares a party wall—a wall that separates and is common to adjoining buildings—that separates buildings owned by different parties.

Where both building owners plan to repair or rebuild, the policy would pay its proportionate share of the damage to the party wall. Where the insured wants to rebuild but the other owner does not, the insurer will pay the full value of the party wall, subject to all applicable policy provisions, with the right to subrogate against the adjoining building owner.

Recovered Property

If either the insurer or the insured were to recover any property after loss settlement, that party must give the other prompt notice. At the insured's option, the property will be returned to it.

If the insured exercises this option, it must return the amount already received from the insurer for the property. Returning the property to the insurer will satisfy the principle of indemnity, as the insured is not allowed to profit from any loss.

Unit-Owner's Insurance

This provision supports the act's requirement that the association policy be primary.

Vacancy

This provision first defines the terms "building" and "vacant."

For a tenant, "building" means the unit or suite rented or leased to the tenant. Such building is vacant when it does not contain enough business personal property to conduct customary operations.

For the building owner or general lessee, "building" means the entire building. Such building is vacant unless at least 31 percent of its total square footage is rented to a lessee or sublessee to conduct its customary operations or used by the building owner to conduct customary operations.

The provision emphasizes that buildings under construction or renovation are not considered vacant.

The vacancy provisions point out the losses that will not be paid if the building where loss or damage occurs has been vacant for more than sixty consecutive days. The following causes of loss are excluded:

- Vandalism
- Sprinkler leakage, unless the insured protected the system against freezing
- Building glass breakage
- Water damage
- Theft
- Attempted theft

With respect to covered causes of loss other than those listed, the insurer will reduce the amount it would otherwise pay for loss or damage by 15 percent.

The exclusions and limitations are the insurer's way of limiting its exposure to losses that it deems to be high risk.

Valuation

The value of covered property is determined at actual cash value, except if the limit of insurance for building satisfies the coinsurance provision, or the cost to repair or replace the damaged building property is $2,500 or less. In those circumstances, the insurer will pay the cost of building repairs or replacement. The insurer is essentially offering the insured a waiver of coinsurance in the foregoing circumstances.

Additionally, the cost of building repairs or replacement does not include the increased cost attributable to enforcement of any ordinance or law.

For items such as awnings; floor coverings; appliances for refrigerating, ventilating, cooking, dishwashing, or laundering; or outdoor equipment or furniture, settlement is on an actual cash basis. For glass, replacement is at the cost of replacement with safety-glazing material if required by law.

Waiver of Rights of Recovery

In keeping with the act, the insurer waives its rights of subrogation against any unit-owner of thc condominium shown in the declarations.

Subrogation is applicable to liable third parties. Since the unit-owner is an owner of the condominium and a first party, even in the absence of legislation requiring the waiver, its application makes sense.

Additional Conditions

The policy contains conditions that apply in addition to the common policy conditions and the commercial property conditions.

Coinsurance

The coinsurance condition requires the insured to carry insurance at least to the percentage shown in the declarations. That limit must be adequate not just at the inception of the policy, but more importantly at the time of loss. It is at the time of loss that the adequacy test is performed. If the insured fails the adequacy test, it will incur a penalty. For example, the coinsurance percentage is 80 percent, the value of the property at the time of loss is $500,000, and the coverage A amount at the time of loss is $300,000, and the loss is $200,000. In order to be properly insured the coverage A amount should be $400,000; that is 80 percent of $500,000.

Since coverage A is less than the 80 percent, the coverage A amount, $300,000 is divided by the value of the property, $500,000, yielding .6. The amount of loss is then multiplied by .6, so that what will be paid out is $120,000 less whatever deductible applies. The insured is paying a penalty because the property was underinsured.

Mortgageholders

The term "mortgageholder" includes a trustee. This makes allowance for provisions in any act that requires payment be made to a trustee. Damage from covered causes of loss are paid to each mortgageholder in order of precedence, meaning the mortgageholder listed first is paid first according to its financial interest. Each succeeding mortgageholder is paid according to its position on the list. Even if the mortgageholder has commenced foreclosure proceedings, it still has the right to receive loss payment.

The mortgageholder agreement confers special status on the mortgageholder. The mortgageholder retains the right to be paid for a covered loss, even in circumstances where the insured is denied payment. This special status carries with it certain responsibilities. As a condition for receiving payment, the mortgageholder must do the following:

- Pay any premium due if the insured has failed to do so
- Submit a signed, sworn proof of loss within sixty days after receiving notice from the insurer of the insured's failure to file said proof
- Notify the insurer of any change of ownership, occupancy, or substantial change in risk known to the mortgageholder

If the insurer pays the mortgageholder for any loss denied the insured because of the insured's acts, the following will happen:

- The mortgageholder's rights will be transferred to the insurer, to the extent of its payment to the mortgageholder.
- The rights of the mortgageholder to recover the full amount of its claim will not be impaired.

At its option, the insurer may pay the mortgageholder the full principal on the mortgage plus accrued interest. In that event, the mortgage and note will be transferred to the insurer and the insured will pay its remaining mortgage debt to the insurer.

The mortgageholder/insurer agreement also places responsibility on the insurer. If the insurer cancels the policy it will give the mortgageholder notice of at least:

- ten days before the effective date of cancellation for nonpayment of premium, or
- thirty days before effective date of cancellation if the insurer cancels for other reasons.

If the insurer elects not to renew the policy, it will give the mortgageholder at least ten days written notice before the expiration date of the policy.

Optional Coverages

The optional coverages apply separately to each item and must be shown as applicable in the declarations.

Agreed Value

If the insurer and the insured agree to this settlement option, then the agreed value option replaces the coinsurance clause. A condition for this option is the requirement that the insured submits documentation to verify the values chosen at inception as well as at renewal time. If this option is chosen, the following apply:

- The insurer will pay no more than the proportion that the limit of insurance bears to the agreed value shown in the declarations.
- An expiration date must be shown for this optional coverage. If the expiry date is not extended, the coinsurance condition is reinstated.
- The terms of this optional coverage apply only to loss or damage that occurs on or after the effective date of this optional coverage or before the agreed value expiration date or the policy expiration date, whichever occurs first.

Inflation Guard

As the name suggests, this coverage part guards the insured against the upward spiraling of real property values during inflationary periods.

Once an inflation percentage is chosen, the insurance limit automatically increases by that percentage rate during the course of the year.

b. The amount of the increase will be:

(1) The Limit of Insurance that applied on the most recent of the policy inception date, the policy anniversary date, or any other policy change amending the Limit of Insurance, multiplied by

(2) The percentage of annual increase shown in the Declarations, expressed as a decimal (example: 8% is .08), multiplied by

(3) The number of days since the beginning of the current policy year or the effective date of the most recent policy change amending the Limit of Insurance, divided by 365.

Once the right limits and inflation percentage are set at the beginning, the automatic increases give the insured the necessary peace of mind that the right limit of insurance will be available at time of loss.

Replacement Cost

The insured's choice of the replacement cost option in evaluating a loss replaces the actual cash value method that would apply normally.

This Optional Coverage does not apply to:

(1) Personal property of others;

(2) Contents of a residence; or

(3) Works of art, antiques or rare articles, including etchings, pictures, statuary, marbles, bronzes, porcelains and bric-a-brac.

This subsection is careful to draw the boundaries around property it is not intended to cover.

Additionally, the provision points out that property indivisibly owned by all unit-owners is not considered to be personal property of others and is subject to replacement cost coverage.

The insured is offered the option of making a claim on an actual cash value basis. This option gives the insured flexibility in how it wants its loss settled if, for example, it is advantageous for the insured to do so. Even after the insured makes a claim on an actual cash basis the insured has

180 days to give the insurer a claim for replacement cost. As long as the notice is within that 180 days, the insured will get replacement cost.

In order for the insured to get replacement cost coverage, it must meet certain conditions:

- The lost or damaged property must actually be repaired or replaced.
- The repairs or replacement must be made as soon as reasonably possible after the loss or damage.

In the absence of these conditions, the insured could easily take the money and replace the damaged or destroyed property at actual cash value and pocket the difference, thereby profiting from the loss. Additionally, any delay could result in increased cost of construction materials that could easily cause the costs to balloon.

In an attempt to balance fairness of settlement with true indemnity for the insured, where the replacement cost valuation method is used payout is limited to the least of the following:

- The limit of insurance applicable to the lost or damaged property.
- The cost to replace the lost or damaged property with other property of comparable material and quality and used for the same purpose.
- The amount actually spent that is necessary to repair or replace the lost or damaged property.

If a building is to be rebuilt at new premises, the cost would be that which would have applied to the original premises.

Any increased costs attributable to enforcement of any ordinance or law regulating the construction, use, or repair of any property is not covered.

Extension of Replacement Cost to Personal Property of Others

The insured has the option to extend replacement cost to property of others. If this option is exercised, the section of the replacement cost optional coverage that excludes replacement coverage for personal property of others is deleted.

There is one limitation governing this extension of replacement cost to property of others: if a personal property item is governed by a contract outlining the insured's liability for loss, the valuation for loss will be governed by said contract, but the payout will not exceed the lesser of the replacement cost of the property or the applicable limit of insurance.

Definitions

The policy defines the following terms:

1. "Fungus" means any type or form of fungus, including mold or mildew, and any mycotoxins, spores, scents or by-products produced or released by fungi.
2. "Pollutants" means any solid, liquid, gaseous or thermal irritant or contaminant, including smoke, vapor, soot, fumes, acids, alkalis, chemicals and waste. Waste includes materials to be recycled, reconditioned or reclaimed.
3. "Stock" means merchandise held in storage or for sale, raw materials and in-process or finished goods, including supplies used in their packing or shipping.

These definitions clearly identify what is meant by the terms so that coverage, if any, can be clearly identified.

The detailed journey through the Condominium Association Coverage Form – CP 00 17 10 12 reflects a coverage form that perfectly marries the requirement of the act to coverage and coverage intent.

Through coverage and coverage extensions, balanced by limitations and exclusions, the form draws clear boundaries around who is insured, what is insured, and the extent of coverage afforded. Through this balancing act the form also affords coverage that reflects the realities of the condominium world as well as helps the insurer manage its exposures, all while adhering to the principle of indemnity underlying the insurance contract.

CP 00 17 10 12 and CP 00 18 10 12—a Comparison

With an understanding of the coverage provided by the association form in relation to the act, the discussion's focus is now of CP 00 17, the association form, and CP 00 18, the commercial unit-owners form. The following areas will be examined:

- Covered Property—Building
- Covered Property—Business Personal Property

- Covered Property—Personal Property of Others
- Property Not Covered
- Additional Coverages
- Coverage Extensions
- Loss Conditions
- Additional Condition
- Definitions

Covered Property—Building

The coverage wording under A. Coverage and 1. Covered Property is the same for both forms: they both pay for "direct physical loss of or damage to Covered Property at the premises described in the Declarations caused by or resulting from any Covered Cause of Loss."

The meaning and description of covered property is also the same in both forms. Where the two forms differ is in the subject matter of coverage: CP 00 17 provides building coverage; CP 00 18 does not except for fixtures, improvements, and betterments that make up part of the building and owned by the unit-owner. The absence of building coverage on one and not the other draws an invisible line of coverage around the appropriate property to be covered under both forms.

For example, if a unit-owner receives an umpire's award to replace a cement layer of texture on outer walls that cover all of the building, the unit-owner form still would not provide coverage. Parts of the building—including textured outer wall treatments—are the subject of the association policy. Even if the association bylaws require the unit-owner to be responsible for this surface, coverage would not be available on the CP 00 18 because this would not be considered an improvement or betterment solely owned by the unit-owners.

Covered Property—Business Personal Property

Both forms cover business personal property in or on the described building, in the open, or in a vehicle within 100 feet of the described building, or additionally, in the case of CP 00 18, property insured includes property listed on the Your Business Personal Property–Separation Of Coverage form.

CP 00 17 describes the coverage this way:

b. Your Business Personal Property located in or on the building or structure described in the Declarations or in the open (or in a vehicle) within 100 feet of the described premises, consisting of the following:

(1) Personal property owned by you or owned indivisibly by all unit-owner;

(2) Your interest in the labor, materials or services furnished or arranged by you on personal property of others; and

(3) Leased personal property for which you have a contractual responsibility to insure, unless otherwise provided for under Personal Property Of Others

But your business personal property does not include personal property owned only by a unit owner.

The coverage description is careful to take into consideration the indivisible property of all commercial unit-owners while clearly excluding property owned separately by unit-owners, ensuring there is no overlap in coverage intent.

CP 00 18 frames coverage for this section for the individual unit-owner so as to ensure coverage is clear between the two forms. Here is how CP 00 18 details coverage:

a. Your Business Personal Property consists of the following property located in or on the building or structure described in the Declarations or in the open (or in a vehicle) within 100 feet of the building or structure or within 100 feet of the premises described in the Declarations, whichever distance is greater:

(1) Furniture;

(2) Fixtures, improvements and alterations making up part of the building and owned by you;

(3) Machinery and equipment;

(4) "Stock";

(5) All other personal property owned by you and used in your business;

(6) Labor, materials or services furnished or arranged by you on personal property of others;

(7) Leased personal property for which you have a contractual responsibility to insure, unless otherwise provided for under Personal Property Of Others.

The items considered business personal property in CP 00 18 reflect perfectly the items a commercial unit-owner would have as part of its business operations, while at the same time making a distinction between unit-owned and association-owned items through the description of property covered.

In cases of bare walls ownership by the unit-owners in common, the unit-owner may be sole owner of and be responsible for insuring the entire interior of the unit inside the unfinished exterior walls, floor, and ceiling of the unit. The form extends the personal property item to include this property and in the process makes the value of this property, along with the unit-owner's personal property, subject to the coinsurance provision. It is important in writing property insurance for a commercial unit-owner that the unit-owner's responsibility for insuring any portion of the building is identified and its value taken into account when calculating an adequate limit of insurance.

Covered Property—Personal Property of Others

The wording and extent of coverage under this section are similar under both forms. The CP 00 18 contains the updated wording from the 2012 revision stating that property is covered within 100 feet of the building or structure or within 100 feet of the premises described in the declarations, whichever is greater. This wording was added to accommodate multiple tenants or occupants in one building, for which 100 feet from the premises might not be very far if they are located on the thirtieth floor.

Property Not Covered

Under this section of coverage all but six types of property mentioned are in both forms. The exceptions found in CP 00 17 and not in CP 00 18 are:

d. Bridges, roadways, walks, patios or other paved surfaces;

f. The cost of excavations, grading, back filling or filling;

g. Foundations of buildings, structures, machinery or boilers if their foundations are below:

   (1) The lowest basement floor; or

   (2) The surface of the ground if there is no basement.

j. Bulkheads, pilings, piers, wharves or docks;

l. Retaining walls that are not part of a building;

m. Underground pipes, flues or drains;

These exceptions are perfect examples of dovetailing of coverage under both forms. Since all of the exceptions are building-related items, it makes sense that they are excluded in the condominium association form and not mentioned in the condominium commercial unit-owner form, where unit-owners should have no such items.

In addition to these exclusions, there are slight variations under both forms for property excluded under both forms. For example, under the association form, animals are not covered unless owned by others and boarded. The unit-owners form includes this exclusion and provides coverage for animals "if owned by you, only as 'stock' while inside of buildings."

Another variation relates to 2. e. under the unit-owners form and 2.h. under the association form. The association form says, "Land (including land on which the property is located), water, growing crops or lawns (other than lawns which are part of a vegetated roof)."

The unit-owners form, though, states, "Water, growing crops or lawns."

The former includes land, whereas the latter does not, each item being reflective of the kind of property that would be relevant to each type of insured. The association form also makes an exception for lawns that are part of a vegetated roofs, which are considered part of a building. Vegetated roofs are not mentioned in the unit-owner form.

Additional Coverages

The coverage extensions under CP 00 17 and CP 00 18 are identical, with only one exception: CP 00 17 contains an increased cost of construction clause and CP 00 18 does not; this clause relates to buildings, which has application for CP 00 17 and not for CP 00 18.

Coverage Extensions

The coverage extensions under both forms are identical, save for one difference: under the newly acquired property extension, the CP 00 17 form makes reference to building as follows:

a. Newly Acquired Or Constructed Property

(1) Buildings

You may extend the insurance that applies to Building to apply to:

> (a) Your new buildings while being built on the described premises; and
>
> (b) Buildings you acquire at locations, other than the described premises, intended for:
>
> (i) Similar use as the building described in the Declarations; or
>
> (ii) Use as a warehouse.
>
> The most we will pay for loss or damage under this Extension is $250,000 at each building.

The CP 00 18 form has no such extension.

Loss Conditions

The loss conditions in both forms are identical except that CP 00 18 has the following clause:

> 3. Condominium Association Insurance
>
> The Condominium Association may have other insurance covering the same property as this insurance. This insurance is intended to be excess, and not to contribute with that other insurance.

And CP 00 17 the following:

> 6. Unit-Owner's Insurance
>
> A unit-owner may have other insurance covering the same property as this insurance. This insurance is intended to be primary, and not to contribute with such other insurance.

The two forms are so constructed to match exactly the requirements of the act, which stipulates that association coverage is primary.

CP 00 17 contains a waiver of rights of recovery condition, whereby the association waives its right to recover payment from any unit owner of the condominium that is shown in the declarations:

> 9. Waiver Of Rights Of Recovery
>
> We waive our rights to recover payment from any unit owner of the condominium that is shown in the Declarations.

CP 00 18 contains no such waiver, so the unit-owner retains its rights to recover from the condominium association.

CP 00 17 refers to settlement of losses with an insurance trustee. CP 00 18 has no such condition.

CP 00 17 also makes reference to a party wall. CP 00 18 does not have any reference to a party wall as there is no building coverage.

Additional Condition

As discussed earlier, CP 00 17 contains a mortgageholders condition that confers rights and responsibilities on the mortgageholder.

CP 00 18 does not include a mortgageholders condition. This has serious implications for the unit-owner because the unit-owner can obtain a mortgage on its property. If the unit-owner fails to protect the mortgageholder's interest as is done under CP 00 17, in the event of a loss the mortgageholder could be out of pocket.

If the unit-owner does indeed have a mortgage on its condominium unit, then CP 12 18 – Loss Payable Provision, should be attached to the unit-owners policy. For unit-owners who have a mortgage, this will certainly be a requirement of the financial institution.

Definitions

In CP 00 17 the term "fungus" is defined, but there is no "fungus" definition under CP 00 18.

Summary

The journey through the Condominium Association Coverage Form – CP 00 17 and the Condominium Commercial Unit-Owners Coverage Form – CP 00 18 has been in part to demystify commercial unit-owners coverage to show that coverage application is similar whether the building owner or the unit-owner is being insured.

The act remains the foundation for all coverage; the unit-owner and association coverage balance each other in a relationship that ensures that all parties, whether association or unit-owner, have the right coverage that suits their needs.

The similarities and differences shown in the selected coverage areas provide excellent examples of the marriage between association coverage and unit-owners coverage. Where gaps appear as in the mortgageholders condition, a simple endorsement is all that is needed to fill it in.

Chapter 5

Commercial General & Directors and Officers Liability Coverage

Commercial General Liability Coverage

Nearly all commercial businesses, whether profit or not-for-profit, need general liability insurance. One of the advantages of the HO 00 06 Personal (homeowners) Unit-Owners form discussed in Chapter 3, is the fact that it includes both property (Section 1), and liability coverage (Section II). By definition, the ISO homeowners policy is a true "package" policy including both coverage parts, which cannot be separated. Since ISO does not have a similar package for commercial condominium owners or condominium associations, general liability must be purchased under a separate form. The ISO form used for this is CG 00 01 04 13 (current edition). This same form would be used for both commercial unit-owners and condominium associations. It is not the intent of this Chapter to analyze the ISO General Liability form in its entirety; we will merely point out how this form is used by commercial condominium unit owners and condominium associations.

The structure of Section II liability coverage was annotated in our discussion of the personal unit-owners form in a previous chapter. Liability coverage is protection for "bodily injury" or "property damage" to others that the insured is legally liable for that is due to an "occurrence." "Bodily injury" means bodily injury, sickness, or disease sustained by a person, including death, resulting from any of these at any time. "Property damage" means physical injury to tangible property, including loss of use. Loss of use can occur even if the property is not physically injured. An "occurrence" means an accident, including continuous or repeated exposure to substantially the same general harmful conditions.

Since commercial unit-owners and condominium associations are businesses, they have many general liability exposures that are different than what a personal unit-owner might have. However, some are similar (guests or customers tripping or falling on their premises resulting in an injury to a person). Businesses must not only address these sorts of premises exposures, but also products liability if they manufacture, sell, or distribute a product that causes bodily injury or property damage. Furthermore, since the condominium association is responsible for all common areas, they have additional exposures which could include swimming pools, tennis courts, exercise facilities, parking garages, dog parks, green spaces, sidewalks, security, etc. While unit-owners may bear some shared responsibility for these amenities, the condominium association is vested with maintaining these areas and thus assumes primary legal responsibility for them. Because a common element benefits all unit owners, the association is nearly always going to be ultimately responsible for covering the cost of any bodily injury or property damage that occurs in or on a common element. This is true even if a unit owner in some way contributed to the injury or damage.

The two most significant differences between the liability coverage provided in the HO 00 06 and the Commercial General Liability form, is the addition of "personal & advertising injury," and "products and completed operations coverage." "Personal & advertising injury" provides coverage beyond bodily injury and property damage. Personal injury when applied to commercial insurance includes the torts of false arrest, libel, slander, copyright infringement, etc. Advertising injury includes copyright infringement or use of another's advertising idea in an insureds advertisement. "Products & completed operations" include liability arising form any good or products manufactured or sold by the insured, or work or operations performed by the insured or on the insureds behalf, as well as liability they may assume by contract (as long as it falls under the definition of "insured contract.") Depending on the commercial operation, an entity may have more or less exposure to any of these sorts of torts.

Another liability form difference between the personal unit-owner and commercial condominium or association, are how limits of coverage are handled. The commercial general liability policy includes separate occurrence limits for a bodily injury/property damage and personal injury/ advertising injury. In addition, there is a general aggregate and products/ completed operations aggregate. The occurrence limit is the most a policy will pay for any one occurrence; the aggregates are the most that the policy will pay out during the entire policy year, regardless of the number of occurrences. A typical occurrence limit for a commercial general liability policy is $1,000,000 and the aggregates are usually double that limit ($2,000,000).

Commercial condominium unit-owners are non-residential and could technically be running any sort of commercial operation. However, most tend to fall under the category of offices, small retail, warehouses, and possibly light manufacturing. Since the types of business operations will vary, the general liability policy would use the ISO classification of the business to promulgate premium. However, the types of operations permitted in a commercial condominium units would be governed by the condominium association by-laws, and these could significantly limit what type of operations can be performed in a commercial condominium unit.

Commercial condominium associations can govern residential, non-residential, or mixed-use properties. ISO uses the following "association risk only" general liability classifications:

62000 Condominiums–Commercial–Bank or Mercantile, Mfg. or Office (Association Risk Only)

62001 Condominiums–Commercial Shopping Centers (Association Risk Only)

62002 Condominiums–Commercial Warehouses–Mfg. or Private (Association Risk Only)

620003 Condominiums–Residential (Association Risk Only)

Note these rating classifications only address the risk of the association entity itself and its offices. All common area exposures, such as a parking lot (and the other amenities mentioned above), would need to be separately classified and rated.

States vary in their definitions of the elements and requirements for which party is to insure what parts of the building. When are patios an individual unit owners responsibility to insure, and when are patios the responsibility of the association? Fortunately, FC&S has a published chart that answers many of those questions by providing state-by-state definitions and regulation requirements needed to determine what part of the structure belongs to the unit owner, what belongs to the association, and how the insurance policies interact. Each state is broken into two main sections, Association and Unit Owner. The text on the left-hand side of each section should be treated as a heading. For example, the first entry under Common Elements is "All portions of a condominium other than the units." That is a general definition of common elements. If an X is to the right of that text, then that state uses that definition of Common Elements. You can find this helpful link here:

http://www.nuco.com/fcs/2023/05/01/condominium-statutes-by-state/

Directors and Officers Liability Coverage

Most homeowner associations, such as condominium, townhouse, and co-operative developments, automatically purchase property, general liability, crime, and possibly workers compensation insurance. Many times such coverage is required by the condominium act or other governing documents. However, those types of insurance policies do not cover the directors, officers, volunteers, committee members, and others for "wrongful acts." These sorts of acts usually include errors and omissions, misstatements, neglect, and breach of duty in their performance of managing the association. To protect these persons, the act, the bylaws, or other governing documents of most associations often require the purchase of directors and officers (D&O) liability insurance. Even when not required to do so, most associations voluntarily choose to purchase the coverage. This chapter explains the need for D&O insurance and what to look for in a good D&O policy.

It is important to understand that not all D&O policies are the same, and the differences between policies can be significant. Some of those major differences are discussed in this chapter.

Obligations of Directors and Officers

Most states have established guidelines regarding the duties and standard of conduct of corporate directors and officers, whether serving for large for-profit corporations or for nonprofit organizations such as homeowner & condominium associations. In general the directors and officers of homeowner associations must exercise the following duties:

- A duty of diligence and care—they must exercise their duties with the same care that an ordinary person would use in similar circumstances. When discussing and deciding issues, they should seek to educate themselves about the issues and approach discussions of those issues in good faith. When they vote, they should do so in a fair and objective manner.

- A duty of loyalty—they must act prudently and perform their duties in a manner they believe to be in the best interest of the association. They must avoid conflicts of interest and are prohibited from using their position of trust and confidence to further their private interests. For example, a director who has a financial interest in a landscaping firm that the board is considering for hire should abstain from any discussion or votes regarding employment of the landscaping firm.

- A duty of obedience—they must perform their duties in accordance with applicable statutes and the terms of the association's charter, bylaws, and other governing documents.

Failure to conduct themselves in the manner prescribed by law or the association's governing documents can result in directors and officers being held personally and sometimes financially liable for their actions.

Personal Liability

Although some states limit the personal financial liability of volunteer directors and officers, many states do not do so. As a consequence, it is sometimes difficult in the absence of insurance for nonprofit organizations such as homeowner associations to get qualified volunteers to serve as directors, officers, or committee members because they are afraid of being sued as the result of performing their duties.

Volunteer Protection Act of 1997

One intended source of noninsurance financial liability protection for volunteers, including those who perform service for nonprofit organizations, is the federal Volunteer Protection Act of 1997. The original intent of the act was to provide immunity from tort claims that might be filed against the volunteers of nonprofit organizations. For purposes of the act, a "volunteer" is defined as anyone (including officers, directors, trustees, and direct service volunteers) who performs services for a nonprofit organization or governmental entity and receives neither no compensation nor anything of value in lieu of compensation, in excess of $500 per year.

Under the Volunteer Protection Act, as long as the volunteer meets certain criteria, such as "acting within the scope of the volunteer's responsibilities," he or she has a complete defense to a lawsuit and has no liability. Even when a volunteer does not meet the criteria, he may still have some protection against awards of noneconomic and punitive damages, as long as the volunteer has not engaged in specific types of prohibited conduct.

Although some homeowner associations may feel that the Volunteer Protection Act provides sufficient protection from D&O lawsuits so that separate insurance is not needed, such is not the case for several reasons. First, the act does not prohibit lawsuits against volunteers; rather, it provides only an argument for the volunteer's defense if and when the volunteer is sued.

Second, the act is designed to protect volunteers from tort liability, usually meaning liability for acts that result in bodily injury or property damage to others. (Most, if not all, homeowner associations already protect themselves and their directors and officers from such liability by purchasing general liability insurance.)

Third, the act does not protect a volunteer director or officer from liability for gross negligence, willful or criminal misconduct, reckless misconduct, or a flagrant indifference to the rights or safety of others—frequent allegations in lawsuits filed against directors and officers.

A further complication is that states can opt out of the Volunteer Protection Act and are allowed to override its provisions with their own legislation. Many states have, in fact, enacted their own laws that limit both the personal liability of volunteer directors and officers and the organization's ability to indemnify directors and officers in the event they are sued.

Because these financial liability laws vary from state to state and may not provide the desired financial protections, most homeowner associations rely on D&O insurance as the best means of providing the funds to defend directors, officers, employees, committee members, and others from lawsuits that are not covered by other types of insurance.

Common Allegations against Directors and Officers

There are many types of situations that can result in lawsuits being filed by homeowners against individual directors and officers or the board of directors as a whole. The following are some common examples of such situations:

- Special assessments. The association's clubhouse has been in need of extensive renovation for years. After months of interviewing decorators, engineers, and contractors, the association's decorations committee recommends a renovation plan that exceeds the budgeted amount for the renovation. The board authorizes the renovation without seeking the approval of the homeowners as required by the association's governing documents. The resulting assessment is challenged by the homeowners, and a D&O claim filed to repeal the assessment and stop the renovation project.

- Violation of election procedures. A candidate for director fails to win the election and challenges both the results and the propriety of the election process. She files a claim alleging that the board failed to properly count the votes and proxies.

- Dishonest acts of employees. One of the association's maintenance workers enters a homeowner's unit without permission to check for the source of a water leak. After the employee leaves, the unit-owner notices that some cash that was on the counter is missing. The unit-owner then sues the association, alleging that the worker illegally entered the unit and stole the money.

- Maintenance issues. The association's alleged failure to properly maintain building roofs results in an early need to replace them, at great cost to the association's reserves and a potential assessment to the homeowners.

- Employment discrimination. A property manager claims he was not hired or was terminated because of his race or age.

- Failure to enforce rules and regulations. A homeowner that lives next to the community pool complains repeatedly about the board's failure to enforce violations of rules that prohibit after-hours use of the pool.

- Defamation, libel, or slander. At a board meeting, one of the directors makes a derogatory comment about a homeowner who frequently complains about the association's rules and regulations. While not at the meeting, the homeowner subsequently hears about the comment and sues the director, alleging the comment was defamatory and caused him emotional distress.

Other situations that can lead to legal action against the board include, but are not limited to, subleasing policies, decisions of an architectural committee, pet rules, failure to address construction defects, and issues involving potential buyers.

Not all claims or lawsuits filed against homeowner associations or their directors and officers, however, are covered by D&O insurance, as illustrated by the following examples.

Joan, the resident property manager for the Hillcrest Homeowners Association, hires Anderson Paving to install speed bumps on the property. The board of directors decided the bumps were necessary to prevent vehicles from driving on the property at excessive speed, thereby endangering persons that walk along the roadways. Unfortunately, one of the speed bumps is too high, and damages the underside of a car owned by Frank, a resident unit-owner. Frank sues both the directors who voted to install the speed bump and Joan, who hired the paving company, to recover the cost of fixing his car's suspension. The lawsuit would not be covered by the D&O policy since it involves property damage that would be payable under the association's general liability insurance policy.

Severe rains have damaged a walkway on the Sunset Hills association property. While walking her dog, a resident unit-owner steps in a depression, falls, and breaks her arm. She sues the board of directors for not repairing the walkway damage in a timely manner in an attempt to recover her medical expenses. This suit would also not be payable under the D&O policy since bodily injury claims are typically excluded and also would be payable under the association's general liability policy.

Regardless of the circumstances that precipitate their filing, most D&O claims have the following features in common:

- They usually seek nonmonetary relief rather than monetary damages. For example, many D&O claims seek equitable relief, such as some activity or practice stopped, suspended, or altered.

- They mostly involve defense fees and costs, which can be substantial. While small settlements may be common, large indemnity payouts are rare.

- They are sometimes petty and motivated by emotion and personal agendas.

Need for Directors and Officers Liability Insurance

Claims containing allegations like those previously described are many times not covered by traditional general liability insurance since they are not the result of accidents that cause physical (bodily) injury or property damage. Consequently, in the absence of insurance that does cover such allegations, the association and/or the directors and officers would be in the position of having to pay the cost of any damages or settlements out of the association's reserves or their own pockets.

In most cases, however, the primary benefit of D&O insurance is that it pays the cost of investigating or defending claims. Even if the directors and officers are ultimately found not to be liable, the cost to defend a claim can run well into six figures. Many board members and/or their associations would be unable to pay these costs in the absence of insurance.

The following examples illustrate a handful of situations where D&O insurance came in handy for a condominium board.

- The Miller Landscaping Company has a five-year contract with the Valley Park Condominium Association. Because several homeowners are unhappy with Miller's work, the board of directors votes to terminate the contract after only three years. Miller subsequently files a lawsuit against Valley Park's board of directors alleging breach of contract. If the association's D&O policy provides coverage for breach of third-party contracts, it will pay the costs incurred in defending the suit but typically will not pay any damages or settlement. Such payment would create a moral hazard by encouraging boards to violate contracts and look to the insurance to pay for their wrongdoing. It should be noted that if the D&O policy excludes coverage for breach of third-party contracts, even the defense costs might not be covered.

- What if a condominium association changes the rules about how and who can rent out their condos when the owner isn't using it? In *Atain Specialty Ins. Co. v. Galvestonian Condo. Ass'n*, 2020 U.S. Dist. LEXIS 59784 (S.D. Tex. 2020), the Board of the Galvestonian Condominium Association voted to restrict how many condo-owners could rent out their condos through an association-sponsored program and fine owners who rented out their condos through an outside company, even though doing so was not explicitly prohibited and had been permitted prior to the amendment. One condo-owner who rented out his condo through an outside company filed "blitzkrieg-style litigation" that accused the association of a price-fixing conspiracy that "exclude[ed] most owners from participating" and also included allegations of negligence, gross negligence, and breach of fiduciary duty. Though the policy would cover negligence claims, Atain maintained that the underlying damages were excluded because the lower courts had not found the association's negligence had caused the owner's injuries. The court said exclusions only mattered when deciding the duty to indemnify, not the duty to defend. Since the negligence claims *could be covered* by the D&O policy, Atain had to defend the association.

- A board generally needs approval from members before making material changes to the property. However, where is the line between material and immaterial? Taking every little decision to the members can slow things down and, frankly, be a hassle for disinterested homeowners. However, going too far the other way opens the board up to lawsuits. In *Lexington Place Condo. Ass'n v. Flint*, 348 So. 3d 650 (Fla. Dist. Ct. App. 2022), a condo association removed two common elements—an on-site dog park and a wallyball court—and enacted stricter pet guidelines, all without getting a vote from the unit owners. A couple who owned multiple units in the condominium sued the association for violations of the Declaration. Regarding the alterations of the common elements, the article granting the association the authority to make certain alterations without prior approval from the unit owners referred only to alterations, not "material alterations"; the section on "Material Alterations" in the Declaration explicitly required prior approval from a majority of the unit owners. For the stricter pet guidelines, the association had not properly amended the Declaration before adopting the new rule. The court ruled in favor of the unit owners, ordered the restoration of the common elements, nullified the new pet restrictions, and awarded attorney's fees to the plaintiffs.

- In some cases, D&O coverage can survive even if the directors and officers declare bankruptcy. In *Hollingsworth v. Landing Condos. of Waukesha Ass'n*, 2014 Wisc. App. LEXIS 178 (Wis. Ct. App. 2014, unpublished), several condominium owners filed suit against individual members of the board for breach of fiduciary duties. Before the case concluded, however, the board members filed for bankruptcy and consequently were dismissed from the suit. The insurer who had issued the D&O endorsement, State Auto Insurance Company, sought judgment that they did not owe coverage because the insured board members had all been dismissed, so there was zero chance of the insured being held liable. The condo owners pointed to a bankruptcy-specific clause in the D&O endorsement that said bankruptcy wouldn't affect State Auto's obligation to pay, but the circuit court awarded declaratory judgment to State Auto. The appellate court, however, sided with the condo owners. The clause stated "the bankruptcy or insolvency of the insured ... will not relieve us of our obligations under this policy," subject to an exclusion that was not implicated in the suit. The charges in the complaint were precisely those that the endorsement was intended to cover. Judgment in favor of State Auto was reversed.

- Unfortunately, homeowners can sometimes be as troublesome, if not more so, than the association. For example, a homeowner in South Carolina has filed multiple lawsuits against his homeowners association. However, rather than suing the association's Board of Directors directly, he sued the board members in their individual capacities in *Wedlake v. Acord*, *Wedlake v. Bashor*, and *Wedlake v. Edwards*; none of these suits, including the one he finally filed against the Board itself (*Wedlake v. Bd. of Dirs. of Woodington Homeowners' Ass'n*) have led to a published court opinion. The problem isn't necessarily the lawsuits themselves, but the costs they incur and the trepidation they inspire. Whether and how the Board chose to fight each suit is not necessarily relevant when considering how each move in this chess match costs thousands of dollars, which may have led to a steep decline in homeowners volunteering to serve on the Board.

Regardless of any statutory limitations on the personal liability of volunteer directors and officers, many associations would find it hard to attract quality board members without D&O insurance in place. Even though the governing documents of many associations have provisions for indemnifying the directors and officers for loss resulting from their mistakes, the association must decide if it wants to insure for this exposure or be self-insured. Most associations choose to purchase insurance. With proper D&O coverage in place, board members can relax and concentrate on doing the best job possible.

The D&O Policy

There are basically two types of directors and officers liability policies for homeowner associations: so-called package policies and stand-alone (monoline) policies. A package policy (sometimes called a master policy or a community association policy) typically provides property, general liability, crime, and possibly other coverages, including D&O liability coverage. While usually less expensive than a stand-alone policy, the D&O coverage that a package policy provides is usually not as broad as coverage provided by a stand-alone policy.

Monoline association D&O policies are tailored to the unique needs of homeowner associations. They are usually offered by insurers that have experience providing the specialized coverage necessary for condominium, townhouse, and co-op associations.

Policy Format

While a few D&O policy forms provide coverage on an occurrence basis (i.e., the policy in effect when the occurrence or offense causing the injury or damage takes place is the policy that pays the claim), the vast majority of D&O liability policies provide coverage on a claims-made basis (i.e., the policy in effect when the claim is presented is the policy that pays the claim, subject to certain limitations). General Liability policies also have a "claims-made" option, but it would be very unusual to see this on a condominium association policy. For D&O policies, claims-made is nearly universal.

To illustrate the claims-made concept, assume two policies are each in effect from January 1 through December 31 of consecutive years. One policy provides coverage on an occurrence basis while the other provides coverage on a claims-made basis. An occurrence takes place in September of the first year that results in a claim being presented six months later, during the second year. With an occurrence policy, the policy in effect during the first year is the policy that pays for the claim (assuming the policy provides coverage). With a claims-made policy, the policy in effect during the second year (when the claim is presented), is usually the policy that pays for the claim.

There are two significant limitations that may have an impact on coverage by governing which claims-made policy should actually pay for the claim. One limitation is the policy's retroactive date, and the other is the policy's claim reporting requirements.

Retroactive Date

A major feature and potential restriction of many claims-made policies is that the circumstances that result in the claim must occur on or after the policy's retroactive date for coverage to apply. The retroactive date is specified on the policy's declarations page and is typically the date the current insurer first provided coverage. For example, if ABC Insurance Company is the current insurer and has provided coverage for consecutive years beginning June 1, 2015, that date will be the retroactive date shown on each of the consecutive policies. A claim based on circumstances that took place on or after that date could be presented and covered by the current policy. However, if the circumstances occurred prior to June 1, 2015, the current policy would not provide coverage for the claim.

When there is a change of insurance company, the new insurer will typically impose a new retroactive date that coincides with the inception of its coverage. When this occurs, and if the insured feels there is the possibility that a claim on the expired policy may be presented at a later date (and consequently not covered by the new policy), there are two options that should be considered:

(1) Request that the new insurer provide prior acts coverage

(2) Purchase an extended reporting period from the expiring insurer

Prior Acts Coverage

Claims-made policies that do not have a specified retroactive date provide prior acts coverage. This means that the policy will cover claims presented during the policy's coverage period, regardless of when the circumstances that resulted in the claim took place. Some D&O insurers will provide this favorable prior acts coverage upon request, thereby allowing the insured to avoid having to purchase an extended reporting period from the prior insurer.

Discovery Period/Extended Reporting Period

The insuring agreement of most D&O policies usually states that for coverage to apply, the claim must be submitted to the insurer within the policy period. However, because claims are often not reported immediately, and because they sometimes result from circumstances that take place near the end of the policy period, most policies also allow coverage if the claim is reported up to a specified time (usually sixty days) after the policy expires. There is no cost associated with this reporting period extension, usually referred to as the discovery period or the automatic extended reporting period.

For situations where the sixty-day reporting period extension is felt to be insufficient, or if coverage is not being renewed with the same insurer, an optional supplemental extended reporting period of up to three years following policy expiration is also usually available for additional premium. This optional reporting period must be requested within a short period of time—usually thirty or sixty days following expiration of the policy—and the required premium can be as much as 200 percent of the annual policy premium for the expiring policy. The optional extended reporting period is usually not available if the current policy is cancelled by the insurer for nonpayment of premium, and it does not increase or reinstate the policy's limit of liability.

Whether the board feels that a claim may be presented more than sixty days after the expiring D&O policy terminates, an attempt should always be made to have the new insurer provide prior acts coverage. If such coverage is unavailable, consideration should then be given to purchase of the optional extended reporting period from the expiring insurer. Certainly from a cost standpoint, prior acts coverage is the preferred option.

Insuring Agreement

The D&O policy insuring agreement specifies the coverage granted by the policy. It affirms the insurer's obligation to pay claims made against the insured during the policy's coverage period, providing the claim is the result of a wrongful act covered by the policy. The term "wrongful" act is usually defined later in the policy to clarify what types of claims are covered.

Most insuring agreements state the insurer will pay claims "on behalf of the insured," although some policies may state the insurer will "pay the loss" or will "reimburse the insured" for losses paid. Policies that pay on behalf or pay the loss are preferred because they do not require the association to first pay a loss and then seek reimbursement from the insurance company.

Also usually included within the insuring agreement is the claim reporting requirement. For most D&O policies, the claim must be reported during the policy period or any applicable extended reporting period. Policies that contain a retroactive date may also require that the claim occurs on or after the specified retroactive date for coverage to apply.

Defense Provisions

As long as the policy provides coverage for at least one of the allegations in a lawsuit, most association D&O insurers are obligated provide a defense even if the allegation is "groundless, false or fraudulent." This wording benefits the association, since it is not necessary to have allegations proven before coverage is triggered, and the policy pays defense costs.

In the absence of the "groundless, false or fraudulent" wording, the insurer could withhold payment of defense expenses until the plaintiff's allegations were proven. If the allegations were subsequently unproven, or proven to be groundless, false, or fraudulent, the association could end up having to pay all of the defense costs out of its own pocket. Fortunately for homeowner associations, most D&O insurers will provide a defense for claims even if the policy is not required to pay damages.

Supplementary Payments

In addition to attorney fees and court costs, most D&O policies also pay other expenses related to the defense of claims. These costs may be described in a separate supplementary payments section of the policy or included within a definition of "defense expenses," and usually include the following:

- Cost of investigations
- Cost of claims adjustment
- Cost of appeals
- Cost of attachment or similar bonds
- Prejudgement and postjudgment interest on awarded damages
- Other costs taxed on the insured by the lawsuit

Typically not covered, however, are salaries, wages, fees, and overhead or benefit expenses of directors, officers, employees, trustees, volunteers, committee members, or other persons covered by the policy.

Most D&O insurers include the cost of both defense and supplementary payments in the policy's limit of liability. A few insurers, however, will pay these costs in addition to the limit of liability. Some insurers offer a separate limit for defense costs that is in addition to the limit that pays for losses. Policies that pay defense expenses in addition to the limit of liability or that have a separate defense cost limit are often, but not always, more expensive than policies that include defense within the policy limits (the commercial general liability policy previously discussed in this chapter pays defense costs in addition to limits).

Policies that obligate the insurance company to defend the insured are called duty to defend policies and are favorable because the insured does not have to seek its own attorney. Policies that do not require the insurer to defend often allow the defense to be tendered to the insurer if the insured so desires. Some insurers will allow the insured to have its own legal counsel either defend the suit or associate with the insurer's attorney in defense of the claim. The fees of an attorney retained by the insured may or may not be paid by the insurer, depending on the policy.

It should be noted that if the policy clearly does not provide coverage for any of the allegations contained in a lawsuit, the insurer will usually not provide a defense either. For example, if a homeowner sues a director for physically damaging his car, the D&O policy will typically not defend the suit, since coverage (and defense) for the suit should be provided by the director's or the association's general liability insurance policy.

Settlements

All association D&O policies contain claim settlement provisions and requirements that apply to both the insurer and the insured. These provisions and requirements may be stated along with the policy's defense provisions or are sometimes contained within the limit of liability section of the policy. Whether the insurer is obligated to provide a defense, the insured usually must avoid admitting liability or incurring any defense costs without the insurer's prior written consent. Any costs incurred without the insurer's approval may not be paid.

Although most D&O policies do not require the insurance company to obtain the insured's consent for a settlement, most insurers will seek to obtain consent. In some policies, if consent is not given, the insurer's obligation is limited to the cost of the recommended settlement (or a percentage of the settlement in excess of the recommended amount) plus the defense costs incurred prior to the refusal. This settlement amount limitation is known as a "hammer clause" and, if present, can be quite restrictive since the association could end up responsible for payment of additional defense costs plus a substantial additional settlement amount. Below is an example of a "hammer" clause:

Consent to Settle

If we recommend a settlement to the insured which is acceptable to the claimant, but to which the insured does not consent, the most we will pay as damages in the event of any later settlement or judgment is the amount for which the "claim" could have been settled, to which the insured did not give consent, plus "claims expenses" incurred as of the date such settlement was proposed in writing by us to the insured. (BP 17 24 01 10)

Some insurers offer an endorsement that requires the insurer to pay both the settlement and defense amounts that are in excess of the original proposed settlement.

Limit of Liability

The D&O policy's limit of liability is shown on the declarations page and applies regardless of the number of insureds covered by the policy, number of claims received, or number of persons or organizations making claims. Two limits are often shown: a per-claim limit, and an annual aggregate limit. The annual aggregate limit is the total amount the insurer will pay for all claims during the policy period. When D&O coverage is provided under a package policy along with other coverages, a separate limit of liability may be shown for each type of coverage provided.

In most cases, limits shown on the declarations include defense costs and apply whether the association itself or the individual directors and/or officers are sued. Once the policy limits are exhausted, the policy will no longer pay either additional claims or defense costs.

Retention

In most association D&O policies, the policy limits apply excess of a retention (deductible) that applies to each claim. The retention applies whether the suit involves one or more individuals and/or the association as an entity and may or may not include defense costs, depending on the policy form. When multiple related claims are involved, usually only one retention applies.

When a retention applies, it can be imposed by the insurer in a variety of ways, such as in these examples:

- Some insurers apply the retention only to claims filed against the association, not to claims against the directors and officers as individuals.

- Some insurers waive the retention if the insured is found innocent and no damages are awarded.

- Some insurers apply the retention only to defense costs, not to awards or settlements.

- Others apply the retention to awards and settlements, but not to defense costs.

- Still others apply the retention to both loss and expenses.

- Some insurers apply the retention only to claims involving specific coverages, such as allegations of wrongful employment practices.

- Some insurers waive or reduce the retention if the suit is settled through arbitration or mediation.

Another variation in policies involves reimbursement to the insurer of paid amounts in certain circumstances. For example, when the association's governing documents require indemnification of the directors and officers if they have to pay damages in a lawsuit, but such indemnification does not happen for reasons other than the association's insolvency, some policies require the association to repay to the insurer any amounts paid under the policy.

Associations that purchase D&O insurance usually buy coverage limits of $1 million per claim and annual aggregate. If higher coverage limits are desired, the association should consider increasing the limits by including the D&O policy on the association's umbrella or excess liability policy's schedule of underlying coverage. If this can be done, the total coverage limit will then be the same as the total general liability coverage limit. The cost for increasing the coverage limits in this manner is usually less than the cost of purchasing separate, higher D&O coverage limits.

Major Policy Definitions

Important policy terms (i.e., terms with special or significant meaning) are usually defined in D&O policies. These terms often appear within quotation marks, are italicized, or may be shown in boldface type. Some policies contain many defined terms, while other policies contain relatively few.

The following defined terms are important and can be found in most D&O policies.

Claim

The definition of "claim" is important because it clarifies the types of losses that are covered by the policy. While almost all D&O policies cover damages the insured is legally obligated to pay as the result of a wrongful act, the claim can itself take many forms, depending on the policy. Typical claim definitions include but are not limited to the following:

- Civil, criminal, or administrative proceedings (such as lawsuits or hearings) commenced by the service of a complaint or similar proceeding

- Written demand for monetary, nonmonetary, or equitable relief

- Requests for arbitration and/or mediation

- Requests to waive the statute of limitations

If the D&O policy also provides coverage for employment-related wrongful acts such as wrongful termination, harassment (sexual or otherwise), or discrimination, the definition usually is expanded to include notice of EEOC or similar state, local, or foreign agency proceedings.

Because this is a claim triggers policy coverage, it is important that the definition be as broad as possible. A narrow "claim" definition (for example, one that does not include EEOC proceedings or demand for nonmonetary relief) could mean that the policy does not provide some of the important coverages for which the policy was purchased.

Interrelated Wrongful Acts

A single set of circumstances may sometimes result in more than one claim, sometimes called "interrelated wrongful acts." For example, an assessment felt to be improper by a group of homeowners may result in the filing of a separate claim by each homeowner, or a separate claim filed against each director who voted for the assessment, even though all of the claims are the result of the same circumstance (e.g., the assessment). When multiple claims arise out of a single circumstance, the policy usually treats all of the claims as if they were a single claim and subjects them to a single deductible or retention.

If the D&O policy does not include an "interrelated claims" definition, the insurer may treat each claim as a separate claim and apply the deductible or retention to each claim, even if they all resulted from the same circumstance. It is therefore preferred that any D&O policy purchased by the association contain a definition of "interrelated claims."

Potential Claims

In addition to requiring the reporting of claims, most policies also require the insured to report potential claims—circumstances that may later result in a claim. Normally, under claims-made policies, there is no coverage for a claim that is reported after the policy expires unless the policy provides prior acts coverage or the claim is presented during an applicable extended reporting period. However, this problem can be avoided if the policy provides for coverage to be triggered by notice to the insurer of a potential claim. Such notice typically must include specific information about the circumstances that may result in the claim, the date of the occurrence, the names of persons involved, and the insured's reason for anticipating the claim. The policy also usually specifies when the potential claim needs to be reported for coverage to apply.

Notice of a potential claim allows the insurer to treat the claim as if it were reported during the policy period and gives the insurer the opportunity to investigate the circumstances surrounding the potential claim before the facts, witnesses, or other information are forgotten or lost.

Insured/Insured Person

The "insured" and, in some policies, "insured person," definition clarifies the individuals and entities covered by the policy. The definition is often found in the definitions section of the policy, although some D&O policies contain a specific who is insured section. By virtue of the definition, a typical D&O policy covers the following (the association is not included in the definition of "insured person" since they are already listed on the declarations as a named insured and are referenced under the Who is An Insured section):

- Duly elected or appointed past, present, and future directors, officers, and their spouses, if the spouse is named in the claim.
- Employees (in some cases, leased and temporary workers may be included)
- Volunteers
- Some policies contain an expanded "insured person" definition that includes trustees; the estates and heirs, legal representatives, and assigns of covered individuals (beneficial in case of the insolvency, incompetency, or death); the developer—covered for acts related to his capacity as board member, rather than in the capacity as the developer; and property managers

While it is usually not necessary to name the specific individuals for whom coverage is desired, coverage for past, present, and future directors and officers is especially important since many claims are filed after a director's or officer's term of service has ended. This "tail," as it is referred to in casualty policies, is why D&O policies are almost always written on a "claims-made" basis. "Claims-made" triggers were developed to limit the "tail" presented by "occurrence" coverage triggers.

Loss

Almost all D&O policies cover amounts the insured is legally obligated to pay for claims to which the insurance applies. However, it is important to review the "loss" definition carefully, as it clarifies and limits any payments made by the insurance company.

Typical D&O policy "loss" definitions include judgments, settlements, and defense costs. In some policies, the definition also includes punitive damages (where permitted by law) and fines and penalties. Some insurers will also pay a percentage (usually 10 percent) of an excise tax imposed upon certain awarded benefits.

The "loss" definition also usually specifies the types of payments that are not considered to be loss and are therefore not payable under the policy. Such payments may include taxes, civil or criminal fines or penalties, punitive damages, the cost of complying with injunctive or nonmonetary relief, multiplied damages, and matters uninsurable under the law.

The inclusion of defense costs within the "loss" definition is significant for two reasons. First, it confirms that defense costs are included in the policy's limit of liability. Second, it means that any policy definition of "defense costs" should be reviewed to fully understand what defense expenses are covered by the policy.

D&O policies that pay for civil or criminal fines and penalties, as well as punitive damages, are much preferred over policies that do not pay for such damages.

Wrongful Act

All D&O policies contain a "wrongful act" definition. The definition is included because it is fundamental to the scope of coverage provided by the policy. While there are variations between policy forms, a typical "wrongful act" definition includes the following offenses, whether actual or alleged:

- Act
- Error
- Omission
- Misstatement
- Misleading statement
- Neglect
- Breach of duty

Most "wrongful act" definitions also include wording that affirms coverage is provided for claims that are filed against insured persons solely by reason of serving in their capacity, or their status, as insured persons. This wording is important because a claim may be made against individuals who might not have had any involvement with the actual circumstances that resulted in the claim. For example, the entire board may be named in a defamation lawsuit even though only one of the directors made the defamatory statement.

Some D&O policies provide coverage for employment-related offenses, including but not limited to wrongful termination, breach of any implied employment contract, employment-related misrepresentation, discrimination, harassment (sexual or otherwise), failure to employ or promote, and illegal retaliatory treatment. When coverage is present, these offenses may be included with the policy's definition of "wrongful act," or enumerated in a separate "employment practices wrongful act" (or similar) definition.

D&O policies that also provide coverage for employment-related offenses are preferred because it is not necessary for the association to purchase a separate employment practices liability policy in order to have wrongful employment practices coverage.

Major Policy Exclusions

All D&O policies contain exclusions that clarify coverage by restricting or eliminating coverage for certain specified types of losses. In some instances, the excluded offense or circumstance is more properly the subject of other insurance. Other exclusions are included because the coverage is precluded by law or contrary to public policy. Some of the most important, and common, D&O policy exclusions are briefly discussed in the following paragraphs.

Bodily Injury/Property Damage/Personal Injury/ Advertising Injury

Losses resulting in bodily injury, property damage, and personal injury or advertising injury are typically excluded in D&O policies because they are the result of specific acts, rather than errors or omissions. Such injury, damage, or offenses are usually covered by the association's general liability insurance, even if the injury or damage results from a negligent decision or other wrongful act.

To illustrate, assume the association's board of directors votes to plant some large trees in the common area between two residential buildings. During a severe windstorm, one of the trees falls and damages a homeowner's balcony. The homeowner subsequently sues the board for making the decision to plant the trees and to recover the cost of fixing his balcony. There would be no coverage under the D&O policy because coverage for property damage is excluded. In this case, if the association were found liable for the damage, the association's general liability policy would pay the claim.

Some D&O policies provide coverage for personal or advertising injury offenses such as libel, slander, defamation, false advertising, breach of contract, or the like, as long as the offense results from a wrongful act as defined in the policy. If such coverage is present, wording of the bodily injury exclusion is usually modified so that the policy provides coverage for mental anguish, emotional distress, or other similar injury.

Similarly, when the D&O policy includes coverage for wrongful employment practices, the bodily injury exclusion is usually modified to provide coverage for claims alleging emotional distress and/or mental anguish.

When personal injury or advertising injury coverage is not provided under the basic D&O policy form, it is sometimes available by endorsement for additional premium.

Breach of Contract

Most D&O policies exclude coverage for liability the insured assumes in a written or oral contract unless the insured would be liable in the absence of the contract. An exception to this exclusion is often made for employment-related contracts, in which case the insurer typically will pay for both defense and awarded damages.

In some policies, the insurer will provide a defense (only) for any claims alleging breach of contract (including third-party, nonemployment contracts) but will not pay for any awarded damages. In most jurisdictions, breach of contract is an illegal act, especially if the breach is intentional. If the insurance company was required to pay the damages, insureds might be motivated to breach a contract and to look to insurance to pay the consequences of the breach. This would create a "moral hazard" and is generally prohibited as a matter of law or public policy.

Intentional Dishonest or Illegal Acts

All D&O policies exclude coverage for claims resulting from intentional dishonest acts committed by directors, officers, and other individual insureds. In some cases, a single exclusion may encompass all such acts, or the policy may contain separate exclusions, such as the following:

- Personal profit or other remuneration to which the person is not legally entitled—for example, this exclusion would preclude coverage for claims alleging a director or officer received an illegal bribe in exchange for voting to hire a particular vendor.

- Intentional fraudulent, dishonest, or criminal acts—precludes coverage if, for example, a director intentionally influences an election by withholding information that would make a board candidate ineligible to run for office.

- Willful or deliberate violations of law—for example, this exclusion would prevent coverage for claims alleging the board was aware of, but refused to comply with, a local building ordinance in order to save the association money when renovating a clubhouse.

Some D&O policies exclude coverage only for intentional dishonest or illegal acts if they are determined by adjudication to have actually occurred. Such policies are preferred because the policy will typically provide defense coverage unless and until such allegations are proven. They are also favored because most D&O litigation is resolved by settlement prior to final adjudication or any admission of wrongdoing.

Many D&O policies incorporate a nonimputation provision in the dishonesty and illegal acts exclusion. The provision is important because it clarifies that only those persons found to have committed the excluded act or offense are affected by the exclusion. Persons who did not commit the act or defense, but who might also be named in the claim or suit would still have the benefit of coverage.

In some policies, the nonimputation provision may appear elsewhere in the policy, such as at the beginning or end of the policy's exclusions section.

Failure to Maintain Insurance

Many D&O policies exclude coverage for claims resulting from the association's failure to purchase or maintain insurance. The types of insurance that are usually the subject of this exclusion are earthquake, flood, mold, and employee dishonesty. If not present in the D&O policy form, the exclusion is sometimes found in an attached endorsement.

Claims for failure to purchase or maintain insurance are usually filed after a loss occurs. The usual reasoning behind such claims is that the association's failure to purchase the insurance (or failure to purchase enough insurance) resulted in the association having to pay for loss or damage out of its own reserves. If insufficient funds were available to pay for the loss, it may have been necessary for the association to impose an assessment on unit-owners.

There are many versions of failure-to-maintain-insurance exclusions. Some policies will not pay for a loss but will pay some or all of the cost to defend insurance-related claims. Other policies exclude both loss and defense costs. Still others limit application of the exclusion to certain types of insurance, such as earthquake or flood coverage.

While many D&O policies will at least defend failure-to-insure claims, few will pay for the loss, even if the defense is unsuccessful. As is the case with breach of contract claims previously discussed, if insurers had to pay such claims, associations would not have to purchase separate insurance coverage and could look to the insurance companies to pay for the loss.

Outside Directorships

Sometimes association directors or officers also serve as a director, officer, or employee of another organization for business or charitable reasons. While not always the case, such service may be at the request of the association. For example, the association may ask one of its directors to serve on the board of a local charity as a matter of community goodwill. In the event the director is subsequently involved in a claim against the outside organization, and if that organization has limited D&O coverage, the director might try to look to his homeowner association's D&O policy for financial protection.

In order to avoid having to pay for claims resulting from the individual's service for another organization, most D&O insurers include an outside directorships exclusion in their policy forms. The exclusion typically states that coverage is excluded for any wrongful act by insured persons in the discharge of their duties in the capacity of, or by reason of their status as, a director, officer, trustee, or employee of any entity other than the insured organization, even if such service is directed or requested by the insured organization.

Some insurers will extend coverage by endorsement for those association directors or officers who also serve other organizations. The coverage may extend to service for any organization or be limited to service for nonprofit organizations. The extended coverage is usually excess of any indemnification or insurance coverage that is available to the individual through the outside organization.

Pollution

Most association D&O policies exclude claims resulting from actual or alleged pollution. What is considered by the insurer to be pollution may be stated in a policy definition of "pollutants" or may be stated within the pollution exclusion.

In most instances, the pollution exclusion not only applies to injury or damage resulting from a pollution incident (such as contamination of a groundwater aquifer that results from the pouring of toxic chemicals down a sewer or drain), but also to the cost of complying with requests or demands by government entities or others for testing or removal of contaminants.

Because pollution incidents typically result in bodily injury or property damage, they are usually the subject of general liability insurance coverage. However, an unendorsed commercial general liability policy provides very limited pollution coverage.

Prior and Pending Litigation and Claims

Almost all D&O policies exclude coverage for claims arising out of any civil, criminal, administrative, regulatory, or investigative proceeding initiated before a pending or prior litigation date that is usually specified on the declarations page of the policy. Even policies that do not contain a prior-and-pending-litigation exclusion often contain an exclusion that precludes coverage for claims arising out of circumstances that were the subject of any notice given under a prior policy. Many association D&O policies contain both exclusions, either within the policy form or stated in an attached endorsement.

The prior-and-pending-litigation and prior-notice exclusions are not usually an issue if the association has had long-term continuous coverage provided by the same insurer, or if a new insurer is willing to remove the exclusions by endorsement. By eliminating the exclusions, the insurer will cover such acts as long as they are not already covered by a prior policy, providing the circumstances resulting in the claim took place on or after any imposed policy retroactive date.

Punitive Damages/Fines/Penalties

Most D&O policies do not cover punitive damages or civil or criminal fines and penalties that may be awarded or charged as the result of the insured's wrongdoing. The exclusion of coverage for such damages is typically found within the policy's definition of "loss," or may be found in separate policy exclusions.

Even if their policy form excludes coverage for punitive damages, fines and penalties, many insurers will remove the exclusions by endorsement (sometimes for additional premium) as long as coverage is not prohibited by law.

Policy Conditions

The conditions section of D&O policy forms usually contains many conditions that are similar or identical to those found in other types of insurance policies. However, note the following two important D&O policy conditions.

Duties in the Event of a Claim

All D&O policies specify when notice of a claim or potential claim (see "claim" definition, discussed previously) is to be reported to the insurance company for coverage to apply. The notice must usually be in writing and given to the insurer "as soon as practicable" or "as soon as possible" after receipt. A few D&O policies state that the claim must be reported within a specified time frame (usually thirty days) after the policy period or any applicable discovery period.

In addition to reporting the claim (or potential claim) in a timely manner, the insured is typically required to cooperate with the insurer and promptly give the insurer a copy of any reports, investigations, pleadings, or other papers it receives in connection with the claim.

It is extremely important that the association be knowledgeable about the policy's claim reporting requirements as failure to comply with the requirements can jeopardize coverage.

Application

Most D&O policy forms contain a condition stating that the statements made in the insured's application for coverage are material representations. The condition typically goes on to state that the policy has been issued in reliance upon those representations, which are then considered to be incorporated in and made a part of the D&O policy. In some cases, the application is attached to the policy when the policy is issued. This is also sometimes referred to as a warranty. In property & casualty insurance, policy applications are not normally made part of the policy (as opposed to life insurance where this is very common). D&O insurance is a notable exception.

Fortunately for insureds, most application conditions also include a statement that the policy will not be voided or coverage rescinded if the statements in the application are untrue, except as to persons who make such statements with knowledge of their falsity. This severability feature is beneficial since it allows coverage to remain in effect with respect to other insureds that did not make intentional wrongful statements.

Coverage can, however, usually be rescinded for the organization if the person who signs the application on behalf of the organization knew of the falsity of statements that are contained in the application.

Summary

As is the case with all insurance, the broader the coverage provided by the D&O policy, the more protection it will afford both the association and its directors, officers, and other insured individuals. Accordingly, the most favorable D&O policy forms contain the following elements:

- Coverage for prior acts (i.e., no retroactive date)
- Coverage for past, present, and future directors and officers
- Coverage for both elected and appointed directors and officers
- Broad definitions of "claim" and "wrongful act"
- Coverage for employees, volunteers, and committee members
- Coverage for personal injury, such as libel, slander, defamation, and invasion of privacy
- Defense coverage for alleged dishonest or criminal acts until such allegations are proven by adjudication
- No settlement hammer clause
- Coverage for employment-related claims
- Coverage for claims seeking both monetary and nonmonetary damages

- Coverage for claims alleging mental anguish and emotional distress

- Coverage for punitive damages, fines, or penalties where permitted by law

- No exclusion for failure to purchase or maintain insurance

- Coverage for property managers and (where applicable) the association's developer

- Coverage for breach of third-party contracts

- Coverage for outside directorships (if applicable)

When seeking to purchase directors and officers liability insurance coverage, associations are well-advised to work with an insurance agent or broker who is thoroughly familiar with the unique exposures present in homeowner associations and should carefully review any proposed policy forms to make sure they provide the desired coverage. Whenever coverage appears vague, or is not understandable, clarification should be requested from the insurance company prior to purchase of the policy.

Chapter 6

The Agent and Underwriter as Partners in Condominium Insurance Coverage

The Agent and Condominium Coverage

The nature of condominiums demands that the sales process be collaborative and educational at the outset.

Condominium unit purchasers are not always aware of the complex world of condominium ownership. Happy to have someone else cut the grass or shovel the snow, they are often unaware of their roles and responsibilities under this arrangement.

The managers of condominium associations are generally more enlightened when it comes to their roles and responsibilities within the confines of the association as well as the insurance requirements of the association. While they may know the bylaws and covenants relating to insurance, they may not always be fully conversant with the language and intricacies of insurance policies, and they too will rely heavily on the insurance professional to guide them and shepherd them through the insurance process.

This chapter examines condominium customer expectations; the agent's role in meeting those expectations; customer coverage needs and those needs within the context of the provisions of the condominium property act and the policy forms reviewed earlier; and coverage limitations and coverage issues including deductibles, loss assessment, and insurance to value.

The agent's role with that of the underwriter's will be followed, and a checklist as a guide to both partners of what to consider when insuring condominiums is included.

Condominium Customer Expectations

When customers approach their agents for condominium insurance, their first expectation is that he knows condominium insurance and all that it entails. They look to their agent to provide them with a clear understanding of how the condominium product will satisfy their needs and safeguard their financial wellbeing. They look to their agent to build and maintain a strong business relationship. Whether it is a first time buyer purchasing a first home or the empty nester who is downsizing from a life of individual homeownership, they both want their agent to function as a business partner in putting together their insurance programs. And that partnership entails several items, including:

- taking a long-term view of that relationship;
- anticipating and responding to any problems they might have;
- providing them the financial security that will allow them to sleep easy at night;
- providing them with ongoing communication with useful and helpful information about the condominium market;
- providing them reliable and consistent service.

This is quite a tall order, but it is nothing less than you would expect if you were that customer. Nor is it all a one-way relationship where the agent is the only one tasked with delivering all the benefits. Remember, this relationship is a partnership in which the agent should enlist the customer's full participation at the outset. The complexity of the product as well as the maze that is the condominium property act and its interrelationship with declarations, bylaws, and policy wordings demands that the customer becomes an equal partner in this relationship.

The customers' enlistment in the role of partner begins with education. The agent must educate them on the complexities of the product they are buying. They must understand what the process looks like when a claim happens. The need to look at different documents in order to determine which policy covers what is important in the client's overall understanding of the coverage.

But why introduce the thought of losses before they happen? The condominium loss settlement process is not always simple. Knowing the requirements to follow after a loss before it happens produces an educated customer who will be a knowledgeable and helpful insured at the time of loss. There will be no surprises when dealing with the subject matter of insurance.

In the event that you are thinking that educating the condominium customer is a burdensome proposition, consider developing a subject matter expert within your agency.

Having a subject matter expert dedicated to condominium insurance within your agency pays high dividends in the handling of condominium insurance. If that individual becomes an expert on the condominium property act of your state along with expertise in the condominium wordings of the companies you represent, her expert knowledge would build strong customer relationships and facilitate the growth of that line of business within your agency. Condominium insurance knowledge as a competitive advantage will allow you to meet your customers' expectations and craft the condominium insurance coverages that best suit the needs of your customers.

Putting It All Together for the Condo Unit Owner

Once the unit owner has the condominium documents in hand, he is ready to discuss his coverage needs. Also of value in this meeting is a home inventory; many people underestimate the value of their belongings, and this is a good opportunity to establish proper coverage from the beginning. There are many ways to create an inventory, including smartphone apps that allow insureds to photograph belongings. Many people may not keep receipts, and a good inventory provides evidence that the property existed. This meeting must result in a complete understanding of the unit owner's needs, an analysis of exposures, and the identification and resolution of any coverage gaps.

This exercise must begin with an examination of the condominium declaration, its bylaws, and the state's laws governing condominium insurance. Not only must the policy meet the requirements under the association's declaration and covenants, but it must also comply with state law.

This first step in the coverage assessment process will help identify the boundaries of coverage and resolve the "what" of insurance. It will identify the building elements not covered by the association's policy and therefore needing coverage under the unit owner's policy. This preliminary assessment will paint a picture of the scope of coverage needed. Remember that many unit owners' policies will have a clause that states that property which is the insured's responsibility under a corporation or association of property owner's agreement is covered. Those elements must still be identified so insureds know what is covered under their policy, and what their responsibilities are.

From this picture, make a list of the items within the unit owner's purview of coverage, and with the unit owner's help, establish a replacement value for each. The sum total of those individual values should represent an adequate Coverage A limit. During this process, be sure to identify any coverage gaps and close them.

The second step in the process includes establishing the value of moveable personal property, including items of unique value, like paintings or stamp and coin collections that need to be specifically valued and insured at their true replacement costs. This is where the completed home inventory is essential; it allows the agent to establish the proper coverage limit and identify any specific items that may need to be scheduled separately. Remember when scheduling specific items that appraisals are often needed; make sure the insured has current, accurate appraisals from reputable appraisers to ensure items are covered properly. For individuals with higher valued condominiums, it may be wise to work with an agent and insurer that provides "private client" programs. "Private client" is a term the insurance industry uses to describe those who have more assets – either in quantity or higher valued ones – that exceed the maximum coverage limit of standard insurance carriers. Private client insurance offers comprehensive coverage with higher liability limits, to protect those in the higher-end market.

Once the true value for Coverage A – Dwelling and Coverage C – Personal Property exposures is established, the addition of special perils coverage for contents coverage may be needed. An insured should also consider adding ISO HO 17 31, Unit-Owners Coverage C, which adds special cause of loss for contents and HO 17 32, Unit-Owners Coverage A Special Coverage, which adds special causes of loss for property coverage.; The forms expand the covered perils and provide the broadest coverage available to the client. Here too state law should be consulted to ensure that scope of coverage requirements are being met.

In addition to the structural and contents coverage requirements, the unit owner will also have a liability exposure relating to bodily injury and property damage to third parties. Again, the condominium declaration and covenants, together with state law governing requirements, should be consulted to properly assess boundaries and responsibilities.

Once the proper assessment is made, set the proper limits of liability. In addition to the underlying limits of coverage, it is good practice to also offer umbrella coverage, as well as Directors and Officers Liability (D&O) coverage in the event that your client serves on the condominium association's board.

Although the association should carry its own D&O coverage to protect its board members, the additional protection the client carries is helpful. Of course it is important to know how this coverage dovetails with any association coverage or state law requirements.

With the exposures for building, contents, and liability assessed and covered, it is paramount that any gaps in coverage be identified and resolved at the inception stage of the policy construction. Examining the condominium instruments, understanding the condominium property act for the state, together with knowledge and understanding of coverage wordings of the companies represented, will provide an excellent picture of any coverage gaps faced by the client. The two most glaring areas would likely be loss assessment and deductible.

Loss Assessment

Loss assessment provides the insured with protection for assessments made by the condominium association against the insured for loss to collectively owned property. That assessment could be for direct damage by a covered cause of loss or for legal liability arising out of collectively owned property.

In each case the ISO policy affords a $2,000 limit of coverage. This low limit is an obvious exposure for the client, since under both property and liability, the exposure to loss is usually much higher. Providing limits that more adequately reflect the customer's true exposure is paramount. This could be done through ISO HO 04 35 Supplemental Loss Assessment Coverage. The cost of increasing those limits is usually quite affordable. The increased limits of cover combined with the special cause of loss forms gives the customer both higher limits for a wider scope of coverage, all at a very affordable price. That is true value for money.

With the loss assessment limit gap assessed and closed, attention should be turned to the other contentious coverage issue: the assumption of the master policy deductible by the unit owner.

Deductible

As seen in the chapter dealing with coverage wordings, the deductible clauses of both the association form and the unit owners forms are crafted to read and function as any normal deductible clause would: to pay covered losses that are in excess of the policy deductible. What is unwritten is the response of the unit owner's policy to the association's master policy deductible in the event of loss.

The agent's first assessment regarding the deductible is determining the unit owner's responsibility for the association's deductible. This is determined through examination of the condominium association's documents, including its declaration and bylaws.

If the association's responsibility for coverage includes individual units, and if the association, under its official documents, assumes responsibility for the deductible for losses affecting individual units, then there is little or no argument concerning deductibles following a loss.

But what if the association rules place responsibility for deductibles for loss originating from the insured's unit solely on the insured? And what if the association has an inordinately high deductible as is customary today? Then the issue should be resolved at this stage in the construction of coverage.

Resolution of this problem sometimes lies in the manner in which insurance carriers choose to handle deductibles in such cases. Some may allow the application of the Coverage A limit to settle the deductible if condo rules allow and Coverage A limits are high enough.

Others may take a more punitive approach by allowing only $2,000 of coverage under the standard policy. This more often than not leaves insureds out-of-pocket in loss situations occurring in their units.

This deductible gap exposure should be carefully explained to clients, as this is one of the challenges of condominium ownership that they may not have contemplated. Closing that gap could be achieved through the purchase of deductible insurance if available. If it is not and the insured is still willing to accept this gap, then an explanation and written confirmation of this shortfall should be given to the client. Failure to do so could result in future errors and omissions claims.

Closing this deductible coverage gap remains problematic in the insurance industry, and will persist as long as there are pressures on associations (sometimes brought on by unit owners to reduce costs and therefore condo fees) to reduce costs while optimizing coverage. And this responsibility to balance cost and value for money spills over to the insurance requirements of the condominium association.

Putting It All Together for the Condominium Association

In putting together coverage for the condominium association, three sets of documents provide the basis for the scope and extent of coverage.

(1) The condominium property act of the association's state

(2) The condominium declaration

(3) Bylaws and other instruments

(4) Information regarding the condominium property manager

The condominium act, to which the declaration is subject, defines the boundaries of coverage responsibility. Additionally, the condominium instruments could further clarify scope, extent, and type of coverage as permitted under the act.

Armed with these documents, it becomes easy to identify and itemize the coverage areas and to add limits to each area and item subject to coverage. The Illinois Condominium Property Act used in a previous example dictates coverage obligations of the association. Section 12. clearly lays out the coverage requirements.

(1) Property insurance must be placed on both common elements and units, including limited common elements. The act clearly defines those, making it easy to ascribe limits and values to them.

(2) Coverage must be for special form causes of loss.

(3) The total amount of coverage must be for the full replacement cost of the property less deductible, but including coverage for increased costs of construction due to building code requirements.

(4) General liability insurance at a minimum of $1,000,000 is required or greater if a larger limit is mandated by the board of managers.

(5) The act mandates fidelity and D&O coverage.

(6) The act spells out how deductibles are to be applied.

(7) Insured parties, waiver of subrogation, which policy is to be primary, and how losses are to be settled are all defined.

Such specificity regarding insurance requirements makes it easy to structure condominium association coverage. It is one of the reasons to be conversant with the condominium property act or the horizontal property act for your state.

Adding the requirements of the declaration and other instruments of the condominium association to the requirements under the act provides a perfect picture of the interrelationship between the association coverage requirements and the unit owner requirements. Doing so also produces insights into the deductible assessment and other assessment requirements placed on unit owners. This is especially helpful for insuring both unit owner and association and will provide the unique ability to properly craft coverage for both parties that dovetail with each other. It is also important to know who is managing the condominium. In some condominium associations, the condominium owners themselves manage the complex; in most, the condominium management is handled by a professional property manager. An agent should be very wary of a condominium managed by its owners and not a reputable, experienced property manager.

Even without insuring both stakeholders, understanding state act requirements and condominium instruments requirements in structuring insurance coverage puts the agent ahead of the curve in providing value to condominium customers. And that value includes the perfect balance among price, product, and service. It also includes adequacy of limits and insurance to value.

Insurance to Value

As discussed earlier, the declaration, bylaws, and relevant state act will help define elements of coverage for both the condominium unit owner and the condominium association. In each case, an itemization of the objects of coverage and assignment of replacement value for each with help from the respective insureds will yield the proper limits of coverage.

Summary

It is important to understand the states' acts and condominium instruments in structuring insurance coverage for both unit owners and condominium associations; from determining the unit owner's responsibility for building structure items, to his responsibility under condominium association assessments, to the association's roles and responsibilities for coverage; these documents are key.

Once the secrets of the act and the condominium instruments are unlocked to gather all that is needed to determine the objects of coverage, the scope of coverage and the exposures inherent in serving condominium customers, an agent will have done an excellent job in getting the submission ready for presentation to the underwriter for binding coverage and providing the best possible policy coverage for clients.

The Underwriter and Condominium Coverage

An underwriter of condominium insurance is tasked to deliver long-term profit and growth in this segment and consequently deliver value to shareholders. In order to achieve these two objectives, an underwriter must attract and retain profitable condominium customers by satisfying their need for the best possible insurance product at an affordable price.

It is this balancing act of satisfying customer need and providing value for shareholders amid sometimes tumultuous and difficult market conditions that will prove to be the biggest test of an underwriter of condominium insurance. The good news is, there is a way to successfully meet both requirements that in the end will allow the underwriter to satisfy all stakeholders by providing a product that properly balances price, product, and service for the insured. On a day-to-day basis, underwriters measure the value they provide to shareholders by **underwriting profit**. Are the risks in the portfolio the underwriter is responsible for profitable? Underwriting profit (sometimes called underwriting gain) is calculated through a combined ratio, which signifies the amount of money earned for each dollar of premium collected. A combined ratio of 95%, for example, means that for every $100 of premium collected, the insurer retains $5, after paying losses and expenses of $95. The goal is to always achieve a combined ratio less than 100% to achieve a desired underwriting gain.

How is the underwriter able to achieve these two mandates? By exploring an approach to underwriting condominium insurance that uses the condominium property act as context and that provides a roadmap to successfully underwriting condominium insurance.

This chapter ends by examining the two main problem issues encountered by insureds: deductibles and assessments, and explores ways underwriters, in collaboration with agents or brokers, can alleviate those two challenges.

Underwriting Condominium Association Coverage

The first step in the process is to ensure that the risk meets the company's strategic objectives—primarily to make sure that it is a risk that meets the company's guidelines with respect to type of risk and profit potential.

Understanding the Object of Insurance

Given the diversity in the types of condominiums in the market—high rises, town houses, stand-alone homes—the type of risk needs to be established. Once the type of risk has been established, establish the coverage boundaries. This is where the agent comes in. The agent should be conversant with the provisions of the state's condominium property act or horizontal property act, as well as the content of the condominium declaration and bylaws. The expert knowledge that both the agent and the underwriter possess together with the combined knowledge of condominiums as a market segment will allow the underwriter to establish the objects of insurance as well as the limits of insurance.

If the underwriter is heavily reliant on the agent in placing business, it is of paramount importance that the agent also has expert knowledge of that particular risk from within that condominium segment. Using an agent puts the underwriter one-step removed from the customer, so any lack of knowledge on the part of the agent about the risk being placed magnifies any lack of knowledge the underwriter has about the risk. This knowledge gap will jeopardize the chances of meeting the company's first requirement of underwriters: to write profitable business. The first step to underwriting profitable business is to have a clear and full understanding of any risks reviewed.

Understanding the Needs of the Condominium Association

Early collaboration with the agent in establishing the boundaries around the objects of insurance places the underwriter in the optimal position of being able to understand the needs of the customer. Knowing the insurance requirements under the laws of both in the condominium property act and the condominium instruments enables the underwriter to properly match insurance coverage to the insured's needs. This is the ultimate requirement for customer satisfaction and ultimately risk retention—matching the proper coverage to the insured's needs, thereby providing customer value. However, providing customer value achieves only one part of the mandate of underwriter. The other part of the mandate is achieving underwriting profit.

Achieving Underwriting Profit

Attaining an underwriting profit requires an examination of the exposures the underwriter assumes on the company's behalf and an assessment of how well those exposures are controlled so as to mitigate loss. This requires a rigorous examination of the **C**onstruction, **O**ccupancy, **P**rotection, and **E**xposure (COPE) elements of the risk along with any moral hazards that might be inherent in the risk. Over the last decade, digital tools (smart home devices for example) as well as predictive underwriting and pricing models have made this process much more efficient for underwriters.

The underwriter will also be able to understand exposures to loss in the various coverage lines assumed. For example, in the Illinois Act, coverage must be included for the following.

- Property
- General Liability
- Fidelity Bond
- Directors & Officers Liability

The underwriter must decide what this means to the company in the aggregate if one or more lines of coverage are attached in the event of a loss. This requires a thorough understanding of the company's underwriting capacity and the underwriter's personal underwriting authority.

Authority and Capacity

Once the exposures are assessed, and the underwriter deems the controls enough to safeguard profitability, he must attend to the company's ability to assume the condominium risk in question. This hinges on both the company's financial capability as well as on its reinsurance treaty arrangements. Once the ability to assume the risk is verified under either or both of these requirements, the underwriter is in a position to properly price the risk.

Price Commensurate with Exposure

Just as balance was struck between need and coverage for the customer, it must now be stuck between price and exposure for the insurer. And because the underwriter clearly understands the objects of insurance, the exposures to be assumed, and the controls in place to mitigate loss, achieving an underwriting profit through proper pricing becomes possible. Although the ultimate price could be tempered by prevailing market conditions and the customer's expectation around pricing, through the underwriter's depth of knowledge of the condominium market and the specific condominium risk before him, he will be able to make an objective and informed decision about the ultimate price. In the end, the twin objectives of value for the customer and underwriting profit will have been achieved.

Underwriting Condominium Unit Owners Coverage

Examining the act and the condominium instruments will give the underwriter the information needed to determine the unit owner's insurance needs. The underwriter will know whether, for example, the association is responsible for insuring the unit, not insuring it, or whether it is given the option to insure it. Until being able to establish the coverage boundaries, the underwriter will not be able to assess the insured's needs or the exposures assumed in issuing a policy for the unit owner.

Although it is not customary for underwriters to do this kind of assessment, and instead rely solely on the coverage requests made by agents, it is clear that in order to properly serve customer and shareholder, this type of assessment is paramount. The underwriter also will have "cost estimator" tools available which can accurately determine the replacement cost of the unit structure.

How else will the underwriter know what Coverage A under HO 06 should cover? How will the underwriter determine the responsibility of the unit owner versus that of the association? Understanding and clarifying the scope and boundaries of coverage at the inception stage of the policy minimizes problems around loss settlement at the back end of the underwriting process.

There is no question that taking this approach to underwriting takes time. But time should not really be the issue. Achieving underwriting profit while providing value for customers are the important issues. And if a little extra time is needed at the front end of the underwriting process, take the time to do it right.

That time, of course, should be taken in collaboration with the agent because it is at this stage that both should resolve potential problems around deductibles and assessments.

Working to Resolve the Deductible Issue

At some point the industry must come to terms with the problem of deductibles in condominium insurance.

There is currently a hodgepodge approach with different companies and markets taking different approaches depending on the circumstances. An underwriter's approach will be mandated by the company, but it should not be so skewed as to protect the company's interest to the detriment of the insured. There must be balance and a sense of fairness in the construction of the policy.

The approach to deductibles must start with the act and the condominium instruments. As seen in the Illinois example, the act clearly states how deductibles are to be handled:

> (c) Deductibles. The board of directors of the association may, in the case of a claim for damage to a unit or the common elements, (i) pay the deductible amount as a common expense, (ii) after notice and an opportunity for a hearing, assess the deductible amount against the owners who caused the damage or from whose units the damage or cause of loss originated, or (iii) require the unit owners of the units affected to pay the deductible amount. [Sec. 12. Insurance]

We know from this subsection that leeway is given the association in handling deductibles. Because of this flexibility, the underwriter must look to the condominium instruments to see what options the association has exercised in dealing with deductibles. Once this is established, the underwriter and the agent should then decide how the policy should be structured to take care of any deductible obligation the unit owner is to assume in the event of a loss.

The inception stage of the underwriting process is when the deductible issue is resolved, not at the time of loss. It is unfair for the customer to be faced with an association's deductible that could on occasion reach as high as $50,000 or more at the time of loss while insurers for the unit owner and insurers for the association argue about who should pay and for what amount.

What would be helpful to unit owners is to have loss assessment coverage both on the standard ISO HO OO 06 and on the HO 04 35 03 22 endorsement; include this coverage for more than the $2,000 offered by either form. After all, it is unfair to have a personal insurance customer (the unit owner) pay for commercial coverage, which is what the association deductible represents. Not only that, in this scenario the unit owner is being asked to pay insurance twice: once as an assessment by the association on unit owners as part of its costs, and twice at claim time. This is usually an out-of-pocket cost for the unit owner.

Resolving the deductible issue requires collaboration between the underwriter and agent at the very beginning of the process. All should decide at the outset how deductibles would be handled at the time of loss, with one possible settlement option being the provision of higher limits for paying deductibles within loss assessment coverage.

Loss Assessment Coverage

Outside of the deductible issue, the primary coverage challenge for unit owners is the loss assessment limits of coverage afforded under both the property and liability sections of the policy.

Under Coverage A, loss assessment coverage responds to the unit owner's share of losses assessed by the association as a result of a covered loss to collectively owned property.

Under the liability section of the policy, the coverage responds to assessment on the insured by the association for liability arising out of the use of collectively owned property.

In both cases, Coverage A and Coverage D, Section II, the limit afforded is only $2,000, clearly insufficient coverage. Underwriter and agent should work together to ensure that proper limits are established and the policy is written accordingly. Closing the loss assessment coverage gap as well as the deductible coverage gap would go a long way in satisfying customer requirements under the policy. And once those two major requirements are satisfied, the other coverage needs are easy to establish and satisfy. Using the act and the condominium instruments, the coverage boundaries are established, making it easy to:

- identify and understand the objects of coverage;
- understand the controls necessary to mitigate loss;
- properly price the risk;
- provide the customer with value;
- achieve an underwriting profit.

Agents and underwriters of condominium insurance have only one customer and owe it to that customer to provide the best value without forgetting the need to balance customer value with shareholder value.

The following checklist will help in making acquisition and underwriting decisions that facilitate the balance needed to satisfy all stakeholders.

Things to Consider When Insuring Condominiums

	Agent	Underwriter	Coverage
Contents	Have the insured provide a valuation of his contents; remember to include special items, such as baseball cards, for specialized coverage.	Assess exposure, provide coverage.	Coverage for replacement cost; add special perils coverage where needed.

	Agent	Underwriter	Coverage
Building	Get a copy of bylaws and association documents showing unit owners and association responsibilities. Obtain information about the condominium property manager (years of experience, level of expertise managing condominiums, etc.) Get a copy of the deed. Determine (a) what the unit owner actually owns; (b) what thc unit owner is required to insure; (c) what the association is required to insure. Work with unit owner to determine what it would cost to replace and fully install all he is responsible for.	1. Establish with agent that bylaws and condominium instruments have been consulted in establishing coverage. 2. Request a copy of bylaws to ensure boundaries and exposures are well understood. 3. Consult state condominium act to verify boundaries, if necessary.	1. Establish full Coverage A limit. 2. Add special perils coverage where needed, including replacement cost.
Loss Assessment	Increase loss assessment limit to the maximum possible.	Work with agent to ensure adequacy of coverage.	Maximize coverage.
Deductible	Find out current master policy deductible as well as maximum deductible authorized in the declaration; choose the higher, in the event the association raises its deductible at a later date.	1. Establish with the agent how the master policy deductible will apply in a loss situation. 2. Come to a mutual agreement at the outset.	Write the agreement into the policy to avoid disputes or confusion when a loss occurs.

	Agent	Underwriter	Coverage
Liability	1. Sell adequate underlying liability limits. 2. Add umbrella liability coverage.	1. Ensure limits are sufficient to cover exposures. 2. Ensure that capacity is available.	Ensure coverage meets state act requirements.
D&O	Sell adequate limits.	Assess exposure, including: 1. The extent of powers that directors and officers have. 2. If proper controls are in place to prevent mismanagement of funds. 3. Adequacy of the reserve fund compared to the age of the building. 4. Whether the duties and powers afforded the directors and officers by the association are reasonable. 5. Financial viability. 6. D&O loss history. 7. Frequency in turnover of directors and officers. 8. Occupancy percentage. 9. Residency of officers and directors.	After complete assessment, provide needed coverage.

	Agent	Underwriter	Coverage
Other Coverages	1. Add sewer backup coverage. 2. Assess the need for flood and earthquake coverage. 3. Assess wind damage coverage availability.	Assess state requirements and company capacity.	Provide best possible coverage in both scope and limits.

Summary

In using the outlined approach of using the condominium property act and the condominium instruments as a basis for establishing coverage to sell and underwrite condominium insurance, agents and underwriters will have taken the time to do all the right things for all stakeholders in the process, so as to minimize or eliminate claims issues at the back end of the process. Condominium claims are not always straightforward and can provide huge challenges for the claims adjuster.

Chapter 7

Condominium Insurance and Claims Settlement

A claims adjuster's job would be a great deal easier if agents and underwriters used the condominium property act in conjunction with the condominium instruments to define and structure coverage. The many challenges that arise at the back end of the process would be alleviated. Unfortunately, this approach to risk acquisition and underwriting is not always followed, and oftentimes claims adjusters are left to battle a host of issues including scope of coverage and coverage intent. Regardless of what happened at the front end, adjusters must embrace their own responsibilities at the back end. To help adjusters perform effectively in delivering on their end of the bargain, the chapter presents a series of claims scenarios to help in honing skills and knowledge in dealing with similar circumstances.

The chapter closes by examining how adjusters can help underwriters and agents avoid coverage problems by collaborating with them at the front end of the process—sharing information on what the stakeholders can do to facilitate customer satisfaction at the moment of truth, where claims happen.

Condominium Claims Settlement

From First Notice to Settlement—Unit Owner's Property

The first notice of loss always signals an upcoming moment of truth: the time for the insurance company to deliver on the promise made to its customer. On straightforward claims the process could take the following form:

- Report
- Coverage verification
- Investigation
- Assessment and resolution
- Settlement

- Recovery
- Closure

Report

The first notice of loss generally comes from the insured, agent, or broker. A brief description usually accompanies the report. At this early stage, the adjuster should get as clear a picture as possible about the circumstance surrounding the loss. The picture should include answers to the 4Ws of coverage: establish the true insured (who), the objects involved in the loss (what), verification of the location of loss (where), and date and time of loss (when). At this stage the loss settlement process and what is expected should be explained to the insured. The insured should also be able to get a sense that the adjuster understands his plight, is empathetic toward his circumstance, and understands his needs.

Armed with the information from the initial report, the adjuster is now in a position to establish what coverage is available, if any. This process would include checking.

Coverage Verification

- The policy declarations and unit-owners policy need to be reviewed to determine what coverage is available, what limits are in place, and what exclusions may apply.
- Policy term
- Location
- Loss payees
- Mortgages
- Endorsements
- Exclusions/limitations
- Limits of coverage
- Deductible

Once you have done the necessary checks to verify coverage, then the investigation can begin in earnest.

Investigation

There are two other documents that should form part of the investigation: a copy of the condominium declarations and a copy of the condominium bylaws. Just as they were essential in establishing objects of coverage at the inception of the policy, so are they equally essential in establishing the objects of loss. They are paramount in establishing the boundaries of coverage thereby making it easy to determine where coverage begins and where it ends. These two documents, in addition to the unit-owners policy and information generated in the coverage verification process, will help determine:

- any coverage issues;
- scope of the claim (coverage sections of the policy affected);
- any subrogation potential;
- indicators of the insured's involvement in the loss;
- any potential liability exposure.

On the straightforward claim, these two documents do the due diligence as respects:

- documentation;
- assignment of vendors/contractors;
- advice to underwriting;
- collaboration with all stakeholders;
- provision of ongoing reports to the claimant in accordance with an earlier explanation to the insured of the claims settlement process.

Assessment and Resolution of the Claim

In assessing the claim, continue to:

- provide support and progress reports to the insured;
- use vendors/contractors to assess the loss;

- review the results of the assessment with the insured to ensure that he agrees with repairs or replacement of items;
- determine what items are salvageable;
- promptly value and negotiate settlement, if any, with insured.

Settlement

Once value has been established and confirmed, settlement should proceed promptly.

Recovery

Recovery could take two forms: salvage or subrogation. Once the claim has been resolved with the insured, contractors could be approached about purchasing any salvage. If there is an opportunity for subrogation, then the responsible party should be pursued for recovery.

Closure

Closure of the process means ensuring that:

- all payments have been made;
- all reserves are closed;
- all recoveries have been considered, pursued, and realized;
- you have contacted the insured to ensure that the claim is indeed wrapped up;
- all required notification has been sent as needed;
- moment of truth has been fulfilled.

From First Notice to Settlement— Unit Owners Liability

The liability claims settlement process looks very much like the property claims settlement process with the differences reflected only in the nature of the claims the two processes intend to resolve. Like the process for property, it too deals with the critical stages of:

- report;
- coverage verification;
- investigation;
- assessment and resolution;
- settlement;
- recovery;
- closure.

Report

The first notice of liability claims could come from different sources including the insured, agent, broker, or third party. As with property losses, adjusters must get as clear a picture as possible of the loss circumstances, including the parties involved, location of loss, date and time, nature of injuries and/or damage, and preventive or protective actions to protect persons or property.

Coverage Verification

Again the unit owners policy must be reviewed in order to verify coverage. This verification includes:

- policy term;
- location;
- endorsements, including additional insureds or hold harmless agreements;
- exclusions/limitations;
- limits of coverage;
- deductibles.

If there are coverage issues, these must be dealt with immediately in accordance with the company's policy regarding such issues. If there are no coverage issues, the investigation proper may begin.

Investigation

Key considerations in the investigation process include:

- control and reduction of the loss potential;
- determination of the amount of investigation required as well as the scope of documentation;
- the expenses to be incurred vis-à-vis the loss potential;
- proper compliance with the company's file documentation standards.

The cause of loss is imperative in a liability claim. Along with the policy itself, the condominium declarations and bylaws are two key instruments in the investigation process. As with property losses, these two documents will help to determine the boundaries of coverage between the association or the unit owner. They will help ferret out any coverage issues and whether to proceed on a "without prejudice" basis through a reservation of rights letter to forestall any estoppel that could result without it.

The investigation process will help determine:

- who is liable;
- whether there is any contributory negligence;
- whether any other party should be put on notice;
- if proscription is at play;
- amount of exposure.

Due diligence is also necessary with respect to:

- obtaining detailed loss information from the insured, third parties, and witnesses;
- scene investigation;
- retention of experts;
- use of any other investigation tools and/or methodologies required.

Assessment and Resolution of the Claim

The goals of the assessment stage are to:

- seek appraisals from contractors in property damage losses;
- collect data, such as medical reports, income loss documentation, and other evidence needed to assess the amount of loss in bodily injury losses;
- select and retain experts as necessary to help determine amount of loss;
- provide clear and concise instructions to defense counsel;
- review case law as needed.

Settlement

At this point in the process the amount of the loss will start becoming clear. If the amount is beyond the adjuster's settlement authority, it is mandatory to receive the necessary sign-off from superiors. If a settlement agreement cannot be reached, mediation is always an option. Once settlement is achieved, all good adjusters should look for opportunities for recovery.

Recovery

If there is an opportunity to subrogate, the responsible third party should be pursued. If the loss was a property damage loss and the policy has a property damage deductible, the deductible should be recoverable. If legal action is contemplated, the company's guidelines will provide a roadmap for that process.

Closure

Closure includes making sure that:

- all payments have been made;
- reserves have been finalized;
- final releases have been signed;
- all required notification has been sent.

This outline of what would be a simple and straightforward liability claim should result in the fulfillment of the company's moment of truth to the insured.

From First Notice to Settlement—Condominium Association Property and Liability

The loss settlement process for the condominium association would essentially be the same as that of the unit owner for property and liability. The process should begin the same way: examination of both the condominium declarations and the condominium bylaws, and the insurance policy. Additionally, examine the requirements of the act for the appropriate state as it may contain certain important insurance requirements needed to consider as part of the loss settlement process.

For example, the Illinois Condominium Property Act places the following claims settlement requirements on insurers:

> (k) Settlement of claims. Any insurer defending a liability claim against a condominium association must notify the association of the terms of the settlement no less than 10 days before settling the claim. The association may not veto the settlement unless otherwise provided by contract or statute. [Sec. 12. Insurance]

It places an important obligation on the insurer and adjuster with which they must comply. Additionally, the Illinois Act places the following certificates of insurance requirements for contractors and vendors doing business with the condominium association:

> (i) Certificates of insurance. Contractors and vendors (except public utilities) doing business with a condominium association under contracts exceeding $10,000 per year must provide certificates of insurance naming the association, its board of directors, and its managing agent as additional insured parties. [Sec. 12. Insurance]

This requirement is important to be aware of as it could produce subrogation opportunities in liability claims situations. Having contractors and vendors insured prevents the association from assuming responsibility for liability resulting from the actions of others.

The condominium property act also mandates the following guidelines regarding mandatory unit owner coverage:

> (h) Mandatory unit owner coverage. The board of directors may, under the declaration and bylaws or by rule, require condominium

> unit owners to obtain insurance covering their personal liability and compensatory (but not consequential) damages to another unit caused by the negligence of the owner or his or her guests, residents, or invitees, or regardless of any negligence originating from the unit. The personal liability of a unit owner or association member must include the deductible of the owner whose unit was damaged, any damage not covered by insurance required by this subsection, as well as the decorating, painting, wall and floor coverings, trim, appliances, equipment, and other furnishings. [Sec.12. Insurance]

This subsection mandates coverage. Regardless of the loss situation and whether the loss is caused by the negligence of the owner, guests, residents, or invitees, the association cannot be held responsible for lack of coverage by the unit owner.

The importance of being in possession of and conversant with the condominium property act, and the declarations and bylaws of the condominium association during a loss, cannot be overemphasized. These documents, together with an effective and efficient loss settlement process, provide the perfect roadmap for settling condominium losses.

Although a rather straightforward claims settlement process for condominium loss settlement has been sketched, its central purpose is to help develop an understanding of the essential tools and steps necessary for condominium claims. The stage is set for examination of some of the challenges real life claims could pose. The following are some claims examples and the interplay among unit owner, the association, and the adjusting process.

In the first case, think about what you would do the same or differently. Be attentive to the process and think about how it could be improved. Reflect on the adjuster's decisions and the timing of certain actions. Would you have taken them sooner or later?

Call to mind the coverage issues and assess their importance in the current scenario. How important was coverage and policy response, given the stance taken by the association?

Put yourself in the shoes of the insured; feel the angst and pressure that he feels as he is squeezed between the time pressures imposed by the association to get repairs done, the coverage uncertainty he faces, and the mounting costs of attorney's fees as well as additional costs and assessments.

Reflect too on the importance of knowing the relevant act, and what it means to the settlement process. What difference would it have made to the speed and timeliness of the settlement process?

In the final analysis, reflect on the lessons learned from this scenario and the application of those lessons to your world.

Condominium Water Loss

Mrs. Minerva, unit owner, has a pipe burst, flooding her unit and the one beneath. The water soaks the unit owner's floor, the ceiling, walls, and the carpet of the unit owner beneath the insured, and soaks the floor of the common hallway. How should this loss be covered?

First, the state's condominium act needs to be reviewed to determine what is the unit owner's property and what is a common or limited common element. For the sake of the example, walls, floors, and ceilings designated as boundaries of a separate unit and halls, stairs, and lobbies are all considered to be common elements. Further, all lath, furring, wallboard, and finished floors are part of the unit.

Based on the act, Mrs. Minerva's finished floor is considered to be part of her unit. The flooring beneath Mrs. Minerva's finished floor, the ceiling, and walls of the next unit owner from the finished surface out, and the common hallway are common elements. The carpet of the next unit owner and the finished walls of that unit are considered parts of that unit.

In this state, the association policy is not primary over an individual unit-owners policy. The damage to Mrs. Minerva's finished floor is covered by her unit-owners policy. Since the walls, floors, ceilings, halls, and lobbies are considered to be common elements, these are covered by the association policy.

Coverage for damage to the other unit can be found under Mrs. Minerva's policy's damage to property of others section. No liability needs to be determined; the coverage is for damage to property of others caused by an insured. The limit for this coverage is $5,000. The other unit owner's policy will cover any remaining damage to the finished surfaces of the ceiling, walls, and carpet although the nonfinished areas are covered by the association policy.

The limit was raised with the last update to the HO 00 06 form in 2022.

This case is merely a snapshot of the world of condominium claims. Yet in this snapshot, the roles and responsibilities of all stakeholders are abundantly clear. Just as important is the need for each stakeholder to understand his role and responsibility and to execute accordingly.

Additionally, the importance of taking care of things at the front end of the process to alleviate problems at the back end is clearly demonstrated in this example. It highlights the need for attention to detail in some key areas, such as the following:

- Condominium unit purchasers should do painstaking research to ensure that they are buying into the condominium complex where the construction is excellent, the condominium instruments fair and reasonable from their perspective, and that the board of managers is reasonable.
- The purchasers must be fully cognizant of their responsibilities and the consequences of failing to meet those responsibilities.
- The purchasers must be conversant with the declarations and bylaws of the prospective communities in order to know whether they will be able to live within the tenets of the instruments that will govern their conduct as owners.
- They should also be aware of their insurance requirements and work with their brokers to understand those requirements.
- Brokers must be the best insurance guides and educators they could be, ensuring that from a scope and limits standpoint, their clients are covered.
- Underwriters must know what they insure, which requires a good knowledge of the territory in which they write business. Knowledge of the projects they insure and the quality of the construction of those projects along with the fundamental underwriting requirements is paramount.
- Adjusters must know the products, the process, and how to execute effectively.

These precautions are by no means exhaustive, but as a bare minimum, they act as introductory steps to safeguarding all stakeholders.

Yet, every condominium association is different; declarations are different, as are bylaws; even for the same developer. So knowing the instruments of one association does not equal knowing the instruments of all associations. Each has to be studied, analyzed, and judged on its own merits.

The example case could have turned out very differently with a different association, different bylaws, and a different board of managers. As the facts show, all of these elements can make a huge difference.

Beyond possibly purchasing a poorly constructed condominium unit, did the unit owner meet what would be deemed critical insurance tests? Did the unit owner meet the coverage criteria required by the act? Were boundaries of coverage reasonably clear to allow for proper calculation of limits? Did he purchase the right scope and limits of coverage?

By all accounts, the unit owner appears to have met the mandatory personal liability under the act and responsibly purchased both personal liability and umbrella liability at reasonable limits.

The uncomplicated claims are routinely settled. When cause of loss meets coverage there is usually never a problem. Every now and then, however, it is good for the adjuster to encounter claims that are not so clear cut. When such claims arise, it is helpful to the adjuster if the loss circumstance is not complicated by coverage issues. When both cause of loss and coverage are in doubt, the insured's position could be doubly jeopardized.

It is always helpful when the agent and underwriter have crafted the right coverage at the front end. In this case they seemed to have done so. Yet, in spite of their best efforts, the client still suffered.

Truth is, no matter how well-crafted a policy, dilemmas and difficulties may still be unavoidable from time to time. However, it is better to have a well-crafted policy than a poorly-crafted one when such dilemmas and difficulties arise.

Condominium Fire Loss

A fire occurred at the Four Star Condominiums. Many of the ceilings collapsed, and the ceilings had an asbestos-based, sprayed-on finish. Plaster and asbestos dust settled on the personal property of the unit owners. The act states that the association policy is primary over the unit-owners policy and that the insurance must include the units but not the improvements or betterments. Therefore, the ceilings are covered by the association policy. The personal property is covered by the unit-owners policy.

However, the debris were from the ceiling, which is covered by the association policy. The standard policy language states that the insurer pays for "your expense to remove debris of Covered Property caused by or resulting from a Covered Cause of Loss that occurs during the policy period." Since the ceiling is covered property and fire is a covered cause of loss, it is the association policy that should pay for the cleanup of the debris off of the unit owner's property. The HO 00 06 promises to pay for the removal of debris of covered property, and in this instance the debris is not from covered property of the unit owner, although it is on property of the unit owner, which is different altogether.

Condominium Assessment Claim

A homeowner received a loss assessment charge from the condo association regarding damages caused by Hurricane Maria. The date of the actual physical loss to the condominium caused by Hurricane Maria was 9/20/2017. The homeowner had a homeowner policy, HO 00 06 05 11, with Oneness Insurance Company, with a policy period of 7/1/2017 to 7/1/2018. The additional coverage of loss assessment states that "We will pay up to $1,000 for your share of loss assessment charged during the policy period against you…" The homeowner did not renew the homeowner insurance policy with Oneness Insurance Company. The date of the loss assessment was 8/15/2018. The homeowner presented the loss assessment claim to Oneness Insurance Company. Oneness Insurance Company denied the claim based on the loss assessment policy language that the loss assessment had to be charged during the policy period. Since the date of the loss assessment was after the policy period Oneness Insurance Company denied the loss assessment claim.

The policy (prior to the 2022 update) clearly states that up to $1,000 is paid for assessment charged during the policy period against you. Based on that wording, the carrier is correct that there is no coverage under that policy. Had the policy stated that coverage was for an assessment for a loss that occurred during the policy, then there would have been coverage. But, the policy ties the coverage for loss assessment to the assessment itself, and the assessment did not occur until after the policy had expired.

Claim for Recovery of Carpet and Wallpaper

In this claim, the unit owner, insured under HO 00 06, sustained fire damage to the unit, including damage to carpets and wallpaper.

A review of the master deed and bylaws of the condominium complex revealed that the association was required to insure the common elements, limited common elements, and all units. The insurer for the unit owner denied the claim under the unit-owner's policy and referred the unit owner to the association policy on the following grounds:

Coverage is available under CP 00 17, A. Coverage, 1. Covered Property:

> Any of the following types of property contained within a unit, regardless of ownership, if your Condominium Association Agreement requires you to insure it:
>
> (a) Fixtures, improvements and alterations that are a part of the building or structure; and
>
> (b) Appliances, such as those used for refrigerating, ventilating, cooking, dishwashing, laundering, security or housekeeping.
>
> But Building does not include personal property owned by, used by or in the care, custody or control of a unit-owner.

Not only that, continued the insurer, the association's policy was primary as outlined under section 6. Unit-Owner's Insurance.

Condo Association, Unit Owner, and ALE (Additional Living Expenses)

This claim involves an HOA and HO6 policy. A collapsed sewer line caused black water damage to the interior of the insured risk. The HOA and homeowner carriers are arguing about who is primary and responsible for damages. The sewer line is under the slab in the middle of the unit. It will require cutting the slab to repair. The HOA insurance company took over 55 days to deny the claim. The homeowner filed a lawsuit against the HOA – the homeowner carrier advised they would try to get an agreement with the HOA carrier. Eight months later no settlement from either carrier and the ALE had been exhausted. The insured felt since no agreement has been reached that the ALE should not be tolled until there is an agreement from their carrier. To date over 30k had been incurred. They realize that some or all may be recovered from the HOA carrier.

The ISO HO 00 06 03 22 clearly states that ALE is paid for the shortest time to repair or replace the damage, or until the insured permanently relocates, whichever is shorter. Since the property is uninhabitable, the insured should continue to receive ALE.

As far as who should pay to repair the damages, the HO 06 states that the policy covers real property that pertains exclusively to the "residence premises" – "residence premises" is defined as the unit where the insured resides and is shown in the declarations.

It needed to be determined if the sewer line exclusively serves the unit – if it does not, there is no coverage under this section.

Also the HO 06 provides coverage to property which is the insured's responsibility to insure under a corporation or association of property owners agreement. So the insured/carrier need to look at the condominium master agreement between the insured and the association. This will indicate what the insured and the association are responsible for. Most often the association is responsible for anything used in common with other unit owners. Likewise many states make the association primary on such things, so the state statutes should be checked as well.

Unit-Owners Insurance

A unit owner may have other insurance covering the same property as this insurance. This insurance is intended to be primary and not to contribute with such other insurance.

Additionally, the unit-owner's policy was excess in any covered cause of loss situation as outlined in Condition G. of HO 00 06 – Other Insurance And Service Agreement:

2. Subject to Paragraph G.1., if, at the time of loss, there is other insurance or a service agreement in the name of a corporation or association of property owners covering the same property covered by this Policy, this insurance is:

   a. Excess over the amount due under such other insurance or service agreement, whether the corporation or association of property owners has collected that amount or not; and

   b. Primary with respect to any amount of the loss covered by this Policy and not due under such other insurance or service agreement because of the application of a deductible. And although the covered property was clearly within the purview of coverage of the association's policy, the HO 00 06 makes clear how coverage should apply.

The unit owner's insurer got it right in this claim. But everything starts with boundaries as laid out in the bylaws and condominium instruments.

Because the boundaries of both property covered and perils insured fell within the boundaries of coverage of the association's policy, coverage fell to the association.

In some instances the unit owners may be deemed to purchase "air space," meaning everything from bare walls out would be considered the unit owner's responsibility to insure. In this instance, however, the association is responsible for what would be considered fixtures, improvements, and alterations that are part of the building structure. Improvements and alterations that are part of the building would include, but are not limited to, paint, wallpaper, lighting fixtures, and counters.

Coverage for carpeting follows the same logic. If wall-to-wall carpeting is included in the mortgage, it is part of the realty and thus falls under the improvements and alterations that are part of the building structure. If not so designated, then generally where carpet is laid over an unfinished floor it is considered part of the building and would be covered as such.

If the carpet is laid over a finished floor and its removal would not materially damage the floor, courts have generally held it to be contents. Coverage would therefore be found under the HO 00 06 policy.

Master Deductible Claim

The unit owner of a large condo complex was assessed his share of the association's deductible of $200,000, following a hurricane. The unit owner had Coverage C insurance but no Coverage A, since the bylaws and declaration did not require it. The agent filed a claim for $2,000, the amount allowed under HO 00 06, but the insurer denied the claim on grounds that the unit owner did not purchase any Coverage A insurance.

> The loss assessment amount was raised to $2,000 in the March 2022 update of the HO 00 06 form.

Nowhere under Section 7. Loss Assessment does it say that the unit owner is required to carry Coverage A insurance; the coverage reads as follows:

6. Loss Assessment

   a. We will pay up to $2,000 for your share of loss assessment charged during the policy period against you, as owner or tenant of the "residence premises", by a corporation or association of property owners. The assessment must be made as a result of direct loss to property, owned by all members collectively, of the type that would be covered by this Policy if owned by you, caused by a Peril Insured Against under Coverage A, other than:

(1) Earthquake; or

(2) Land shock waves or tremors before, during or after a volcanic eruption.

The limit of $2,000 is the most we will pay with respect to any one loss, regardless of the number of assessments. We will only apply one deductible, per unit, to the total amount of any one loss to the property described above, regardless of the number of assessments.

b. We do not cover assessments charged against you or a corporation or association of property owners by any governmental body.

c. Paragraph Q. Policy Period under Section I – Conditions does not apply to this coverage.

This coverage is additional insurance.

The condominium unit owner does not have to carry Coverage A in order for loss assessment coverage to apply. The coverage applies as long as the loss is caused by a coverage A peril. Because wind is a coverage A peril, loss assessment would apply for the unit owner's share of the master policy deductible, to a maximum of $2,000.

Summary

Various claims situations have been explored at length to demonstrate how some of the issues could be confounding in certain claims situations. Truth is, adjusting the claims does not have to be this confounding. The starting point of condo claims settlement has to be the establishment of boundaries. Once the boundaries of both property covered and covered causes of loss are established, who pays what should be a matter of course. If there is confusion, check the condominium instruments for clarification. If there is still confusion, the state act is the final authority. Check the policy wording not only for coverage but also for coverage intent.

Throughout all deliberations, the overriding approach should be to do the right thing by the customer. The business of insurance, and particularly condominium insurance, should not be a tug-of-war between insurers over who pays, while the customer suffers on the sidelines. If all stakeholders take a solutions-oriented approach to condominium insurance from acquisition to claims settlement, in the end the customer will see value in the product purchased.

Forms

COMMERCIAL PROPERTY
CP 00 17 10 12

CONDOMINIUM ASSOCIATION COVERAGE FORM

Various provisions in this policy restrict coverage. Read the entire policy carefully to determine rights, duties and what is and is not covered.

Throughout this policy, the words "you" and "your" refer to the Named Insured shown in the Declarations. The words "we", "us" and "our" refer to the company providing this insurance.

Other words and phrases that appear in quotation marks have special meaning. Refer to Section **H.** Definitions.

A. Coverage

We will pay for direct physical loss of or damage to Covered Property at the premises described in the Declarations caused by or resulting from any Covered Cause of Loss.

1. Covered Property

Covered Property, as used in this Coverage Part, means the type of property described in this section, **A.1.**, and limited in **A.2.** Property Not Covered, if a Limit Of Insurance is shown in the Declarations for that type of property.

a. Building, meaning the building or structure described in the Declarations, including:

(1) Completed additions;

(2) Fixtures, outside of individual units, including outdoor fixtures;

(3) Permanently installed:

(a) Machinery; and

(b) Equipment;

(4) Personal property owned by you that is used to maintain or service the building or structure or its premises, including:

(a) Fire-extinguishing equipment;

(b) Outdoor furniture;

(c) Floor coverings; and

(d) Appliances used for refrigerating, ventilating, cooking, dishwashing or laundering that are not contained within individual units;

(5) If not covered by other insurance:

(a) Additions under construction, alterations and repairs to the building or structure;

(b) Materials, equipment, supplies, and temporary structures, on or within 100 feet of the described premises, used for making additions, alterations or repairs to the building or structure; and

(6) Any of the following types of property contained within a unit, regardless of ownership, if your Condominium Association Agreement requires you to insure it:

(a) Fixtures, improvements and alterations that are a part of the building or structure; and

(b) Appliances, such as those used for refrigerating, ventilating, cooking, dishwashing, laundering, security or housekeeping.

But Building does not include personal property owned by, used by or in the care, custody or control of a unit-owner except for personal property listed in Paragraph **A.1.a.(6)** above.

b. Your Business Personal Property located in or on the building or structure described in the Declarations or in the open (or in a vehicle) within 100 feet of the described premises, consisting of the following:

(1) Personal property owned by you or owned indivisibly by all unit-owners;

(2) Your interest in the labor, materials or services furnished or arranged by you on personal property of others; and

(3) Leased personal property for which you have a contractual responsibility to insure, unless otherwise provided for under Personal Property Of Others.

But Your Business Personal Property does not include personal property owned only by a unit-owner.

c. **Personal Property Of Others** that is:

(1) In your care, custody or control; and

(2) Located in or on the building or structure described in the Declarations or in the open (or in a vehicle) within 100 feet of the described premises.

However, our payment for loss of or damage to personal property of others will only be for the account of the owner of the property.

2. **Property Not Covered**

Covered Property does not include:

a. Accounts, bills, currency, food stamps or other evidences of debt, money, notes or securities. Lottery tickets held for sale are not securities;

b. Animals, unless owned by others and boarded by you;

c. Automobiles held for sale;

d. Bridges, roadways, walks, patios or other paved surfaces;

e. Contraband, or property in the course of illegal transportation or trade;

f. The cost of excavations, grading, backfilling or filling;

g. Foundations of buildings, structures, machinery or boilers if their foundations are below:

(1) The lowest basement floor; or

(2) The surface of the ground if there is no basement;

h. Land (including land on which the property is located), water, growing crops or lawns (other than lawns which are part of a vegetated roof);

i. Personal property while airborne or waterborne;

j. Bulkheads, pilings, piers, wharves or docks;

k. Property that is covered under this or any other policy in which it is more specifically described, except for the excess of the amount due (whether you can collect on it or not) from that other insurance;

l. Retaining walls that are not part of a building;

m. Underground pipes, flues or drains;

n. Electronic data, except as provided under the Additional Coverage, Electronic Data. Electronic data means information, facts or computer programs stored as or on, created or used on, or transmitted to or from computer software (including systems and applications software), on hard or floppy disks, CD-ROMs, tapes, drives, cells, data processing devices or any other repositories of computer software which are used with electronically controlled equipment. The term computer programs, referred to in the foregoing description of electronic data, means a set of related electronic instructions which direct the operations and functions of a computer or device connected to it, which enable the computer or device to receive, process, store, retrieve or send data. This paragraph, **n.**, does not apply to electronic data which is integrated in and operates or controls the building's elevator, lighting, heating, ventilation, air conditioning or security system;

o. The cost to replace or restore the information on valuable papers and records, including those which exist as electronic data. Valuable papers and records include but are not limited to proprietary information, books of account, deeds, manuscripts, abstracts, drawings and card index systems. Refer to the Coverage Extension for Valuable Papers And Records (Other Than Electronic Data) for limited coverage for valuable papers and records other than those which exist as electronic data;

p. Vehicles or self-propelled machines (including aircraft or watercraft) that:

(1) Are licensed for use on public roads; or

(2) Are operated principally away from the described premises.

This paragraph does not apply to:

(a) Vehicles or self-propelled machines or autos you manufacture or warehouse;

(b) Vehicles or self-propelled machines, other than autos, you hold for sale;

(c) Rowboats or canoes out of water at the described premises; or

(d) Trailers, but only to the extent provided for in the Coverage Extension for Non-owned Detached Trailers; or

q. The following property while outside of buildings:

(1) Grain, hay, straw or other crops; or

(2) Fences, radio or television antennas (including satellite dishes) and their lead-in wiring, masts or towers, trees, shrubs or plants (other than trees, shrubs or plants which are "stock" or are part of a vegetated roof), all except as provided in the Coverage Extensions.

3. Covered Causes Of Loss

See applicable Causes Of Loss form as shown in the Declarations.

4. Additional Coverages

a. Debris Removal

(1) Subject to Paragraphs **(2)**, **(3)** and **(4)**, we will pay your expense to remove debris of Covered Property and other debris that is on the described premises, when such debris is caused by or results from a Covered Cause of Loss that occurs during the policy period. The expenses will be paid only if they are reported to us in writing within 180 days of the date of direct physical loss or damage.

(2) Debris Removal does not apply to costs to:

(a) Remove debris of property of yours that is not insured under this policy, or property in your possession that is not Covered Property;

(b) Remove any property that is Property Not Covered, including property addressed under the Outdoor Property Coverage Extension;

(c) Remove property of others of a type that would not be Covered Property under this Coverage Form;

(d) Remove deposits of mud or earth from the grounds of the described premises;

(e) Extract "pollutants" from land or water; or

(f) Remove, restore or replace polluted land or water.

(3) Subject to the exceptions in Paragraph **(4)**, the following provisions apply:

(a) The most we will pay for the total of direct physical loss or damage plus debris removal expense is the Limit of Insurance applicable to the Covered Property that has sustained loss or damage.

(b) Subject to **(a)** above, the amount we will pay for debris removal expense is limited to 25% of the sum of the deductible plus the amount that we pay for direct physical loss or damage to the Covered Property that has sustained loss or damage. However, if no Covered Property has sustained direct physical loss or damage, the most we will pay for removal of debris of other property (if such removal is covered under this Additional Coverage) is $5,000 at each location.

(4) We will pay up to an additional $25,000 for debris removal expense, for each location, in any one occurrence of physical loss or damage to Covered Property, if one or both of the following circumstances apply:

(a) The total of the actual debris removal expense plus the amount we pay for direct physical loss or damage exceeds the Limit of Insurance on the Covered Property that has sustained loss or damage.

(b) The actual debris removal expense exceeds 25% of the sum of the deductible plus the amount that we pay for direct physical loss or damage to the Covered Property that has sustained loss or damage.

Therefore, if **(4)(a)** and/or **(4)(b)** applies, our total payment for direct physical loss or damage and debris removal expense may reach but will never exceed the Limit of Insurance on the Covered Property that has sustained loss or damage, plus $25,000.

(5) Examples

The following examples assume that there is no Coinsurance penalty.

Example 1

Limit of Insurance:	$ 90,000
Amount of Deductible:	$ 500
Amount of Loss:	$ 50,000
Amount of Loss Payable:	$ 49,500
	($50,000 – $500)
Debris Removal Expense:	$ 10,000
Debris Removal Expense Payable:	$ 10,000

($10,000 is 20% of $50,000.)

The debris removal expense is less than 25% of the sum of the loss payable plus the deductible. The sum of the loss payable and the debris removal expense ($49,500 + $10,000 = $59,500) is less than the Limit of Insurance. Therefore, the full amount of debris removal expense is payable in accordance with the terms of Paragraph **(3).**

Example 2

Limit of Insurance:	$ 90,000
Amount of Deductible:	$ 500
Amount of Loss:	$ 80,000
Amount of Loss Payable:	$ 79,500
	($80,000 – $500)
Debris Removal Expense:	$ 40,000
Debris Removal Expense Payable	
Basic Amount:	$ 10,500
Additional Amount:	$ 25,000

The basic amount payable for debris removal expense under the terms of Paragraph **(3)** is calculated as follows: $80,000 ($79,500 + $500) x .25 = $20,000, capped at $10,500. The cap applies because the sum of the loss payable ($79,500) and the basic amount payable for debris removal expense ($10,500) cannot exceed the Limit of Insurance ($90,000).

The additional amount payable for debris removal expense is provided in accordance with the terms of Paragraph **(4),** because the debris removal expense ($40,000) exceeds 25% of the loss payable plus the deductible ($40,000 = 50% of $80,000), and because the sum of the loss payable and debris removal expense ($79,500 + $40,000 = $119,500) would exceed the Limit of Insurance ($90,000). The additional amount of covered debris removal expense is $25,000, the maximum payable under Paragraph **(4).** Thus, the total payable for debris removal expense in this example is $35,500; $4,500 of the debris removal expense is not covered.

b. Preservation Of Property

If it is necessary for you to move Covered Property from the described premises to preserve it from loss or damage by a Covered Cause of Loss, we will pay for any direct physical loss or damage to that property:

(1) While it is being moved or while temporarily stored at another location; and

(2) Only if the loss or damage occurs within 30 days after the property is first moved.

c. Fire Department Service Charge

When the fire department is called to save or protect Covered Property from a Covered Cause of Loss, we will pay up to $1,000 for service at each premises described in the Declarations unless a higher limit is shown in the Declarations. Such limit is the most we will pay regardless of the number of responding fire departments or fire units, and regardless of the number or type of services performed.

This Additional Coverage applies to your liability for fire department service charges:

(1) Assumed by contract or agreement prior to loss; or

(2) Required by local ordinance.

No Deductible applies to this Additional Coverage.

d. Pollutant Clean-up And Removal

We will pay your expense to extract "pollutants" from land or water at the described premises if the discharge, dispersal, seepage, migration, release or escape of the "pollutants" is caused by or results from a Covered Cause of Loss that occurs during the policy period. The expenses will be paid only if they are reported to us in writing within 180 days of the date on which the Covered Cause of Loss occurs.

This Additional Coverage does not apply to costs to test for, monitor or assess the existence, concentration or effects of "pollutants". But we will pay for testing which is performed in the course of extracting the "pollutants" from the land or water.

The most we will pay under this Additional Coverage for each described premises is $10,000 for the sum of all covered expenses arising out of Covered Causes of Loss occurring during each separate 12-month period of this policy.

e. Increased Cost Of Construction

(1) This Additional Coverage applies only to buildings to which the Replacement Cost Optional Coverage applies.

(2) In the event of damage by a Covered Cause of Loss to a building that is Covered Property, we will pay the increased costs incurred to comply with the minimum standards of an ordinance or law in the course of repair, rebuilding or replacement of damaged parts of that property, subject to the limitations stated in **e.(3)** through **e.(9)** of this Additional Coverage.

(3) The ordinance or law referred to in **e.(2)** of this Additional Coverage is an ordinance or law that regulates the construction or repair of buildings or establishes zoning or land use requirements at the described premises and is in force at the time of loss.

(4) Under this Additional Coverage, we will not pay any costs due to an ordinance or law that:

(a) You were required to comply with before the loss, even when the building was undamaged; and

(b) You failed to comply with.

(5) Under this Additional Coverage, we will not pay for:

(a) The enforcement of or compliance with any ordinance or law which requires demolition, repair, replacement, reconstruction, remodeling or remediation of property due to contamination by "pollutants" or due to the presence, growth, proliferation, spread or any activity of "fungus", wet or dry rot or bacteria; or

(b) Any costs associated with the enforcement of or compliance with an ordinance or law which requires any insured or others to test for, monitor, clean up, remove, contain, treat, detoxify or neutralize, or in any way respond to, or assess the effects of "pollutants", "fungus", wet or dry rot or bacteria.

(6) The most we will pay under this Additional Coverage, for each described building insured under this Coverage Form, is $10,000 or 5% of the Limit of Insurance applicable to that building, whichever is less. If a damaged building is covered under a blanket Limit of Insurance which applies to more than one building or item of property, then the most we will pay under this Additional Coverage, for that damaged building, is the lesser of $10,000 or 5% times the value of the damaged building as of the time of loss times the applicable Coinsurance percentage.

The amount payable under this Additional Coverage is additional insurance.

(7) With respect to this Additional Coverage:

(a) We will not pay for the Increased Cost of Construction:

(i) Until the property is actually repaired or replaced, at the same or another premises; and

(ii) Unless the repair or replacement is made as soon as reasonably possible after the loss or damage, not to exceed two years. We may extend this period in writing during the two years.

(b) If the building is repaired or replaced at the same premises, or if you elect to rebuild at another premises, the most we will pay for the Increased Cost of Construction, subject to the provisions of **e.(6)** of this Additional Coverage, is the increased cost of construction at the same premises.

(c) If the ordinance or law requires relocation to another premises, the most we will pay for the Increased Cost of Construction, subject to the provisions of **e.(6)** of this Additional Coverage, is the increased cost of construction at the new premises.

(8) This Additional Coverage is not subject to the terms of the Ordinance Or Law Exclusion to the extent that such Exclusion would conflict with the provisions of this Additional Coverage.

(9) The costs addressed in the Loss Payment and Valuation Conditions and the Replacement Cost Optional Coverage, in this Coverage Form, do not include the increased cost attributable to enforcement of or compliance with an ordinance or law. The amount payable under this Additional Coverage, as stated in **e.(6)** of this Additional Coverage, is not subject to such limitation.

f. Electronic Data

(1) Under this Additional Coverage, electronic data has the meaning described under Property Not Covered, Electronic Data. This Additional Coverage does not apply to electronic data which is integrated in and operates or controls the building's elevator, lighting, heating, ventilation, air conditioning or security system.

(2) Subject to the provisions of this Additional Coverage, we will pay for the cost to replace or restore electronic data which has been destroyed or corrupted by a Covered Cause of Loss. To the extent that electronic data is not replaced or restored, the loss will be valued at the cost of replacement of the media on which the electronic data was stored, with blank media of substantially identical type.

(3) The Covered Causes of Loss applicable to Your Business Personal Property apply to this Additional Coverage, Electronic Data, subject to the following:

(a) If the Causes Of Loss – Special Form applies, coverage under this Additional Coverage, Electronic Data, is limited to the "specified causes of loss" as defined in that form and Collapse as set forth in that form.

(b) If the Causes Of Loss – Broad Form applies, coverage under this Additional Coverage, Electronic Data, includes Collapse as set forth in that form.

(c) If the Causes Of Loss form is endorsed to add a Covered Cause of Loss, the additional Covered Cause of Loss does not apply to the coverage provided under this Additional Coverage, Electronic Data.

(d) The Covered Causes of Loss include a virus, harmful code or similar instruction introduced into or enacted on a computer system (including electronic data) or a network to which it is connected, designed to damage or destroy any part of the system or disrupt its normal operation. But there is no coverage for loss or damage caused by or resulting from manipulation of a computer system (including electronic data) by any employee, including a temporary or leased employee, or by an entity retained by you or for you to inspect, design, install, modify, maintain, repair or replace that system.

(4) The most we will pay under this Additional Coverage, Electronic Data, is $2,500 (unless a higher limit is shown in the Declarations) for all loss or damage sustained in any one policy year, regardless of the number of occurrences of loss or damage or the number of premises, locations or computer systems involved. If loss payment on the first occurrence does not exhaust this amount, then the balance is available for subsequent loss or damage sustained in but not after that policy year. With respect to an occurrence which begins in one policy year and continues or results in additional loss or damage in a subsequent policy year(s), all loss or damage is deemed to be sustained in the policy year in which the occurrence began.

6. Coverage Extensions

Except as otherwise provided, the following Extensions apply to property located in or on the building described in the Declarations or in the open (or in a vehicle) within 100 feet of the described premises.

If a Coinsurance percentage of 80% or more is shown in the Declarations, you may extend the insurance provided by this Coverage Part as follows:

a. Newly Acquired Or Constructed Property

(1) Buildings

You may extend the insurance that applies to Building to apply to:

(a) Your new buildings while being built on the described premises; and

(b) Buildings you acquire at locations, other than the described premises, intended for:

(i) Similar use as the building described in the Declarations; or

(ii) Use as a warehouse.

The most we will pay for loss or damage under this Extension is $250,000 at each building.

(2) Your Business Personal Property

(a) If this policy covers Your Business Personal Property, you may extend that insurance to apply to:

(i) Business personal property, including such property that you newly acquire, at any location you acquire other than at fairs, trade shows or exhibitions; or

(ii) Business personal property, including such property that you newly acquire, located at your newly constructed or acquired buildings at the location described in the Declarations.

The most we will pay for loss or damage under this Extension is $100,000 at each building.

(b) This Extension does not apply to:

(i) Personal property of others that is temporarily in your possession in the course of installing or performing work on such property; or

(ii) Personal property of others that is temporarily in your possession in the course of your manufacturing or wholesaling activities.

(3) Period Of Coverage

With respect to insurance provided under this Coverage Extension for Newly Acquired Or Constructed Property, coverage will end when any of the following first occurs:

(a) This policy expires;

(b) 30 days expire after you acquire the property or begin construction of that part of the building that would qualify as covered property; or

(c) You report values to us.

We will charge you additional premium for values reported from the date you acquire the property or begin construction of that part of the building that would qualify as covered property.

b. Personal Effects And Property Of Others

You may extend the insurance that applies to Your Business Personal Property to apply to:

(1) Personal effects owned by you, your officers, your partners or members, your managers or your employees. This Extension does not apply to loss or damage by theft.

(2) Personal property of others in your care, custody or control.

The most we will pay for loss or damage under this Extension is $2,500 at each described premises. Our payment for loss of or damage to personal property of others will only be for the account of the owner of the property.

c. Valuable Papers And Records (Other Than Electronic Data)

(1) You may extend the insurance that applies to Your Business Personal Property to apply to the cost to replace or restore the lost information on valuable papers and records for which duplicates do not exist. But this Extension does not apply to valuable papers and records which exist as electronic data. Electronic data has the meaning described under Property Not Covered, Electronic Data.

(2) If the Causes Of Loss – Special Form applies, coverage under this Extension is limited to the "specified causes of loss" as defined in that form and Collapse as set forth in that form.

(3) If the Causes Of Loss – Broad Form applies, coverage under this Extension includes Collapse as set forth in that form.

(4) Under this Extension, the most we will pay to replace or restore the lost information is $2,500 at each described premises, unless a higher limit is shown in the Declarations. Such amount is additional insurance. We will also pay for the cost of blank material for reproducing the records (whether or not duplicates exist) and (when there is a duplicate) for the cost of labor to transcribe or copy the records. The costs of blank material and labor are subject to the applicable Limit of Insurance on Your Business Personal Property and, therefore, coverage of such costs is not additional insurance.

d. Property Off-premises

(1) You may extend the insurance provided by this Coverage Form to apply to your Covered Property while it is away from the described premises, if it is:

(a) Temporarily at a location you do not own, lease or operate;

(b) In storage at a location you lease, provided the lease was executed after the beginning of the current policy term; or

(c) At any fair, trade show or exhibition.

(2) This Extension does not apply to property:

(a) In or on a vehicle; or

(b) In the care, custody or control of your salespersons, unless the property is in such care, custody or control at a fair, trade show or exhibition.

(3) The most we will pay for loss or damage under this Extension is $10,000.

e. Outdoor Property

You may extend the insurance provided by this Coverage Form to apply to your outdoor fences, radio and television antennas (including satellite dishes), trees, shrubs and plants (other than trees, shrubs or plants which are "stock" or are part of a vegetated roof), including debris removal expense, caused by or resulting from any of the following causes of loss if they are Covered Causes of Loss:

(1) Fire;

(2) Lightning;

(3) Explosion;

(4) Riot or Civil Commotion; or

(5) Aircraft.

The most we will pay for loss or damage under this Extension is $1,000, but not more than $250 for any one tree, shrub or plant. These limits apply to any one occurrence, regardless of the types or number of items lost or damaged in that occurrence.

Subject to all aforementioned terms and limitations of coverage, this Coverage Extension includes the expense of removing from the described premises the debris of trees, shrubs and plants which are the property of others.

f. Non-owned Detached Trailers

(1) You may extend the insurance that applies to Your Business Personal Property to apply to loss or damage to trailers that you do not own, provided that:

(a) The trailer is used in your business;

(b) The trailer is in your care, custody or control at the premises described in the Declarations; and

(c) You have a contractual responsibility to pay for loss or damage to the trailer.

(2) We will not pay for any loss or damage that occurs:

(a) While the trailer is attached to any motor vehicle or motorized conveyance, whether or not the motor vehicle or motorized conveyance is in motion;

(b) During hitching or unhitching operations, or when a trailer becomes accidentally unhitched from a motor vehicle or motorized conveyance.

(3) The most we will pay for loss or damage under this Extension is $5,000, unless a higher limit is shown in the Declarations.

(4) This insurance is excess over the amount due (whether you can collect on it or not) from any other insurance covering such property.

g. Business Personal Property Temporarily In Portable Storage Units

(1) You may extend the insurance that applies to Your Business Personal Property to apply to such property while temporarily stored in a portable storage unit (including a detached trailer) located within 100 feet of the described premises.

(2) If the applicable Covered Causes of Loss form or endorsement contains a limitation or exclusion concerning loss or damage from sand, dust, sleet, snow, ice or rain to property in a structure, such limitation or exclusion also applies to property in a portable storage unit.

(3) Coverage under this Extension:

(a) Will end 90 days after the business personal property has been placed in the storage unit;

(b) Does not apply if the storage unit itself has been in use at the described premises for more than 90 consecutive days, even if the business personal property has been stored there for 90 or fewer days as of the time of loss or damage.

(4) Under this Extension, the most we will pay for the total of all loss or damage to business personal property is $10,000 (unless a higher limit is indicated in the Declarations for such Extension) regardless of the number of storage units. Such limit is part of, not in addition to, the applicable Limit of Insurance on Your Business Personal Property. Therefore, payment under this Extension will not increase the applicable Limit of Insurance on Your Business Personal Property.

(5) This Extension does not apply to loss or damage otherwise covered under this Coverage Form or any endorsement to this Coverage Form or policy, and does not apply to loss or damage to the storage unit itself.

Each of these Extensions is additional insurance unless otherwise indicated. The Additional Condition, Coinsurance, does not apply to these Extensions.

B. Exclusions And Limitations

See applicable Causes Of Loss form as shown in the Declarations.

C. Limits Of Insurance

The most we will pay for loss or damage in any one occurrence is the applicable Limit Of Insurance shown in the Declarations.

The most we will pay for loss or damage to outdoor signs, whether or not the sign is attached to a building, is $2,500 per sign in any one occurrence.

The amounts of insurance stated in the following Additional Coverages apply in accordance with the terms of such coverages and are separate from the Limit(s) Of Insurance shown in the Declarations for any other coverage:

1. Fire Department Service Charge;

2. Pollutant Clean-up And Removal;

3. Increased Cost Of Construction; and

4. Electronic Data.

Payments under the Preservation Of Property Additional Coverage will not increase the applicable Limit of Insurance.

D. Deductible

In any one occurrence of loss or damage (hereinafter referred to as loss), we will first reduce the amount of loss if required by the Coinsurance Condition or the Agreed Value Optional Coverage. If the adjusted amount of loss is less than or equal to the Deductible, we will not pay for that loss. If the adjusted amount of loss exceeds the Deductible, we will then subtract the Deductible from the adjusted amount of loss and will pay the resulting amount or the Limit of Insurance, whichever is less.

When the occurrence involves loss to more than one item of Covered Property and separate Limits of Insurance apply, the losses will not be combined in determining application of the Deductible. But the Deductible will be applied only once per occurrence.

Example 1

(This example assumes there is no Coinsurance penalty.)

Deductible:	$ 250
Limit of Insurance – Building 1:	$ 60,000
Limit of Insurance – Building 2:	$ 80,000
Loss to Building 1:	$ 60,100
Loss to Building 2:	$ 90,000

The amount of loss to Building 1 ($60,100) is less than the sum ($60,250) of the Limit of Insurance applicable to Building 1 plus the Deductible.

The Deductible will be subtracted from the amount of loss in calculating the loss payable for Building 1:

$ 60,100
– 250
$ 59,850 Loss Payable – Building 1

The Deductible applies once per occurrence and therefore is not subtracted in determining the amount of loss payable for Building 2. Loss payable for Building 2 is the Limit of Insurance of $80,000.

Total amount of loss payable:

$59,850 + $80,000 = $139,850

Example 2

(This example, too, assumes there is no Coinsurance penalty.)

The Deductible and Limits of Insurance are the same as those in Example 1.

Loss to Building 1:	$ 70,000
(Exceeds Limit of Insurance plus Deductible)	
Loss to Building 2:	$ 90,000
(Exceeds Limit of Insurance plus Deductible)	
Loss Payable – Building 1:	$ 60,000
(Limit of Insurance)	
Loss Payable – Building 2:	$ 80,000
(Limit of Insurance)	
Total amount of loss payable:	$ 140,000

E. Loss Conditions

The following conditions apply in addition to the Common Policy Conditions and the Commercial Property Conditions:

1. Abandonment

There can be no abandonment of any property to us.

2. Appraisal

If we and you disagree on the value of the property or the amount of loss, either may make written demand for an appraisal of the loss. In this event, each party will select a competent and impartial appraiser. The two appraisers will select an umpire. If they cannot agree, either may request that selection be made by a judge of a court having jurisdiction. The appraisers will state separately the value of the property and amount of loss. If they fail to agree, they will submit their differences to the umpire. A decision agreed to by any two will be binding. Each party will:

a. Pay its chosen appraiser; and

b. Bear the other expenses of the appraisal and umpire equally.

If there is an appraisal, we will still retain our right to deny the claim.

3. Duties In The Event Of Loss Or Damage

a. You must see that the following are done in the event of loss or damage to Covered Property:

(1) Notify the police if a law may have been broken.

(2) Give us prompt notice of the loss or damage. Include a description of the property involved.

(3) As soon as possible, give us a description of how, when and where the loss or damage occurred.

(4) Take all reasonable steps to protect the Covered Property from further damage, and keep a record of your expenses necessary to protect the Covered Property, for consideration in the settlement of the claim. This will not increase the Limit of Insurance. However, we will not pay for any subsequent loss or damage resulting from a cause of loss that is not a Covered Cause of Loss. Also, if feasible, set the damaged property aside and in the best possible order for examination.

(5) At our request, give us complete inventories of the damaged and undamaged property. Include quantities, costs, values and amount of loss claimed.

(6) As often as may be reasonably required, permit us to inspect the property proving the loss or damage and examine your books and records.

Also, permit us to take samples of damaged and undamaged property for inspection, testing and analysis, and permit us to make copies from your books and records.

(7) Send us a signed, sworn proof of loss containing the information we request to investigate the claim. You must do this within 60 days after our request. We will supply you with the necessary forms.

(8) Cooperate with us in the investigation or settlement of the claim.

b. We may examine any insured under oath, while not in the presence of any other insured and at such times as may be reasonably required, about any matter relating to this insurance or the claim, including an insured's books and records. In the event of an examination, an insured's answers must be signed.

4. Loss Payment

a. In the event of loss or damage covered by this Coverage Form, at our option, we will either:

(1) Pay the value of lost or damaged property;

(2) Pay the cost of repairing or replacing the lost or damaged property, subject to **b.** below;

(3) Take all or any part of the property at an agreed or appraised value; or

(4) Repair, rebuild or replace the property with other property of like kind and quality, subject to **b.** below.

We will determine the value of lost or damaged property, or the cost of its repair or replacement, in accordance with the applicable terms of the Valuation Condition in this Coverage Form or any applicable provision which amends or supersedes the Valuation Condition.

b. The cost to repair, rebuild or replace does not include the increased cost attributable to enforcement of or compliance with any ordinance or law regulating the construction, use or repair of any property.

c. We will give notice of our intentions within 30 days after we receive the sworn proof of loss.

d. We will not pay you more than your financial interest in the Covered Property.

e. We may adjust losses with the owners of lost or damaged property if other than you. If we pay the owners, such payments will satisfy your claims against us for the owners' property. We will not pay the owners more than their financial interest in the Covered Property.

f. We may elect to defend you against suits arising from claims of owners of property. We will do this at our expense.

g. We will pay for covered loss or damage to Covered Property within 30 days after we receive the sworn proof of loss, if you have complied with all of the terms of this Coverage Part, and:

(1) We have reached agreement with you on the amount of loss; or

(2) An appraisal award has been made.

If you name an insurance trustee, we will adjust losses with you, but we will pay the insurance trustee. If we pay the trustee, the payments will satisfy your claims against us.

h. A party wall is a wall that separates and is common to adjoining buildings that are owned by different parties. In settling covered losses involving a party wall, we will pay a proportion of the loss to the party wall based on your interest in the wall in proportion to the interest of the owner of the adjoining building. However, if you elect to repair or replace your building and the owner of the adjoining building elects not to repair or replace that building, we will pay you the full value of the loss to the party wall, subject to all applicable policy provisions including Limits of Insurance, the Valuation and Coinsurance Conditions and all other provisions of this Loss Payment Condition. Our payment under the provisions of this paragraph does not alter any right of subrogation we may have against any entity, including the owner or insurer of the adjoining building, and does not alter the terms of the Transfer Of Rights Of Recovery Against Others To Us Condition in this policy.

5. Recovered Property

If either you or we recover any property after loss settlement, that party must give the other prompt notice. At your option, the property will be returned to you. You must then return to us the amount we paid to you for the property. We will pay recovery expenses and the expenses to repair the recovered property, subject to the Limit of Insurance.

6. Unit-owner's Insurance

A unit-owner may have other insurance covering the same property as this insurance. This insurance is intended to be primary and not to contribute with such other insurance.

7. Vacancy

a. Description Of Terms

(1) As used in this Vacancy Condition, the term building and the term vacant have the meanings set forth in **(1)(a)** and **(1)(b)** below:

(a) When this policy is issued to a tenant, and with respect to that tenant's interest in Covered Property, building means the unit or suite rented or leased to the tenant. Such building is vacant when it does not contain enough business personal property to conduct customary operations.

(b) When this policy is issued to the owner or general lessee of a building, building means the entire building. Such building is vacant unless at least 31% of its total square footage is:

(i) Rented to a lessee or sublessee and used by the lessee or sublessee to conduct its customary operations; and/or

(ii) Used by the building owner to conduct customary operations.

(2) Buildings under construction or renovation are not considered vacant.

b. Vacancy Provisions

If the building where loss or damage occurs has been vacant for more than 60 consecutive days before that loss or damage occurs:

(1) We will not pay for any loss or damage caused by any of the following even if they are Covered Causes of Loss:

(a) Vandalism;

(b) Sprinkler leakage, unless you have protected the system against freezing;

(c) Building glass breakage;

(d) Water damage;

(e) Theft; or

(f) Attempted theft.

(2) With respect to Covered Causes of Loss other than those listed in **b.(1)(a)** through **b.(1)(f)** above, we will reduce the amount we would otherwise pay for the loss or damage by 15%.

8. Valuation

We will determine the value of Covered Property in the event of loss or damage as follows:

a. At actual cash value as of the time of loss or damage, except as provided in **b.** and **c.** below.

b. If the Limit of Insurance for Building satisfies the Additional Condition, Coinsurance, and the cost to repair or replace the damaged building property is $2,500 or less, we will pay the cost of building repairs or replacement.

The cost of building repairs or replacement does not include the increased cost attributable to enforcement of or compliance with any ordinance or law regulating the construction, use or repair of any property. However, the following property will be valued at the actual cash value, even when attached to the building:

(1) Awnings or floor coverings;

(2) Appliances for refrigerating, ventilating, cooking, dishwashing or laundering; or

(3) Outdoor equipment or furniture.

c. Glass at the cost of replacement with safety-glazing material if required by law.

9. Waiver Of Rights Of Recovery

We waive our rights to recover payment from any unit-owner of the condominium that is shown in the Declarations.

F. Additional Conditions

The following conditions apply in addition to the Common Policy Conditions and the Commercial Property Conditions:

1. Coinsurance

If a Coinsurance percentage is shown in the Declarations, the following condition applies:

a. We will not pay the full amount of any loss if the value of Covered Property at the time of loss times the Coinsurance percentage shown for it in the Declarations is greater than the Limit of Insurance for the property.

Instead, we will determine the most we will pay using the following steps:

(1) Multiply the value of Covered Property at the time of loss by the Coinsurance percentage;

(2) Divide the Limit of Insurance of the property by the figure determined in Step **(1)**;

(3) Multiply the total amount of loss, before the application of any deductible, by the figure determined in Step **(2)**; and

(4) Subtract the deductible from the figure determined in Step **(3)**.

We will pay the amount determined in Step **(4)** or the Limit of Insurance, whichever is less. For the remainder, you will either have to rely on other insurance or absorb the loss yourself.

Example 1 (Underinsurance)

When:	The value of the property is:	$ 250,000
	The Coinsurance percentage for it is:	80%
	The Limit of Insurance for it is:	$ 100,000
	The Deductible is:	$ 250
	The amount of loss is:	$ 40,000
Step **(1)**:	$250,000 x 80% = $200,000 (the minimum amount of insurance to meet your Coinsurance requirements)	
Step **(2)**:	$100,000 ÷ $200,000 = .50	
Step **(3)**:	$40,000 x .50 = $20,000	
Step **(4)**:	$20,000 – $250 = $19,750	

We will pay no more than $19,750. The remaining $20,250 is not covered.

Example 2 (Adequate Insurance)

When:	The value of the property is:	$ 250,000
	The Coinsurance percentage for it is:	80%
	The Limit of Insurance for it is:	$ 200,000
	The Deductible is:	$ 250
	The amount of loss is:	$ 40,000

The minimum amount of insurance to meet your Coinsurance requirement is $200,000 ($250,000 x 80%). Therefore, the Limit of Insurance in this example is adequate and no penalty applies. We will pay no more than $39,750 ($40,000 amount of loss minus the deductible of $250).

b. If one Limit of Insurance applies to two or more separate items, this condition will apply to the total of all property to which the limit applies.

Example 3

When:	The value of the property is:	
	Building at Location 1:	$ 75,000
	Building at Location 2:	$ 100,000
	Personal Property at Location 2:	$ 75,000
		$ 250,000
	The Coinsurance percentage for it is:	90%
	The Limit of Insurance for Buildings and Personal Property at Locations 1 and 2 is:	$ 180,000
	The Deductible is:	$ 1,000
	The amount of loss is:	
	Building at Location 2:	$ 30,000
	Personal Property at Location 2:	$ 20,000
		$ 50,000
Step **(1)**:	$250,000 x 90% = $225,000 (the minimum amount of insurance to meet your Coinsurance requirements and to avoid the penalty shown below)	
Step **(2)**:	$180,000 ÷ $225,000 = .80	
Step **(3)**:	$50,000 x .80 = $40,000	
Step **(4)**:	$40,000 – $1,000 = $39,000	

We will pay no more than $39,000. The remaining $11,000 is not covered.

2. Mortgageholders

a. The term mortgageholder includes trustee.

b. We will pay for covered loss of or damage to buildings or structures to each mortgageholder shown in the Declarations in their order of precedence, as interests may appear.

c. The mortgageholder has the right to receive loss payment even if the mortgageholder has started foreclosure or similar action on the building or structure.

d. If we deny your claim because of your acts or because you have failed to comply with the terms of this Coverage Part, the mortgageholder will still have the right to receive loss payment if the mortgageholder:

(1) Pays any premium due under this Coverage Part at our request if you have failed to do so;

(2) Submits a signed, sworn proof of loss within 60 days after receiving notice from us of your failure to do so; and

(3) Has notified us of any change in ownership, occupancy or substantial change in risk known to the mortgageholder.

All of the terms of this Coverage Part will then apply directly to the mortgageholder.

e. If we pay the mortgageholder for any loss or damage and deny payment to you because of your acts or because you have failed to comply with the terms of this Coverage Part:

(1) The mortgageholder's rights under the mortgage will be transferred to us to the extent of the amount we pay; and

(2) The mortgageholder's right to recover the full amount of the mortgageholder's claim will not be impaired.

At our option, we may pay to the mortgageholder the whole principal on the mortgage plus any accrued interest. In this event, your mortgage and note will be transferred to us and you will pay your remaining mortgage debt to us.

f. If we cancel this policy, we will give written notice to the mortgageholder at least:

(1) 10 days before the effective date of cancellation if we cancel for your nonpayment of premium; or

(2) 30 days before the effective date of cancellation if we cancel for any other reason.

g. If we elect not to renew this policy, we will give written notice to the mortgageholder at least 10 days before the expiration date of this policy.

G. Optional Coverages

If shown as applicable in the Declarations, the following Optional Coverages apply separately to each item:

1. Agreed Value

a. The Additional Condition, Coinsurance, does not apply to Covered Property to which this Optional Coverage applies. We will pay no more for loss of or damage to that property than the proportion that the Limit of Insurance under this Coverage Part for the property bears to the Agreed Value shown for it in the Declarations.

b. If the expiration date for this Optional Coverage shown in the Declarations is not extended, the Additional Condition, Coinsurance, is reinstated and this Optional Coverage expires.

c. The terms of this Optional Coverage apply only to loss or damage that occurs:

(1) On or after the effective date of this Optional Coverage; and

(2) Before the Agreed Value expiration date shown in the Declarations or the policy expiration date, whichever occurs first.

2. Inflation Guard

a. The Limit of Insurance for property to which this Optional Coverage applies will automatically increase by the annual percentage shown in the Declarations.

b. The amount of increase will be:

(1) The Limit of Insurance that applied on the most recent of the policy inception date, the policy anniversary date, or any other policy change amending the Limit of Insurance, times

(2) The percentage of annual increase shown in the Declarations, expressed as a decimal (example: 8% is .08), times

(3) The number of days since the beginning of the current policy year or the effective date of the most recent policy change amending the Limit of Insurance, divided by 365.

Example

If:	The applicable Limit of Insurance is:	$ 100,000
	The annual percentage increase is:	8%
	The number of days since the beginning of the policy year (or last policy change) is:	146
	The amount of increase is: $100,000 x .08 x 146 ÷ 365 =	$ 3,200

3. Replacement Cost

a. Replacement Cost (without deduction for depreciation) replaces Actual Cash Value in the Loss Condition, Valuation, of this Coverage Form.

b. This Optional Coverage does not apply to:

(1) Personal property of others;

(2) Contents of a residence; or

(3) Works of art, antiques or rare articles, including etchings, pictures, statuary, marbles, bronzes, porcelains and bric-a-brac.

Under the terms of this Replacement Cost Optional Coverage, personal property owned indivisibly by all unit-owners, and the property covered under Paragraph **A.1.a.(6)** of this Coverage Form, are not considered to be the personal property of others.

c. You may make a claim for loss or damage covered by this insurance on an actual cash value basis instead of on a replacement cost basis. In the event you elect to have loss or damage settled on an actual cash value basis, you may still make a claim for the additional coverage this Optional Coverage provides if you notify us of your intent to do so within 180 days after the loss or damage.

d. We will not pay on a replacement cost basis for any loss or damage:

(1) Until the lost or damaged property is actually repaired or replaced; and

(2) Unless the repair or replacement is made as soon as reasonably possible after the loss or damage.

e. We will not pay more for loss or damage on a replacement cost basis than the least of **(1)**, **(2)** or **(3)**, subject to **f.** below:

(1) The Limit of Insurance applicable to the lost or damaged property;

(2) The cost to replace the lost or damaged property with other property:

(a) Of comparable material and quality; and

(b) Used for the same purpose; or

(3) The amount actually spent that is necessary to repair or replace the lost or damaged property.

If a building is rebuilt at a new premises, the cost described in **e.(2)** above is limited to the cost which would have been incurred if the building had been rebuilt at the original premises.

f. The cost of repair or replacement does not include the increased cost attributable to enforcement of or compliance with any ordinance or law regulating the construction, use or repair of any property.

4. Extension Of Replacement Cost To Personal Property Of Others

a. If the Replacement Cost Optional Coverage is shown as applicable in the Declarations, then this Extension may also be shown as applicable. If the Declarations show this Extension as applicable, then Paragraph **3.b.(1)** of the Replacement Cost Optional Coverage is deleted and all other provisions of the Replacement Cost Optional Coverage apply to replacement cost on personal property of others.

b. With respect to replacement cost on the personal property of others, the following limitation applies:

If an item(s) of personal property of others is subject to a written contract which governs your liability for loss or damage to that item(s), then valuation of that item(s) will be based on the amount for which you are liable under such contract, but not to exceed the lesser of the replacement cost of the property or the applicable Limit of Insurance.

H. Definitions

1. "Fungus" means any type or form of fungus, including mold or mildew, and any mycotoxins, spores, scents or by-products produced or released by fungi.

2. "Pollutants" means any solid, liquid, gaseous or thermal irritant or contaminant, including smoke, vapor, soot, fumes, acids, alkalis, chemicals and waste. Waste includes materials to be recycled, reconditioned or reclaimed.

3. "Stock" means merchandise held in storage or for sale, raw materials and in-process or finished goods, including supplies used in their packing or shipping.

CONDOMINIUM COMMERCIAL UNIT-OWNERS COVERAGE FORM

Various provisions in this policy restrict coverage. Read the entire policy carefully to determine rights, duties and what is and is not covered.

Throughout this policy, the words "you" and "your" refer to the Named Insured shown in the Declarations. The words "we", "us" and "our" refer to the company providing this insurance.

Other words and phrases that appear in quotation marks have special meaning. Refer to Section **H.** Definitions.

A. Coverage

We will pay for direct physical loss of or damage to Covered Property at the premises described in the Declarations caused by or resulting from any Covered Cause of Loss.

1. Covered Property

Covered Property, as used in this Coverage Part, means the type of property described in this section, **A.1.**, and limited in **A.2.** Property Not Covered, if a Limit Of Insurance is shown in the Declarations for that type of property.

a. Your Business Personal Property consists of the following property located in or on the building or structure described in the Declarations or in the open (or in a vehicle) within 100 feet of the building or structure or within 100 feet of the premises described in the Declarations, whichever distance is greater:

(1) Furniture;

(2) Fixtures, improvements and alterations making up part of the building and owned by you;

(3) Machinery and equipment;

(4) "Stock";

(5) All other personal property owned by you and used in your business;

(6) Labor, materials or services furnished or arranged by you on personal property of others;

(7) Leased personal property for which you have a contractual responsibility to insure, unless otherwise provided for under Personal Property Of Others.

b. Personal Property Of Others that is:

(1) In your care, custody or control; and

(2) Located in or on the building or structure described in the Declarations or in the open (or in a vehicle) within 100 feet of the building or structure or within 100 feet of the premises described in the Declarations, whichever distance is greater.

However, our payment for loss of or damage to personal property of others will only be for the account of the owner of the property.

2. Property Not Covered

Covered Property does not include:

a. Accounts, bills, currency, food stamps or other evidences of debt, money, notes or securities. Lottery tickets held for sale are not securities;

b. Animals, unless owned by others and boarded by you, or if owned by you, only as "stock" while inside of buildings;

c. Automobiles held for sale;

d. Contraband, or property in the course of illegal transportation or trade;

e. Water, growing crops or lawns;

f. Personal property while airborne or waterborne;

g. Property that is covered under another Coverage Form of this or any other policy in which it is more specifically described, except for the excess of the amount due (whether you can collect on it or not) from that other insurance;

h. Electronic data, except as provided under the Additional Coverage, Electronic Data. Electronic data means information, facts or computer programs stored as or on, created or used on, or transmitted to or from computer software (including systems and applications software), on hard or floppy disks, CD-ROMs, tapes, drives, cells, data processing devices or any other repositories of computer software which are used with electronically controlled equipment. The term computer programs, referred to in the foregoing description of electronic data, means a set of related electronic instructions which direct the operations and functions of a computer or device connected to it, which enable the computer or device to receive, process, store, retrieve or send data. This paragraph, **h.,** does not apply to your "stock" of prepackaged software, or to electronic data which is integrated in and operates or controls the building's elevator, lighting, heating, ventilation, air conditioning or security system;

i. The cost to replace or restore the information on valuable papers and records, including those which exist as electronic data. Valuable papers and records include but are not limited to proprietary information, books of account, deeds, manuscripts, abstracts, drawings and card index systems. Refer to the Coverage Extension for Valuable Papers And Records (Other Than Electronic Data) for limited coverage for valuable papers and records other than those which exist as electronic data;

j. Vehicles or self-propelled machines (including aircraft or watercraft) that:

(1) Are licensed for use on public roads; or

(2) Are operated principally away from the described premises.

This paragraph does not apply to:

(a) Vehicles or self-propelled machines or autos you manufacture, process or warehouse;

(b) Vehicles or self-propelled machines, other than autos, you hold for sale;

(c) Rowboats or canoes out of water at the described premises; or

(d) Trailers, but only to the extent provided for in the Coverage Extension for Non-owned Detached Trailers;

k. The following property while outside of buildings:

(1) Grain, hay, straw or other crops; or

(2) Fences, radio or television antennas (including satellite dishes) and their lead-in wiring, masts or towers, trees, shrubs or plants (other than "stock" of trees, shrubs or plants), all except as provided in the Coverage Extensions;

l. Any of the following types of property contained within a unit, regardless of ownership, if your Condominium Association Agreement requires the Association to insure it:

(1) Fixtures, improvements and alterations that are a part of the building; and

(2) Appliances, such as those used for refrigerating, ventilating, cooking, dishwashing, laundering, security or housekeeping.

3. Covered Causes Of Loss

See applicable Causes Of Loss form as shown in the Declarations.

4. Additional Coverages

a. Debris Removal

(1) Subject to Paragraphs **(2), (3)** and **(4),** we will pay your expense to remove debris of Covered Property and other debris that is on the described premises, when such debris is caused by or results from a Covered Cause of Loss that occurs during the policy period. The expenses will be paid only if they are reported to us in writing within 180 days of the date of direct physical loss or damage.

(2) Debris Removal does not apply to costs to:

(a) Remove debris of property of yours that is not insured under this policy, or property in your possession that is not Covered Property;

(b) Remove any property that is Property Not Covered, including property addressed under the Outdoor Property Coverage Extension;

(c) Remove property of others of a type that would not be Covered Property under this Coverage Form;

(d) Remove deposits of mud or earth from the grounds of the described premises;

(e) Extract "pollutants" from land or water; or

(f) Remove, restore or replace polluted land or water.

(3) Subject to the exceptions in Paragraph **(4),** the following provisions apply:

(a) The most we will pay for the total of direct physical loss or damage plus debris removal expense is the Limit of Insurance applicable to the Covered Property that has sustained loss or damage.

(b) Subject to **(a)** above, the amount we will pay for debris removal expense is limited to 25% of the sum of the deductible plus the amount that we pay for direct physical loss or damage to the Covered Property that has sustained loss or damage. However, if no Covered Property has sustained direct physical loss or damage, the most we will pay for removal of debris of other property (if such removal is covered under this Additional Coverage) is $5,000 at each location.

(4) We will pay up to an additional $25,000 for debris removal expense, for each location, in any one occurrence of physical loss or damage to Covered Property, if one or both of the following circumstances apply:

(a) The total of the actual debris removal expense plus the amount we pay for direct physical loss or damage exceeds the Limit of Insurance on the Covered Property that has sustained loss or damage.

(b) The actual debris removal expense exceeds 25% of the sum of the deductible plus the amount that we pay for direct physical loss or damage to the Covered Property that has sustained loss or damage.

Therefore, if **(4)(a)** and/or **(4)(b)** applies, our total payment for direct physical loss or damage and debris removal expense may reach but will never exceed the Limit of Insurance on the Covered Property that has sustained loss or damage, plus $25,000.

(5) Examples

The following examples assume that there is no Coinsurance penalty.

Example 1

Limit of Insurance:	$ 90,000
Amount of Deductible:	$ 500
Amount of Loss:	$ 50,000
Amount of Loss Payable:	$ 49,500
	($50,000 – $500)
Debris Removal Expense:	$ 10,000
Debris Removal Expense Payable:	$ 10,000

($10,000 is 20% of $50,000.)

The debris removal expense is less than 25% of the sum of the loss payable plus the deductible. The sum of the loss payable and the debris removal expense ($49,500 + $10,000 = $59,500) is less than the Limit of Insurance. Therefore the full amount of debris removal expense is payable in accordance with the terms of Paragraph **(3).**

Example 2

Limit of Insurance:	$ 90,000
Amount of Deductible:	$ 500
Amount of Loss:	$ 80,000
Amount of Loss Payable:	$ 79,500
	($80,000 – $500)
Debris Removal Expense:	$ 40,000
Debris Removal Expense Payable:	
Basic Amount:	$ 10,500
Additional Amount:	$ 25,000

The basic amount payable for debris removal expense under the terms of Paragraph **(3)** is calculated as follows: $80,000 ($79,500 + $500) x .25 = $20,000; capped at $10,500. The cap applies because the sum of the loss payable ($79,500) and the basic amount payable for debris removal expense ($10,500) cannot exceed the Limit of Insurance ($90,000).

The additional amount payable for debris removal expense is provided in accordance with the terms of Paragraph **(4)**, because the debris removal expense ($40,000) exceeds 25% of the loss payable plus the deductible ($40,000 is 50% of $80,000), and because the sum of the loss payable and debris removal expense ($79,500 + $40,000 = $119,500) would exceed the Limit of Insurance ($90,000). The additional amount of covered debris removal expense is $25,000, the maximum payable under Paragraph **(4)**. Thus, the total payable for debris removal expense in this example is $35,500; $4,500 of the debris removal expense is not covered.

b. Preservation Of Property

If it is necessary to move Covered Property from the described premises to preserve it from loss or damage by a Covered Cause of Loss, we will pay for any direct physical loss or damage to that property:

(1) While it is being moved or while temporarily stored at another location; and

(2) Only if the loss or damage occurs within 30 days after the property is first moved.

c. Fire Department Service Charge

When the fire department is called to save or protect Covered Property from a Covered Cause of Loss, we will pay up to $1,000 for service at each premises described in the Declarations, unless a higher limit is shown in the Declarations. Such limit is the most we will pay regardless of the number of responding fire departments or fire units, and regardless of the number or type of services performed.

This Additional Coverage applies to your liability for fire department service charges:

(1) Assumed by contract or agreement prior to loss; or

(2) Required by local ordinance.

No Deductible applies to this Additional Coverage.

d. Pollutant Clean-up And Removal

We will pay your expense to extract "pollutants" from land or water at the described premises if the discharge, dispersal, seepage, migration, release or escape of the "pollutants" is caused by or results from a Covered Cause of Loss that occurs during the policy period. The expenses will be paid only if they are reported to us in writing within 180 days of the date on which the Covered Cause of Loss occurs.

This Additional Coverage does not apply to costs to test for, monitor or assess the existence, concentration or effects of "pollutants". But we will pay for testing which is performed in the course of extracting the "pollutants" from the land or water.

The most we will pay under this Additional Coverage for each described premises is $10,000 for the sum of all covered expenses arising out of Covered Causes of Loss occurring during each separate 12-month period of this policy.

e. Electronic Data

(1) Under this Additional Coverage, electronic data has the meaning described under Property Not Covered, Electronic Data. This Additional Coverage does not apply to your "stock" of prepackaged software, or to electronic data which is integrated in and operates or controls the building's elevator, lighting, heating, ventilation, air conditioning or security system.

(2) Subject to the provisions of this Additional Coverage, we will pay for the cost to replace or restore electronic data which has been destroyed or corrupted by a Covered Cause of Loss. To the extent that electronic data is not replaced or restored, the loss will be valued at the cost of replacement of the media on which the electronic data was stored, with blank media of substantially identical type.

(3) The Covered Causes of Loss applicable to Your Business Personal Property apply to this Additional Coverage, Electronic Data, subject to the following:

(a) If the Causes Of Loss – Special Form applies, coverage under this Additional Coverage, Electronic Data, is limited to the "specified causes of loss" as defined in that form and Collapse as set forth in that form.

(b) If the Causes Of Loss – Broad Form applies, coverage under this Additional Coverage, Electronic Data, includes Collapse as set forth in that form.

(c) If the Causes Of Loss form is endorsed to add a Covered Cause of Loss, the additional Covered Cause of Loss does not apply to the coverage provided under this Additional Coverage, Electronic Data.

(d) The Covered Causes of Loss include a virus, harmful code or similar instruction introduced into or enacted on a computer system (including electronic data) or a network to which it is connected, designed to damage or destroy any part of the system or disrupt its normal operation. But there is no coverage for loss or damage caused by or resulting from manipulation of a computer system (including electronic data) by any employee, including a temporary or leased employee, or by an entity retained by you or for you to inspect, design, install, modify, maintain, repair or replace that system.

(4) The most we will pay under this Additional Coverage, Electronic Data, is $2,500 (unless a higher limit is shown in the Declarations) for all loss or damage sustained in any one policy year, regardless of the number of occurrences of loss or damage or the number of premises, locations or computer systems involved. If loss payment on the first occurrence does not exhaust this amount, then the balance is available for subsequent loss or damage sustained in but not after that policy year. With respect to an occurrence which begins in one policy year and continues or results in additional loss or damage in a subsequent policy year(s), all loss or damage is deemed to be sustained in the policy year in which the occurrence began.

5. Coverage Extensions

Except as otherwise provided, the following Extensions apply to property located in or on the building described in the Declarations or in the open (or in a vehicle) within 100 feet of the described premises.

If a Coinsurance percentage of 80% or more, or a Value Reporting period symbol, is shown in the Declarations, you may extend the insurance provided by this Coverage Part as follows:

a. Newly Acquired Property

(1) You may extend the insurance that applies to Your Business Personal Property to apply to:

(a) Business personal property, including such property that you newly acquire, at any location you acquire other than at fairs, trade shows or exhibitions; or

(b) Business personal property, including such property that you newly acquire, located at your newly constructed or acquired buildings at the location described in the Declarations.

The most we will pay for loss or damage under this Extension is $100,000 at each building.

(2) This Extension does not apply to:

(a) Personal property of others that is temporarily in your possession in the course of installing or performing work on such property; or

(b) Personal property of others that is temporarily in your possession in the course of your manufacturing or wholesaling activities.

(3) Insurance under this Coverage Extension for Newly Acquired Property will end when any of the following first occurs:

(a) This policy expires;

(b) 30 days expire after you acquire the property; or

(c) You report values to us.

We will charge you additional premium for values reported from the date you acquire the property.

b. Personal Effects And Property Of Others

You may extend the insurance that applies to Your Business Personal Property to apply to:

(1) Personal effects owned by you, your officers, your partners or members, your managers or your employees. This Extension does not apply to loss or damage by theft.

(2) Personal property of others in your care, custody or control.

The most we will pay for loss or damage under this Extension is $2,500 at each described premises. Our payment for loss of or damage to personal property of others will only be for the account of the owner of the property.

c. Valuable Papers And Records (Other Than Electronic Data)

(1) You may extend the insurance that applies to Your Business Personal Property to apply to the cost to replace or restore the lost information on valuable papers and records for which duplicates do not exist. But this Extension does not apply to valuable papers and records which exist as electronic data. Electronic data has the meaning described under Property Not Covered, Electronic Data.

(2) If the Causes Of Loss – Special Form applies, coverage under this Extension is limited to the "specified causes of loss" as defined in that form and Collapse as set forth in that form.

(3) If the Causes Of Loss – Broad Form applies, coverage under this Extension includes Collapse as set forth in that form.

(4) Under this Extension, the most we will pay to replace or restore the lost information is $2,500 at each described premises, unless a higher limit is shown in the Declarations. Such amount is additional insurance. We will also pay for the cost of blank material for reproducing the records (whether or not duplicates exist) and (when there is a duplicate) for the cost of labor to transcribe or copy the records. The costs of blank material and labor are subject to the applicable Limit of Insurance on Your Business Personal Property and, therefore, coverage of such costs is not additional insurance.

d. Property Off-premises

(1) You may extend the insurance that applies to Your Business Personal Property to apply to your business personal property while it is away from the described premises, if it is:

(a) Temporarily at a location you do not own, lease or operate;

(b) In storage at a location you lease, provided the lease was executed after the beginning of the current policy term; or

(c) At any fair, trade show or exhibition.

(2) This Extension does not apply to property:

(a) In or on a vehicle; or

(b) In the care, custody or control of your salespersons, unless the property is in such care, custody or control at a fair, trade show or exhibition.

(3) The most we will pay for loss or damage under this Extension is $10,000.

e. Outdoor Property

You may extend the insurance that applies to Your Business Personal Property to apply to your outdoor fences, radio and television antennas (including satellite dishes), trees, shrubs and plants (other than "stock" of trees, shrubs or plants), including debris removal expense, caused by or resulting from any of the following causes of loss if they are Covered Causes of Loss:

(1) Fire;

(2) Lightning;

(3) Explosion;

(4) Riot or Civil Commotion; or

(5) Aircraft.

The most we will pay for loss or damage under this Extension is $1,000, but not more than $250 for any one tree, shrub or plant. These limits apply to any one occurrence, regardless of the types or number of items lost or damaged in that occurrence.

Subject to all aforementioned terms and limitations of coverage, this Coverage Extension includes the expense of removing from the described premises the debris of trees, shrubs and plants which are the property of others.

f. Non-owned Detached Trailers

(1) You may extend the insurance that applies to Your Business Personal Property to apply to loss or damage to trailers that you do not own, provided that:

(a) The trailer is used in your business;

(b) The trailer is in your care, custody or control at the premises described in the Declarations; and

(c) You have a contractual responsibility to pay for loss or damage to the trailer.

(2) We will not pay for any loss or damage that occurs:

(a) While the trailer is attached to any motor vehicle or motorized conveyance, whether or not the motor vehicle or motorized conveyance is in motion;

(b) During hitching or unhitching operations, or when a trailer becomes accidentally unhitched from a motor vehicle or motorized conveyance.

(3) The most we will pay for loss or damage under this Extension is $5,000, unless a higher limit is shown in the Declarations.

(4) This insurance is excess over the amount due (whether you can collect on it or not) from any other insurance covering such property.

g. Business Personal Property Temporarily In Portable Storage Units

(1) You may extend the insurance that applies to Your Business Personal Property to apply to such property while temporarily stored in a portable storage unit (including a detached trailer) located within 100 feet of the building or structure described in the Declarations or within 100 feet of the premises described in the Declarations, whichever distance is greater.

(2) If the applicable Covered Causes of Loss form or endorsement contains a limitation or exclusion concerning loss or damage from sand, dust, sleet, snow, ice or rain to property in a structure, such limitation or exclusion also applies to property in a portable storage unit.

(3) Coverage under this Extension:

(a) Will end 90 days after the business personal property has been placed in the storage unit;

(b) Does not apply if the storage unit itself has been in use at the described premises for more than 90 consecutive days, even if the business personal property has been stored there for 90 or fewer days as of the time of loss or damage.

(4) Under this Extension, the most we will pay for the total of all loss or damage to business personal property is $10,000 (unless a higher limit is indicated in the Declarations for such Extension) regardless of the number of storage units. Such limit is part of, not in addition to, the applicable Limit of Insurance on Your Business Personal Property. Therefore, payment under this Extension will not increase the applicable Limit of Insurance on Your Business Personal Property.

(5) This Extension does not apply to loss or damage otherwise covered under this Coverage Form or any endorsement to this Coverage Form or policy, and does not apply to loss or damage to the storage unit itself.

Each of these Extensions is additional insurance unless otherwise indicated. The Additional Condition, Coinsurance, does not apply to these Extensions.

B. Exclusions And Limitations

See applicable Causes Of Loss form as shown in the Declarations.

C. Limits Of Insurance

The most we will pay for loss or damage in any one occurrence is the applicable Limit Of Insurance shown in the Declarations.

The most we will pay for loss or damage to outdoor signs, whether or not the sign is attached to a building, is $2,500 per sign in any one occurrence.

The amounts of insurance stated in the following Additional Coverages apply in accordance with the terms of such coverages and are separate from the Limit(s) Of Insurance shown in the Declarations for any other coverage:

1. Fire Department Service Charge;
2. Pollutant Clean-up And Removal; and
3. Electronic Data.

Payments under the Preservation Of Property Additional Coverage will not increase the applicable Limit of Insurance.

D. Deductible

In any one occurrence of loss or damage (hereinafter referred to as loss), we will first reduce the amount of loss if required by the Coinsurance Condition or the Agreed Value Optional Coverage. If the adjusted amount of loss is less than or equal to the Deductible, we will not pay for that loss. If the adjusted amount of loss exceeds the Deductible, we will then subtract the Deductible from the adjusted amount of loss and will pay the resulting amount or the Limit of Insurance, whichever is less.

When the occurrence involves loss to more than one item of Covered Property and separate Limits of Insurance apply, the losses will not be combined in determining application of the Deductible. But the Deductible will be applied only once per occurrence.

Example 1

(This example assumes there is no Coinsurance penalty.)

Deductible:	$ 250
Limit of Insurance – Building 1:	$ 60,000
Limit of Insurance – Building 2:	$ 80,000
Loss to Building 1:	$ 60,100
Loss to Building 2:	$ 90,000

The amount of loss to Building 1 ($60,100) is less than the sum ($60,250) of the Limit of Insurance applicable to Building 1 plus the Deductible.

The Deductible will be subtracted from the amount of loss in calculating the loss payable for Building 1:

$ 60,100
– 250
$ 59,850 Loss Payable – Building 1

The Deductible applies once per occurrence and therefore is not subtracted in determining the amount of loss payable for Building 2. Loss payable for Building 2 is the Limit of Insurance of $80,000.

Total amount of loss payable:

$59,850 + $80,000 = $139,850

Example 2

(This example, too, assumes there is no Coinsurance penalty.)

The Deductible and Limits of Insurance are the same as those in Example 1.

Loss to Building 1:	$ 70,000
(Exceeds Limit of Insurance plus Deductible)	
Loss to Building 2:	$ 90,000
(Exceeds Limit of Insurance plus Deductible)	
Loss Payable – Building 1:	$ 60,000
(Limit of Insurance)	
Loss Payable – Building 2:	$ 80,000
(Limit of Insurance)	
Total amount of loss payable:	$ 140,000

E. Loss Conditions

The following conditions apply in addition to the Common Policy Conditions and the Commercial Property Conditions:

1. Abandonment

There can be no abandonment of any property to us.

2. Appraisal

If we and you disagree on the value of the property or the amount of loss, either may make written demand for an appraisal of the loss. In this event, each party will select a competent and impartial appraiser. The two appraisers will select an umpire. If they cannot agree, either may request that selection be made by a judge of a court having jurisdiction. The appraisers will state separately the value of the property and amount of loss. If they fail to agree, they will submit their differences to the umpire. A decision agreed to by any two will be binding. Each party will:

a. Pay its chosen appraiser; and

b. Bear the other expenses of the appraisal and umpire equally.

If there is an appraisal, we will still retain our right to deny the claim.

3. Condominium Association Insurance

The Condominium Association may have other insurance covering the same property as this insurance. This insurance is intended to be excess, and not to contribute with that other insurance.

4. Duties In The Event Of Loss Or Damage

a. You must see that the following are done in the event of loss or damage to Covered Property:

(1) Notify the police if a law may have been broken.

(2) Give us prompt notice of the loss or damage. Include a description of the property involved.

(3) As soon as possible, give us a description of how, when and where the loss or damage occurred.

(4) Take all reasonable steps to protect the Covered Property from further damage, and keep a record of your expenses necessary to protect the Covered Property, for consideration in the settlement of the claim. This will not increase the Limit of Insurance. However, we will not pay for any subsequent loss or damage resulting from a cause of loss that is not a Covered Cause of Loss. Also, if feasible, set the damaged property aside and in the best possible order for examination.

(5) At our request, give us complete inventories of the damaged and undamaged property. Include quantities, costs, values and amount of loss claimed.

(6) As often as may be reasonably required, permit us to inspect the property proving the loss or damage and examine your books and records.

Also permit us to take samples of damaged and undamaged property for inspection, testing and analysis, and permit us to make copies from your books and records.

(7) Send us a signed, sworn proof of loss containing the information we request to investigate the claim. You must do this within 60 days after our request. We will supply you with the necessary forms.

(8) Cooperate with us in the investigation or settlement of the claim.

b. We may examine any insured under oath, while not in the presence of any other insured and at such times as may be reasonably required, about any matter relating to this insurance or the claim, including an insured's books and records. In the event of an examination, an insured's answers must be signed.

5. Loss Payment

a. In the event of loss or damage covered by this Coverage Form, at our option, we will either:

(1) Pay the value of lost or damaged property;

(2) Pay the cost of repairing or replacing the lost or damaged property, subject to **b.** below;

(3) Take all or any part of the property at an agreed or appraised value; or

(4) Repair, rebuild or replace the property with other property of like kind and quality, subject to **b.** below.

We will determine the value of lost or damaged property, or the cost of its repair or replacement, in accordance with the applicable terms of the Valuation Condition in this Coverage Form or any applicable provision which amends or supersedes the Valuation Condition.

b. The cost to repair, rebuild or replace does not include the increased cost attributable to enforcement of or compliance with any ordinance or law regulating the construction, use or repair of any property.

c. We will give notice of our intentions within 30 days after we receive the sworn proof of loss.

d. We will not pay you more than your financial interest in the Covered Property.

e. We may adjust losses with the owners of lost or damaged property if other than you. If we pay the owners, such payments will satisfy your claims against us for the owners' property. We will not pay the owners more than their financial interest in the Covered Property.

f. We may elect to defend you against suits arising from claims of owners of property. We will do this at our expense.

g. We will pay for covered loss or damage within 30 days after we receive the sworn proof of loss, if you have complied with all of the terms of this Coverage Part, and:

(1) We have reached agreement with you on the amount of loss; or

(2) An appraisal award has been made.

6. Recovered Property

If either you or we recover any property after loss settlement, that party must give the other prompt notice. At your option, the property will be returned to you. You must then return to us the amount we paid to you for the property. We will pay recovery expenses to repair the recovered property, subject to the Limit of Insurance.

7. Vacancy

a. Description Of Terms

(1) As used in this Vacancy Condition, the term building and the term vacant have the meanings set forth in **(1)(a)** and **(1)(b)** below:

(a) When this policy is issued to a tenant, and with respect to that tenant's interest in Covered Property, building means the unit or suite rented or leased to the tenant. Such building is vacant when it does not contain enough business personal property to conduct customary operations.

(b) When this policy is issued to the owner or general lessee of a building, building means the entire building. Such building is vacant unless at least 31% of its total square footage is:

(i) Rented to a lessee or sublessee and used by the lessee or sublessee to conduct its customary operations; and/or

(ii) Used by the building owner to conduct customary operations.

(2) Buildings under construction or renovation are not considered vacant.

b. Vacancy Provisions

If the building where loss or damage occurs has been vacant for more than 60 consecutive days before that loss or damage occurs:

(1) We will not pay for any loss or damage caused by any of the following, even if they are Covered Causes of Loss:

(a) Vandalism;

(b) Sprinkler leakage, unless you have protected the system against freezing;

(c) Building glass breakage;

(d) Water damage;

(e) Theft; or

(f) Attempted theft.

(2) With respect to Covered Causes of Loss other than those listed in **b.(1)(a)** through **b.(1)(f)** above, we will reduce the amount we would otherwise pay for the loss or damage by 15%.

8. Valuation

We will determine the value of Covered Property in the event of loss or damage as follows:

a. At actual cash value as of the time of loss or damage, except as provided in **b.** and **c.** below.

b. "Stock" you have sold but not delivered at the selling price less discounts and expenses you otherwise would have had.

c. Glass at the cost of replacement with safety-glazing material if required by law.

F. Additional Condition

COINSURANCE

If a Coinsurance percentage is shown in the Declarations, the following condition applies in addition to the Common Policy Conditions and the Commercial Property Conditions:

a. We will not pay the full amount of any loss if the value of Covered Property at the time of loss times the Coinsurance percentage shown for it in the Declarations is greater than the Limit of Insurance for the property.

Instead, we will determine the most we will pay using the following steps:

(1) Multiply the value of Covered Property at the time of loss by the Coinsurance percentage;

(2) Divide the Limit of Insurance of the property by the figure determined in Step **(1)**;

(3) Multiply the total amount of loss, before the application of any deductible, by the figure determined in Step **(2)**; and

(4) Subtract the deductible from the figure determined in Step **(3)**.

We will pay the amount determined in Step **(4)** or the Limit of Insurance, whichever is less. For the remainder, you will either have to rely on other insurance or absorb the loss yourself.

Example 1 (Underinsurance)

When:	The value of the property is:	$ 250,000
	The Coinsurance percentage for it is:	80%
	The Limit of Insurance for it is:	$ 100,000
	The Deductible is:	$ 250
	The amount of loss is:	$ 40,000

Step **(1)**: $250,000 x 80% = $200,000
(the minimum amount of insurance to meet your Coinsurance requirements)

Step **(2)**: $100,000 ÷ $200,000 = .50

Step **(3)**: $40,000 x .50 = $20,000

Step **(4)**: $20,000 – $250 = $19,750

We will pay no more than $19,750. The remaining $20,250 is not covered.

Example 2 (Adequate Insurance)

When:	The value of the property is:	$ 250,000
	The Coinsurance percentage for it is:	80%
	The Limit of Insurance for it is:	$ 200,000
	The Deductible is:	$ 250
	The amount of loss is:	$ 40,000

The minimum amount of insurance to meet your Coinsurance requirement is $200,000 ($250,000 x 80%). Therefore, the Limit of Insurance in this example is adequate and no penalty applies. We will pay no more than $39,750 ($40,000 amount of loss minus the deductible of $250).

b. If one Limit of Insurance applies to two or more separate items, this condition will apply to the total of all property to which the limit applies.

Example 3

When:	The value of the property is:	
	Personal Property at Location 1:	$ 175,000
	Personal Property at Location 2:	$ 75,000
		$ 250,000
	The Coinsurance percentage for it is:	90%
	The Limit of Insurance for Personal Property at Locations 1 and 2 is:	$ 180,000
	The Deductible is:	$ 1,000
	The amount of loss is:	
	Personal Property at Location 1:	$ 30,000
	Personal Property at Location 2:	$ 20,000
		$ 50,000

Step **(1)**: $250,000 x 90% = $225,000
(the minimum amount of insurance to meet your Coinsurance requirements and to avoid the penalty shown below)

Step **(2)**: $180,000 ÷ $225,000 = .80

Step **(3)**: $50,000 x .80 = $40,000

Step **(4)**: $40,000 – $1,000 = $39,000

We will pay no more than $39,000. The remaining $11,000 is not covered.

G. Optional Coverages

If shown as applicable in the Declarations, the following Optional Coverages apply separately to each item:

1. Agreed Value

a. The Additional Condition, Coinsurance, does not apply to Covered Property to which this Optional Coverage applies. We will pay no more for loss of or damage to that property than the proportion that the Limit of Insurance under this Coverage Part for the property bears to the Agreed Value shown for it in the Declarations.

b. If the expiration date for this Optional Coverage shown in the Declarations is not extended, the Additional Condition, Coinsurance, is reinstated and this Optional Coverage expires.

c. The terms of this Optional Coverage apply only to loss or damage that occurs:

(1) On or after the effective date of this Optional Coverage; and

(2) Before the Agreed Value expiration date shown in the Declarations or the policy expiration date, whichever occurs first.

2. Inflation Guard

a. The Limit of Insurance for property to which this Optional Coverage applies will automatically increase by the annual percentage shown in the Declarations.

b. The amount of increase will be:

(1) The Limit of Insurance that applied on the most recent of the policy inception date, the policy anniversary date, or any other policy change amending the Limit of Insurance, times

(2) The percentage of annual increase shown in the Declarations, expressed as a decimal (example: 8% is .08), times

(3) The number of days since the beginning of the current policy year or the effective date of the most recent policy change amending the Limit of Insurance, divided by 365.

Example

If:	The applicable Limit of Insurance is:	$ 100,000
	The annual percentage increase is:	8%
	The number of days since the beginning of the policy year (or last policy change) is:	146
	The amount of increase is: $100,000 x .08 x 146 ÷ 365 =	$ 3,200

3. Replacement Cost

a. Replacement Cost (without deduction for depreciation) replaces Actual Cash Value in the Loss Condition, Valuation, of this Coverage Form.

b. This Optional Coverage does not apply to:

(1) Personal property of others;

(2) Contents of a residence;

(3) Works of art, antiques or rare articles, including etchings, pictures, statuary, marbles, bronzes, porcelains and bric-a-brac; or

(4) "Stock", unless the Including "Stock" option is shown in the Declarations.

c. You may make a claim for loss or damage covered by this insurance on an actual cash value basis instead of on a replacement cost basis. In the event you elect to have loss or damage settled on an actual cash value basis, you may still make a claim for the additional coverage this Optional Coverage provides if you notify us of your intent to do so within 180 days after the loss or damage.

d. We will not pay on a replacement cost basis for any loss or damage:

(1) Until the lost or damaged property is actually repaired or replaced; and

(2) Unless the repairs or replacement are made as soon as reasonably possible after the loss or damage.

e. We will not pay more for loss or damage on a replacement cost basis than the least of **(1), (2)** or **(3),** subject to **f.** below:

(1) The Limit of Insurance applicable to the lost or damaged property;

(2) The cost to replace the lost or damaged property with other property:

(a) Of comparable material and quality; and

(b) Used for the same purpose; or

(3) The amount actually spent that is necessary to repair or replace the lost or damaged property.

If a building is rebuilt at a new premises, the cost described in **e.(2)** above is limited to the cost which would have been incurred if the building had been rebuilt at the original premises.

f. The cost of repair or replacement does not include the increased cost attributable to enforcement of or compliance with any ordinance or law regulating the construction, use or repair of any property.

4. Extension Of Replacement Cost To Personal Property Of Others

a. If the Replacement Cost Optional Coverage is shown as applicable in the Declarations, then this Extension may also be shown as applicable. If the Declarations show this Extension as applicable, then Paragraph **3.b.(1)** of the Replacement Cost Optional Coverage is deleted and all other provisions of the Replacement Cost Optional Coverage apply to replacement cost on personal property of others.

b. With respect to replacement cost on the personal property of others, the following limitation applies:

If an item(s) of personal property of others is subject to a written contract which governs your liability for loss or damage to that item(s), then valuation of that item(s) will be based on the amount for which you are liable under such contract, but not to exceed the lesser of the replacement cost of the property or the applicable Limit of Insurance.

H. Definitions

1. "Pollutants" means any solid, liquid, gaseous or thermal irritant or contaminant, including smoke, vapor, soot, fumes, acids, alkalis, chemicals and waste. Waste includes materials to be recycled, reconditioned or reclaimed.

2. "Stock" means merchandise held in storage or for sale, raw materials and in-process or finished goods, including supplies used in their packing or shipping.

HOMEOWNERS
HO 00 06 03 22

HOMEOWNERS 6 – UNIT-OWNERS FORM

AGREEMENT

We will provide the insurance described in this Policy in return for the premium and compliance with all applicable provisions of this Policy.

DEFINITIONS

A. In this Policy, "you" and "your" refer to the "named insured" shown in the Declarations and the spouse if a resident of the same household. "We", "us" and "our" refer to the company providing this insurance.

B. In addition, certain words and phrases are defined as follows:

1. "Aircraft Liability", "Hovercraft Liability", "Motor Vehicle Liability" and "Watercraft Liability", subject to the provisions in **b.** below, mean the following:

a. Liability for "bodily injury" or "property damage" arising out of the:

(1) Ownership of such vehicle or craft by an "insured";

(2) Maintenance, occupancy, operation, use, loading or unloading of:

(a) An aircraft, hovercraft or watercraft by any person; or

(b) A motor vehicle by an "insured";

(3) Entrustment of such vehicle or craft by an "insured" to any person;

(4) Failure to supervise or negligent supervision of any person involving such vehicle or craft by an "insured"; or

(5) Vicarious liability, whether or not imposed by law, for the actions of a child or minor involving such vehicle or craft.

b. For the purpose of this definition:

(1) Aircraft means any contrivance used or designed for flight except model or hobby aircraft not used or designed to carry people or cargo;

(2) Hovercraft means a self-propelled motorized ground effect vehicle and includes, but is not limited to, flarecraft and air cushion vehicles;

(3) Watercraft means a craft principally designed to be propelled on or in water by wind, engine power or electric motor, except model or hobby watercraft not used or designed to carry people or cargo; and

(4) Motor vehicle means a "motor vehicle" as defined in **11.** below.

2. "Bodily injury" means bodily harm, sickness or disease, including required care, loss of services and death that results.

3. "Business" means:

a. A trade, profession or occupation engaged in on a full-time, part-time or occasional basis;

b. "Home-sharing host activities";

c. The leasing of the mineral rights of an "insured location"; or

d. Any other activity engaged in for money or other compensation, except the following:

(1) One or more activities, not described in **(2)** through **(4)** below, for which no "insured" receives more than $5,000 in total compensation for the 12 months before the beginning of the policy period;

(2) Volunteer activities for which no money is received other than payment for expenses incurred to perform the activity;

(3) Providing home day care services for which no compensation is received, other than the mutual exchange of such services; or

(4) The rendering of home day care services to a relative of an "insured".

4. "Cannabis" means:

a. Any good or product that consists of or contains any amount of Tetrahydrocannabinol (THC) or any other cannabinoid, regardless of whether any such THC or cannabinoid is natural or synthetic.

b. Paragraph **4.a.** above includes, but is not limited to, any of the following containing such THC or cannabinoid:

(1) Any plant of the genus Cannabis L., or any part thereof, such as seeds, stems, flowers, stalks and roots; or

(2) Any compound, by-product, extract, derivative, mixture or combination, such as:

(a) Resin, oil or wax;

(b) Hash or hemp; or

(c) Infused liquid or edible cannabis;

whether or not derived from any plant or part of any plant set forth in Paragraph **4.b.(1)** above.

c. Paragraph **4.a.** above includes, but is not limited to, marijuana.

5. "Employee" means an employee of an "insured", or an employee leased to an "insured" by a labor leasing firm under an agreement between an "insured" and the labor leasing firm, whose duties are other than those performed by a "residence employee".

6. "Home-sharing host activities" means:

a. The:

(1) Rental or holding for rental; or

(2) Mutual exchange of services;

of the "residence premises", in whole or in part, by an "insured" to a "home-sharing occupant" through the use of a "home-sharing network platform"; and

b. Any other related property or services made available by an "insured" for use during such:

(1) Rental; or

(2) Mutual exchange of services;

except those property or services provided by another party.

7. "Home-sharing network platform" means an online-enabled application, web site or digital network that:

a. Is used for the purpose of facilitating, for money, mutual exchange of services or other compensation, the rental of a dwelling or other structure, in whole or in part; and

b. Allows for the agreement and compensation with respect to such rental to be transacted through such online-enabled application, web site or digital network.

8. "Home-sharing occupant" means a person, other than an "insured", who:

a. Has entered into an agreement or arranged compensation with an "insured" through the use of a "home-sharing network platform" for "home-sharing host activities"; or

b. Is accompanying or staying with a person described in Paragraph **8.a.** above under such "home-sharing host activities".

9. "Insured" means:

a. You and residents of your household who are:

(1) Your relatives; or

(2) Other persons under the age of 21 and in your care or the care of a resident of your household who is your relative;

b. A student enrolled in school full-time, as defined by the school, who was a resident of your household before moving out to attend school, provided the student is under the age of:

(1) 24 and your relative; or

(2) 21 and in your care or the care of a resident of your household who is your relative; or

c. Under Section **II:**

(1) With respect to animals or watercraft to which this Policy applies, any person or organization legally responsible for these animals or watercraft which are owned by you or any person described in **9.a.** or **b.** "Insured" does not mean a person or organization using or having custody of these animals or watercraft in the course of any "business" or without consent of the owner; or

(2) With respect to a "motor vehicle" to which this Policy applies:

(a) Persons while engaged in your employ or that of any person described in **9.a.** or **b.;** or

(b) Other persons using the vehicle on an "insured location" with your consent.

Under both Sections **I** and **II,** when the word an immediately precedes the word "insured", the words an "insured" together mean one or more "insureds".

10. "Insured location" means:

a. The "residence premises";

b. The part of other premises, other structures and grounds used by you as a residence; and

(1) Which is shown in the Declarations; or

(2) Which is acquired by you during the policy period for your use as a residence;

c. Any premises used by you in connection with a premises described in **a.** and **b.** above;

d. Any part of a premises:

(1) Not owned by an "insured"; and

(2) Where an "insured" is temporarily residing;

e. Vacant land, other than farm land, owned by or rented to an "insured";

f. Land owned by or rented to an "insured" on which a one-, two-, three- or four-family dwelling is being built as a residence for an "insured";

g. Individual or family cemetery plots or burial vaults of an "insured"; or

h. Any part of a premises occasionally rented to an "insured" for other than "business" use.

11. "Motor vehicle" means:

a. A land or amphibious vehicle that is self-propelled or capable of being self-propelled; or

b. Any trailer or semitrailer which is being carried on, towed by or hitched for towing by a vehicle described in **11.a.** above.

12. "Occurrence" means an accident, including continuous or repeated exposure to substantially the same general harmful conditions, which results, during the policy period, in:

a. "Bodily injury"; or

b. "Property damage".

13. "Property damage" means physical injury to, destruction of or loss of use of tangible property.

14. "Residence employee" means:

a. An employee of an "insured", or an employee leased to an "insured" by a labor leasing firm, under an agreement between an "insured" and the labor leasing firm, whose duties are related to the maintenance or use of the "residence premises", including household or domestic services; or

b. One who performs similar duties elsewhere not related to the "business" of an "insured".

A "residence employee" does not include a temporary employee who is furnished to an "insured" to substitute for a permanent "residence employee" on leave or to meet seasonal or short-term workload conditions.

15. "Residence premises" means the unit where you reside shown as the "residence premises" in the Declarations.

C. In this Policy, the terms:

1. Roomer;

2. Boarder;

3. Tenant; or

4. Guest;

do not include a "home-sharing occupant".

SECTION I – PROPERTY COVERAGES

A. Coverage A – Dwelling

1. We cover:

a. The alterations, appliances, fixtures and improvements which are part of the building contained within the "residence premises";

b. Items of real property which pertain exclusively to the "residence premises";

c. Property which is your insurance responsibility under a corporation or association of property owners agreement; or

d. Structures owned solely by you, other than the "residence premises", at the location of the "residence premises".

2. We do not cover:

a. Land, including land on which the "residence premises", real property or structures are located;

b. Structures rented or held for rental to any person not a tenant of the dwelling, unless used solely as a private garage;

c. Structures from which any "business" is conducted; or

d. Structures used to store "business" property. However, we do cover a structure that contains "business" property solely owned by an "insured" or a tenant of the dwelling, provided that "business" property does not include gaseous or liquid fuel, other than fuel in a permanently installed fuel tank of a vehicle or craft parked or stored in the structure.

B. Coverage C – Personal Property

1. Covered Property

We cover personal property owned or used by an "insured" while it is anywhere in the world. After a loss and at your request, we will cover personal property owned by:

a. Others while the property is on the part of the "residence premises" occupied by an "insured"; or

b. A guest or a "residence employee", while the property is in any residence occupied by an "insured".

2. Limit For Property At Other Locations

a. Other Residences

Our limit of liability for personal property usually located at an "insured's" residence, other than the "residence premises", is 10% of the limit of liability for Coverage **C**, or $1,500, whichever is greater. However, this limitation does not apply to personal property:

(1) Moved from the "residence premises" because it is:

(a) Being remodeled, renovated or repaired; and

(b) Not fit to live in or store property in; or

(2) In a newly acquired principal residence for 30 days from the time you begin to move the property there.

b. Self-storage Facilities

Our limit of liability for personal property owned or used by an "insured" and located in a self-storage facility is 10% of the limit of liability for Coverage **C**, or $1,500, whichever is greater. However, this limitation does not apply to personal property:

(1) Moved from the "residence premises" because it is:

(a) Being remodeled, renovated or repaired; and

(b) Not fit to live in or store property in; or

(2) Usually located in an "insured's" residence, other than the "residence premises".

3. **Special Limits Of Liability**

The special limit for each category shown below is the total limit for each loss for all property in that category. These special limits do not increase the Coverage **C** limit of liability.

a. $300 on money, bank notes, bullion, gold other than goldware, silver other than silverware, platinum other than platinumware, coins, medals, scrip, stored value cards and smart cards.

b. $2,000 on securities, accounts, deeds, evidences of debt, letters of credit, notes other than bank notes, manuscripts, personal records, passports, tickets and stamps. This dollar limit applies to these categories regardless of the medium (such as paper or computer software) on which the material exists.

This limit includes the cost to research, replace or restore the information from the lost or damaged material.

c. $2,000 on watercraft of all types, including their trailers, furnishings, equipment and outboard engines or motors.

d. $2,000 on trailers or semitrailers not used with watercraft of all types.

e. $2,000 for loss by theft of jewelry, watches, furs, precious and semiprecious stones.

f. $3,000 for loss by theft of firearms and related equipment.

g. $3,000 for loss by theft of silverware, silver-plated ware, goldware, gold-plated ware, platinumware, platinum-plated ware and pewterware. This includes flatware, hollowware, tea sets, trays and trophies made of or including silver, gold or pewter.

h. $3,000 on property, on the "residence premises", used primarily for "business" purposes.

i. $1,500 on property, away from the "residence premises", used primarily for "business" purposes. However, this limit does not apply to antennas, tapes, wires, records, disks or other media that are:

(1) Used with electronic equipment that reproduces, receives or transmits audio, visual or data signals; and

(2) In or upon a "motor vehicle".

j. $2,000 on portable electronic equipment that:

(1) Reproduces, receives or transmits audio, visual or data signals;

(2) Is designed to be operated by more than one power source, one of which is a "motor vehicle's" electrical system; and

(3) Is in or upon a "motor vehicle".

k. $300 on antennas, tapes, wires, records, disks or other media that are:

(1) Used with electronic equipment that reproduces, receives or transmits audio, visual or data signals; and

(2) In or upon a "motor vehicle".

l. $2,000 on model or hobby aircraft not used or designed to carry people or cargo.

4. **Property Not Covered**

We do not cover:

a. Articles separately described and specifically insured, regardless of the limit for which they are insured, in this or other insurance;

b. Animals, birds or fish;

c. "Motor vehicles".

This includes a "motor vehicle's" equipment, and parts, that are in or upon the "motor vehicle".

However, this Paragraph **4.c.** does not apply to:

(1) Portable electronic equipment that:

(a) Reproduces, receives or transmits audio, visual or data signals; and

(b) Is designed so that it may be operated from a power source other than a "motor vehicle's" electrical system.

(2) "Motor vehicles" not required to be registered for use on public roads or property which are:

(a) Used solely to service a residence; or

(b) Designed to assist the handicapped;

d. Aircraft, meaning any contrivance used or designed for flight, including any parts whether or not attached to the aircraft.

We do cover model or hobby aircraft not used or designed to carry people or cargo;

e. Hovercraft and parts. Hovercraft means a self-propelled motorized ground effect vehicle and includes, but is not limited to, flarecraft and air cushion vehicles;

f. Property of:

(1) A "home-sharing occupant";

(2) Any other person occupying the "residence premises" as a result of any "home-sharing host activities"; and

(3) Roomers, boarders and other tenants, except property of roomers and boarders related to an "insured";

g. Property in:

(1) A space while rented or primarily held for rental to a "home-sharing occupant"; or

(2) Subject to Paragraph **g.(1),** an apartment regularly rented or held for rental to others by an "insured";

h. Property used primarily for "home-sharing host activities";

i. Property rented or held for rental to others off the "residence premises";

j. "Business" data, including such data stored in:

(1) Books of account, drawings or other paper records; or

(2) Computers and related equipment.

We do cover the cost of blank recording or storage media and of prerecorded computer programs available on the retail market;

k. Credit cards, electronic fund transfer cards or access devices used solely for deposit, withdrawal or transfer of funds;

l. Water or steam;

m. Virtual currency of any kind, by whatever name known, whether actual or fictitious including, but not limited to, digital currency, crypto currency or any other type of electronic currency; or

n. Any:

(1) Controlled Substances, other than "cannabis", as defined by the Federal Food and Drug Law at 21 U.S.C.A. Sections 811 and 812; and

(2) "Cannabis" regardless of whether such "cannabis" is considered a Controlled Substance.

Controlled Substances include but are not limited to cocaine, LSD and all narcotic drugs.

However, this Paragraph **4.n.** does not apply to:

(3) Prescription drugs obtained following the lawful orders of a licensed health care professional; or

(4) Goods or products containing or derived from hemp, including, but not limited to:

(a) Seeds;

(b) Food;

(c) Clothing;

(d) Lotions, oils or extracts;

(e) Building materials; or

(f) Paper.

However, this Paragraph **4.n.(4)** does not apply to the extent any such goods or products are prohibited under an applicable state or local statute, regulation or ordinance in the state where such goods or products are located.

C. Coverage D – Loss Of Use

The limit of liability for Coverage **D** is the total limit for the coverages in **1.** Additional Living Expense, **2.** Fair Rental Value and **3.** Civil Authority Prohibits Use below.

1. Additional Living Expense

If a loss by a Peril Insured Against under this Policy to covered property or the building containing the property makes the "residence premises" not fit to live in, we cover any necessary increase in living expenses incurred by you and residents of your household who are:

a. Your relatives; or

b. Other persons under the age of 21 and in your care or the care of a resident of your household who is your relative;

so that your household can maintain its normal standard of living.

Payment will be for the shortest time required to repair or replace the damaged property or, if your household permanently relocates, the shortest time required for your household to settle elsewhere.

2. Fair Rental Value

If a loss covered under Section **I** makes that part of the "residence premises" rented to others or held for rental by you not fit to live in, we cover the fair rental value of such premises less any expenses that do not continue while it is not fit to live in.

However, we do not cover any fair rental value arising out of or in connection with "home-sharing host activities".

Payment will be for the shortest time required to repair or replace the damaged property.

3. Civil Authority Prohibits Use

If a civil authority prohibits you from use of the "residence premises" as a result of direct damage to neighboring premises by a Peril Insured Against, we cover the loss as provided in **1.** Additional Living Expense and **2.** Fair Rental Value above for no more than two weeks.

4. Loss Or Expense Not Covered

We do not cover loss or expense due to cancellation of a lease or agreement.

The periods of time under **1.** Additional Living Expense, **2.** Fair Rental Value and **3.** Civil Authority Prohibits Use above are not limited by expiration of this Policy.

D. Additional Coverages

1. Debris Removal

a. We will pay your reasonable expense for the removal of:

(1) Debris of covered property if a Peril Insured Against that applies to the damaged property causes the loss; or

(2) Ash, dust or particles from a volcanic eruption that has caused direct loss to a building or property contained in a building.

This expense is included in the limit of liability that applies to the damaged property. If the amount to be paid for the actual damage to the property plus the debris removal expense is more than the limit of liability for the damaged property, an additional 5% of that limit is available for such expense.

b. We will also pay your reasonable expense, up to $3,000, for the removal from the "residence premises" of:

(1) Trees you solely own felled by the peril of Windstorm or Hail or Weight of Ice, Snow or Sleet; or

(2) A neighbor's trees felled by a Peril Insured Against under Coverage **C;**

provided the trees damage a covered structure.

The $3,000 limit is the most we will pay in any one loss, regardless of the number of fallen trees. No more than $1,500 of this limit will be paid for the removal of any one tree.

This coverage is additional insurance.

2. Reasonable Repairs

a. We will pay the reasonable cost incurred by you for the necessary measures taken solely to protect covered property that is damaged by a Peril Insured Against from further damage.

b. If the measures taken involve repair to other damaged property, we will only pay if that property is covered under this Policy and the damage is caused by a Peril Insured Against. This coverage does not:

(1) Increase the limit of liability that applies to the covered property; or

(2) Relieve you of your duties, in case of a loss to covered property, described in **C.3.** under Section **I** – Conditions.

3. Trees, Shrubs And Other Plants

We cover trees, shrubs, plants or lawns, you solely own at the location of the "residence premises", for loss caused by the following Perils Insured Against:

a. Fire or Lightning;

b. Explosion;

c. Riot or Civil Commotion;

d. Aircraft;

e. Vehicles not owned or operated by a resident of the "residence premises";

f. Vandalism or Malicious Mischief; or

g. Theft.

We will pay up to 10% of the limit of liability that applies to Coverage **C** for all trees, shrubs, plants or lawns. No more than $1,500 of this limit will be paid for any one tree, shrub or plant. We do not cover:

h. Property, other than "cannabis", grown for "business" purposes; or

i. "Cannabis", whether or not grown for "business" purposes.

This coverage is additional insurance.

4. Fire Department Service Charge

We will pay up to $500 for your liability assumed by contract or agreement for fire department charges incurred when the fire department is called to save or protect covered property from a Peril Insured Against. We do not cover fire department service charges if the property is located within the limits of the city, municipality or protection district furnishing the fire department response.

This coverage is additional insurance. No deductible applies to this coverage.

5. Property Removed

We insure covered property against direct loss from any cause while being removed from a premises endangered by a Peril Insured Against and for no more than 30 days while removed.

This coverage does not increase the limit of liability that applies to the property being removed.

6. Loss Assessment

a. We will pay up to $2,000 for your share of loss assessment charged during the policy period against you, as owner or tenant of the "residence premises", by a corporation or association of property owners. The assessment must be made as a result of direct loss to property, owned by all members collectively, of the type that would be covered by this Policy if owned by you, caused by a Peril Insured Against under Coverage **A**, other than:

(1) Earthquake; or

(2) Land shock waves or tremors before, during or after a volcanic eruption.

The limit of $2,000 is the most we will pay with respect to any one loss, regardless of the number of assessments. We will only apply one deductible, per unit, to the total amount of any one loss to the property described above, regardless of the number of assessments.

b. We do not cover assessments charged against you or a corporation or association of property owners by any governmental body.

c. Paragraph **Q. Policy Period** under **Section I – Conditions** does not apply to this coverage.

This coverage is additional insurance.

7. Collapse

a. The coverage provided under this Additional Coverage – Collapse applies only to an abrupt collapse.

b. For the purpose of this Additional Coverage – Collapse, abrupt collapse means an abrupt falling down or caving in of a building or any part of a building with the result that the building or part of the building cannot be occupied for its intended purpose.

c. This Additional Coverage – Collapse does not apply to:

(1) A building or any part of a building that is in danger of falling down or caving in;

(2) A part of a building that is standing, even if it has separated from another part of the building; or

(3) A building or any part of a building that is standing, even if it shows evidence of cracking, bulging, sagging, bending, leaning, settling, shrinkage or expansion.

d. We insure for direct physical loss to covered property involving abrupt collapse of a building or any part of a building if such collapse was caused by one or more of the following:

(1) The Perils Insured Against named under Coverage **C;**

(2) Decay, of a building or any part of a building, that is hidden from view, unless the presence of such decay is known to an "insured" prior to collapse;

(3) Insect or vermin damage, to a building or any part of a building, that is hidden from view, unless the presence of such damage is known to an "insured" prior to collapse;

(4) Weight of contents, equipment, animals or people;

(5) Weight of rain which collects on a roof; or

(6) Use of defective material or methods in construction, remodeling or renovation if the collapse occurs during the course of the construction, remodeling or renovation.

e. Loss to an awning, fence, patio, deck, pavement, swimming pool, underground pipe, flue, drain, cesspool, septic tank, foundation, retaining wall, bulkhead, pier, wharf or dock is not included under **d.(2)** through **(6)** above, unless the loss is a direct result of the collapse of a building or any part of a building.

f. This coverage does not increase the limit of liability that applies to the damaged covered property.

8. Glass Or Safety Glazing Material

a. We cover:

(1) The breakage of glass or safety glazing material which is part of a building, storm door or storm window and covered under Coverage **A;**

(2) The breakage of glass or safety glazing material which is part of a building, storm door or storm window and covered under Coverage **A** when caused directly by earth movement; and

(3) The direct physical loss to covered property caused solely by the pieces, fragments or splinters of broken glass or safety glazing material which is part of a building, storm door or storm window.

b. This coverage does not include loss:

(1) To covered property which results because the glass or safety glazing material has been broken, except as provided in **a.(3)** above; or

(2) To the "residence premises" if the building containing the "residence premises" has been vacant for more than 60 consecutive days immediately before the loss, except when the breakage results directly from earth movement as provided in **a.(2)** above. A building being constructed, remodeled, renovated or repaired is not considered vacant.

c. This coverage does not increase the limit of liability that applies to the damaged property.

9. Ordinance Or Law

a. We will pay up to 10% of the limit of liability that applies to Coverage **A** for the increased costs you incur due to the enforcement of any ordinance or law which requires or regulates:

(1) The construction, demolition, remodeling, renovation or repair of that part of property covered under Coverage **A** damaged by a Peril Insured Against;

(2) The demolition and reconstruction of the undamaged part of property covered under Coverage **A,** when that property must be totally demolished because of damage by a Peril Insured Against to another part of that property covered under Coverage **A;** or

(3) The remodeling, removal or replacement of the portion of the undamaged part of property covered under Coverage **A** necessary to complete the remodeling, repair or replacement of that part of the property covered under Coverage **A** damaged by a Peril Insured Against.

b. You may use all or part of this ordinance or law coverage to pay for the increased costs you incur to remove debris resulting from the construction, demolition, remodeling, renovation, repair or replacement of property as stated in **a.** above.

c. We do not cover:

(1) The loss in value to any property covered under Coverage **A** due to the requirements of any ordinance or law; or

(2) The costs to comply with any ordinance or law which requires any "insured" or others to test for, monitor, clean up, remove, contain, treat, detoxify or neutralize, or in any way respond to, or assess the effects of, pollutants in or on any property covered under Coverage **A.**

Pollutants means any solid, liquid, gaseous or thermal irritant or contaminant, including smoke, vapor, soot, fumes, acids, alkalis, chemicals and waste. Waste includes materials to be recycled, reconditioned or reclaimed.

This coverage is additional insurance.

10. Grave Markers

We will pay up to $5,000 for grave markers, including mausoleums, away from the "residence premises" for loss caused by a Peril Insured Against.

This coverage does not increase the limits of liability that apply to the damaged covered property.

SECTION I – PERILS INSURED AGAINST

We insure for direct physical loss to the property described in Coverages **A** and **C** caused by any of the following perils unless the loss is excluded in Section **I** – Exclusions.

1. Fire Or Lightning

2. Windstorm Or Hail

This peril includes loss to watercraft of all types and their trailers, furnishings, equipment, and outboard engines or motors, only while inside a fully enclosed building.

This peril does not include loss to the inside of a building or the property contained in a building caused by rain, snow, sleet, sand or dust unless the direct force of wind or hail damages the building causing an opening in a roof or wall and the rain, snow, sleet, sand or dust enters through this opening.

3. Explosion

4. Riot Or Civil Commotion

5. Aircraft

This peril includes self-propelled missiles and spacecraft.

6. Vehicles

This peril does not include loss to a fence, driveway or walk caused by a vehicle owned or operated by a resident of the "residence premises".

7. Smoke

This peril means sudden and accidental damage from smoke, including the emission or puffback of smoke, soot, fumes or vapors from a boiler, furnace or related equipment.

This peril does not include loss caused by smoke from agricultural smudging or industrial operations.

8. Vandalism Or Malicious Mischief

This peril does not include loss to property which pertains to the "residence premises", and any ensuing loss caused by any intentional and wrongful act committed in the course of the vandalism or malicious mischief, if:

a. The loss arises out of or results from "home-sharing host activities"; or

b. The building containing the "residence premises" has been vacant for more than 60 consecutive days immediately before the loss. A building being constructed, remodeled, renovated or repaired is not considered vacant.

9. Theft

a. This peril includes attempted theft and loss of property from a known place when it is likely that the property has been stolen.

b. This peril does not include loss caused by theft:

(1) Committed by an "insured";

(2) In or to a "residence premises" under construction, or of materials and supplies for use in the construction until the "residence premises" is finished and occupied;

(3) From that part of a "residence premises" rented by an "insured" to someone other than another "insured";

(4) That occurs away from the "residence premises" or the location of the "residence premises" of:

(a) Trailers, semitrailers and campers;

(b) Watercraft of all types, and their furnishings, equipment and outboard engines or motors; or

(c) Property while at any other residence owned by, rented to, or occupied by an "insured", except while an "insured" is temporarily living there. Property of an "insured" who is a student is covered while at the residence the student occupies to attend school as long as the student has been there at any time during the 90 days immediately before the loss; or

(5) If such loss arises out of or results from "home-sharing host activities".

10. Falling Objects

This peril does not include loss to the inside of a building or property contained in the building unless the roof or an outside wall of the building is first damaged by a falling object. Damage to the falling object itself is not included.

11. Weight Of Ice, Snow Or Sleet

This peril means weight of ice, snow or sleet which causes damage to a building or property contained in a building.

This peril does not include loss to an awning, fence, patio, pavement, swimming pool, foundation, retaining wall, bulkhead, pier, wharf or dock.

12. Accidental Discharge Or Overflow Of Water Or Steam

a. This peril means accidental discharge or overflow of water or steam from within a plumbing, heating, air conditioning or automatic fire protective sprinkler system or from within a household appliance. We also pay to tear out and replace any part of a building or other structure owned solely by you which is covered under Coverage **A** and at the location of the "residence premises", but only when necessary to repair the system or appliance from which the water or steam escaped. However, such tear out and replacement coverage only applies to other structures if the water or steam causes actual damage to a building owned solely by you at the location of the "residence premises".

b. This peril does not include loss:

(1) To or within the "residence premises", if the building containing the "residence premises" has been vacant for more than 60 consecutive days immediately before the loss. A building being constructed, remodeled, renovated or repaired is not considered vacant;

(2) To the system or appliance from which the water or steam escaped;

(3) Caused by or resulting from freezing except as provided in Peril Insured Against **14.** Freezing;

(4) To or within the "residence premises" caused by accidental discharge or overflow which occurs away from the building where the "residence premises" is located; or

(5) Caused by mold, fungus or wet rot unless hidden within the walls or ceilings or beneath the floors or above the ceilings of a structure.

c. In this peril, a plumbing system or household appliance does not include a sump, sump pump or related equipment or a roof drain, gutter, downspout or similar fixtures or equipment.

d. Section I – Exclusion 3. Water, Paragraphs a. and c. that apply to surface water and water below the surface of the ground do not apply to loss by water covered under this peril.

13. Sudden And Accidental Tearing Apart, Cracking, Burning Or Bulging

This peril means sudden and accidental tearing apart, cracking, burning or bulging of a steam or hot water heating system, an air conditioning or automatic fire protective sprinkler system, or an appliance for heating water.

This peril does not include loss caused by or resulting from freezing except as provided in Peril Insured Against **14.** Freezing below.

14. Freezing

a. This peril means freezing of a plumbing, heating, air conditioning or automatic fire protective sprinkler system or of a household appliance, but only if you have used reasonable care to:

(1) Maintain heat in the building; or

(2) Shut off the water supply and drain all systems and appliances of water.

However, if the building is protected by an automatic fire protective sprinkler system, you must use reasonable care to continue the water supply and maintain heat in the "residence premises" for coverage to apply.

b. In this peril, a plumbing system or household appliance does not include a sump, sump pump or related equipment or a roof drain, gutter, downspout or similar fixtures or equipment.

15. Sudden And Accidental Damage From Artificially Generated Electrical Current

This peril does not include loss to tubes, transistors, electronic components or circuitry that is a part of appliances, fixtures, computers, home entertainment units or other types of electronic apparatus.

16. Volcanic Eruption

This peril does not include loss caused by earthquake, land shock waves or tremors.

SECTION I – EXCLUSIONS

We do not insure for loss caused directly or indirectly by any of the following. Such loss is excluded regardless of any other cause or event contributing concurrently or in any sequence to the loss. These exclusions apply whether or not the loss event results in widespread damage or affects a substantial area.

1. Ordinance Or Law

Ordinance Or Law means any ordinance or law:

a. Requiring or regulating the construction, demolition, remodeling, renovation or repair of property, including removal of any resulting debris. This Exclusion **1.a.** does not apply to the amount of coverage that may be provided for in **D.9.** Ordinance Or Law under Section I – Property Coverages;

b. The requirements of which result in a loss in value to property; or

c. Requiring any "insured" or others to test for, monitor, clean up, remove, contain, treat, detoxify or neutralize, or in any way respond to, or assess the effects of, pollutants.

Pollutants means any solid, liquid, gaseous or thermal irritant or contaminant, including smoke, vapor, soot, fumes, acids, alkalis, chemicals and waste. Waste includes materials to be recycled, reconditioned or reclaimed.

This Exclusion **1.** applies whether or not the property has been physically damaged.

2. Earth Movement

Earth Movement means:

a. Earthquake, including land shock waves or tremors before, during or after a volcanic eruption;

b. Landslide, mudslide or mudflow;

c. Subsidence or sinkhole; or

d. Any other earth movement including earth sinking, rising or shifting.

This Exclusion **2.** applies regardless of whether any of the above, in **2.a.** through **2.d.**, is caused by an act of nature or is otherwise caused.

However, direct loss by fire, explosion or theft resulting from any of the above, in **2.a.** through **2.d.**, is covered.

3. Water

This means:

a. Flood, surface water, waves, including tidal wave and tsunami, tides, tidal water, overflow of any body of water, or spray from any of these, all whether or not driven by wind, including storm surge;

b. Water which:

(1) Backs up through sewers or drains; or

(2) Overflows or is otherwise discharged from a sump, sump pump or related equipment;

c. Water below the surface of the ground, including water which exerts pressure on, or seeps, leaks or flows through a building, sidewalk, driveway, patio, foundation, swimming pool or other structure; or

d. Waterborne material carried or otherwise moved by any of the water referred to in **3.a.** through **3.c.** of this exclusion.

This Exclusion **3.** applies regardless of whether any of the above, in **3.a.** through **3.d.**, is caused by an act of nature or is otherwise caused.

This Exclusion **3.** applies to, but is not limited to, escape, overflow or discharge, for any reason, of water or waterborne material from a dam, levee, seawall or any other boundary or containment system.

However, direct loss by fire, explosion or theft resulting from any of the above, in **3.a.** through **3.d.**, is covered.

4. Power Failure

Power Failure means the failure of power or other utility service if the failure takes place off the "residence premises". But if the failure results in a loss, from a Peril Insured Against on the "residence premises", we will pay for the loss caused by that peril.

5. Neglect

Neglect means neglect of an "insured" to use all reasonable means to save and preserve property at and after the time of a loss.

6. War

War includes the following and any consequence of any of the following:

a. Undeclared war, civil war, insurrection, rebellion or revolution;

b. Warlike act by a military force or military personnel; or

c. Destruction, seizure or use for a military purpose.

Discharge of a nuclear weapon will be deemed a warlike act even if accidental.

7. Nuclear Hazard

This Exclusion **7.** pertains to Nuclear Hazard to the extent set forth in **N.** Nuclear Hazard Clause under Section **I** – Conditions.

8. Intentional Loss

Intentional Loss means any loss arising out of any act an "insured" commits or conspires to commit with the intent to cause a loss.

In the event of such loss, no "insured" is entitled to coverage, even "insureds" who did not commit or conspire to commit the act causing the loss.

9. Governmental Action

Governmental Action means the destruction, confiscation or seizure of property described in Coverage **A** or **C** by order of any governmental or public authority.

This exclusion does not apply to such acts ordered by any governmental or public authority that are taken at the time of a fire to prevent its spread, if the loss caused by fire would be covered under this Policy.

SECTION I – CONDITIONS

A. Insurable Interest And Limit Of Liability

Even if more than one person has an insurable interest in the property covered, we will not be liable in any one loss:

1. To an "insured" for more than the amount of such "insured's" interest at the time of loss; or

2. For more than the applicable limit of liability.

B. Deductible

Unless otherwise noted in this Policy, the following deductible provision applies:

With respect to any one loss:

1. Subject to the applicable limit of liability, we will pay only that part of the total of all loss payable that exceeds the deductible amount shown in the Declarations.

2. If two or more deductibles under this Policy apply to the loss, the highest deductible amount will apply.

C. Duties After Loss

In case of a loss to covered property, we have no duty to provide coverage under this Policy if the failure to comply with the following duties is prejudicial to us. These duties must be performed either by you, an "insured" seeking coverage or a representative of either:

1. Give prompt notice to us or our agent;

2. Notify the police in case of loss by theft;

3. Protect the property from further damage. If repairs to the property are required, you must:

   a. Make reasonable and necessary repairs to protect the property; and

   b. Keep an accurate record of repair expenses;

4. Cooperate with us in the investigation of a claim;

5. Prepare an inventory of damaged personal property showing the quantity, description, actual cash value and amount of loss. Attach all bills, receipts and related documents that justify the figures in the inventory;

6. As often as we reasonably require:

   a. Show the damaged property;

   b. Provide us with records and documents we request and permit us to make copies; and

   c. Submit to examination under oath, while not in the presence of another "insured", and sign the same;

7. Send to us, within 60 days after our request, your signed, sworn proof of loss which sets forth, to the best of your knowledge and belief:

   a. The time and cause of loss;

   b. The interests of all "insureds" and all others in the property involved and all liens on the property;

   c. Other insurance which may cover the loss;

   d. Changes in title or occupancy of the property during the term of the Policy;

   e. Specifications of damaged buildings and detailed repair estimates;

   f. The inventory of damaged personal property described in **5.** above; and

   g. Receipts for additional living expenses incurred and records that support the fair rental value loss.

D. Loss Settlement

Covered property losses are settled as follows:

1. Personal property and grave markers, including mausoleums, at actual cash value at the time of loss but not more than the amount required to repair or replace.

2. Coverage A – Dwelling:

   a. If the damage is repaired or replaced within a reasonable time, at the actual cost to repair or replace;

   b. If the damage is not repaired or replaced within a reasonable time, at actual cash value but not more than the amount required to repair or replace.

   In this provision, the terms "repaired" or "replaced" do not include the increased costs incurred to comply with the enforcement of any ordinance or law, except to the extent that coverage for these increased costs is provided in **D.9.** Ordinance Or Law under Section **I** – Property Coverages.

E. Loss To A Pair Or Set

In case of loss to a pair or set, we may elect to:

1. Repair or replace any part to restore the pair or set to its value before the loss; or
2. Pay the difference between actual cash value of the property before and after the loss.

F. Appraisal

If you and we fail to agree on the amount of loss, either may demand an appraisal of the loss. In this event, each party will choose a competent and impartial appraiser within 20 days after receiving a written request from the other. The two appraisers will choose an umpire. If they cannot agree upon an umpire within 15 days, you or we may request that the choice be made by a judge of a court of record in the state where the "residence premises" is located. The appraisers will separately set the amount of loss. If the appraisers submit a written report of an agreement to us, the amount agreed upon will be the amount of loss. If they fail to agree, they will submit their differences to the umpire. A decision agreed to by any two will set the amount of loss.

Each party will:

1. Pay its own appraiser; and
2. Bear the other expenses of the appraisal and umpire equally.

G. Other Insurance And Service Agreement

1. If a loss covered by this Policy is also covered by:

   a. Other insurance, except insurance in the name of a corporation or association of property owners, we will pay only the proportion of the loss that the limit of liability that applies under this Policy bears to the total amount of insurance covering the loss; or

   b. A service agreement, except a service agreement in the name of a corporation or association of property owners, this insurance is excess over any amounts payable under any such agreement.

2. Subject to Paragraph **G.1.**, if, at the time of loss, there is other insurance or a service agreement in the name of a corporation or association of property owners covering the same property covered by this Policy, this insurance is:

   a. Excess over the amount due under such other insurance or service agreement, whether the corporation or association of property owners has collected that amount or not; and

   b. Primary with respect to any amount of the loss covered by this Policy and not due under such other insurance or service agreement because of the application of a deductible.

3. As used in this Paragraph **G.**, a service agreement means a service plan, property restoration plan, home warranty or other similar service warranty agreement, even if it is characterized as insurance.

H. Suit Against Us

No action can be brought against us unless there has been full compliance with all of the terms under Section **I** of this Policy and the action is started within two years after the date of loss.

I. Our Option

If we give you written notice within 30 days after we receive your signed, sworn proof of loss, we may repair or replace any part of the damaged property with material or property of like kind and quality.

J. Loss Payment

We will adjust all losses with you. We will pay you unless some other person is named in the Policy or is legally entitled to receive payment. Loss will be payable 60 days after we receive your proof of loss and:

1. Reach an agreement with you;
2. There is an entry of a final judgment; or

3. There is a filing of an appraisal award with us.

K. Abandonment Of Property

We need not accept any property abandoned by an "insured".

L. Mortgage Clause

1. If a mortgagee is named in this Policy, any loss payable under Coverage **A** will be paid to the mortgagee and you, as interests appear. If more than one mortgagee is named, the order of payment will be the same as the order of precedence of the mortgages.
2. If we deny your claim, that denial will not apply to a valid claim of the mortgagee, if the mortgagee:
   a. Notifies us of any change in ownership, occupancy or substantial change in risk of which the mortgagee is aware;
   b. Pays any premium due under this Policy on demand if you have neglected to pay the premium; and
   c. Submits a signed, sworn statement of loss within 60 days after receiving notice from us of your failure to do so. Paragraphs **F.** Appraisal, **H.** Suit Against Us and **J.** Loss Payment under Section **I** – Conditions also apply to the mortgagee.
3. If we decide to cancel or not to renew this Policy, the mortgagee will be notified at least 10 days before the date cancellation or nonrenewal takes effect.
4. If we pay the mortgagee for any loss and deny payment to you:
   a. We are subrogated to all the rights of the mortgagee granted under the mortgage on the property; or
   b. At our option, we may pay to the mortgagee the whole principal on the mortgage plus any accrued interest. In this event, we will receive a full assignment and transfer of the mortgage and all securities held as collateral to the mortgage debt.
5. Subrogation will not impair the right of the mortgagee to recover the full amount of the mortgagee's claim.

M. No Benefit To Bailee

We will not recognize any assignment or grant any coverage that benefits a person or organization holding, storing or moving property for a fee regardless of any other provision of this Policy.

N. Nuclear Hazard Clause

1. "Nuclear Hazard" means any nuclear reaction, radiation, or radioactive contamination, all whether controlled or uncontrolled or however caused, or any consequence of any of these.
2. Loss caused by the nuclear hazard will not be considered loss caused by fire, explosion or smoke, whether these perils are specifically named in or otherwise included within the Perils Insured Against.
3. This Policy does not apply under Section **I** to loss caused directly or indirectly by nuclear hazard, except that direct loss by fire resulting from the nuclear hazard is covered.

O. Recovered Property

If you or we recover any property for which we have made payment under this Policy, you or we will notify the other of the recovery. At your option, the property will be returned to or retained by you or it will become our property. If the recovered property is returned to or retained by you, the loss payment will be adjusted based on the amount you received for the recovered property.

P. Volcanic Eruption Period

One or more volcanic eruptions that occur within a 72-hour period will be considered as one volcanic eruption.

Q. Policy Period

This Policy applies only to loss which occurs during the policy period.

R. Concealment Or Fraud

We provide coverage to no "insureds" under this Policy if, whether before or after a loss, an "insured" has:

1. Intentionally concealed or misrepresented any material fact or circumstance;
2. Engaged in fraudulent conduct; or
3. Made false statements;

relating to this insurance.

S. Loss Payable Clause

If the Declarations shows a loss payee for certain listed insured personal property, the definition of "insured" is changed to include that loss payee with respect to that property.

If we decide to cancel or not renew this Policy, that loss payee will be notified in writing.

SECTION II – LIABILITY COVERAGES

A. Coverage E – Personal Liability

If a claim is made or a suit is brought against an "insured" for damages because of "bodily injury" or "property damage" caused by an "occurrence" to which this coverage applies, we will:

1. Pay up to our limit of liability for the damages for which an "insured" is legally liable. Damages include prejudgment interest awarded against an "insured"; and
2. Provide a defense at our expense by counsel of our choice, even if the suit is groundless, false or fraudulent. We may investigate and settle any claim or suit that we decide is appropriate. Our duty to settle or defend ends when our limit of liability for the "occurrence" has been exhausted by payment of a judgment or settlement.

B. Coverage F – Medical Payments To Others

We will pay the necessary medical expenses that are incurred or medically ascertained within three years from the date of an accident causing "bodily injury". Medical expenses means reasonable charges for medical, surgical, x-ray, dental, ambulance, hospital, professional nursing, prosthetic devices and funeral services. This coverage does not apply to you or regular residents of your household except "residence employees". As to others, this coverage applies only:

1. To a person on the "insured location" with the permission of an "insured"; or
2. To a person off the "insured location", if the "bodily injury":
   a. Arises out of a condition on the "insured location" or the ways immediately adjoining;
   b. Is caused by the activities of an "insured";
   c. Is caused by a "residence employee" in the course of the "residence employee's" employment by an "insured"; or
   d. Is caused by an animal owned by or in the care of an "insured".

SECTION II – EXCLUSIONS

A. Motor Vehicle Liability

1. Coverages **E** and **F** do not apply to any "motor vehicle liability" if, at the time and place of an "occurrence", the involved "motor vehicle":
   a. Is registered for use on public roads or property;
   b. Is not registered for use on public roads or property, but such registration is required by a law, or regulation issued by a government agency, for it to be used at the place of the "occurrence"; or
   c. Is being:
      (1) Operated in, or practicing for, any prearranged or organized race, speed contest or other competition;
      (2) Rented to others;
      (3) Used to carry persons or cargo for a charge; or
      (4) Used for any "business" purpose except for a motorized golf cart while on a golfing facility.
2. If Exclusion **A.1.** does not apply, there is still no coverage for "motor vehicle liability", unless the "motor vehicle" is:
   a. In dead storage on an "insured location";
   b. Used solely to service a residence;
   c. A riding lawn mower that, at the time of the "occurrence", is being used to mow a lawn;
   d. Designed to assist the handicapped and, at the time of an "occurrence", it is:
      (1) Being used to assist a handicapped person; or

(2) Parked on an "insured location";

e. Designed for recreational use off public roads and:

(1) Not owned by an "insured"; or

(2) Owned by an "insured" provided the "occurrence" takes place:

(a) On an "insured location" as defined in Definition **B.10.a., b., d., e.** or **h.**; or

(b) Off an "insured location" and the "motor vehicle" is:

(i) Designed as a toy vehicle for use by children under seven years of age;

(ii) Powered by one or more batteries; and

(iii) Not built or modified after manufacture to exceed a speed of five miles per hour on level ground;

f. A motorized golf cart that is owned by an "insured", designed to carry up to four persons, not built or modified after manufacture to exceed a speed of 25 miles per hour on level ground and, at the time of an "occurrence", is within the legal boundaries of:

(1) A golfing facility and is parked or stored there, or being used by an "insured" to:

(a) Play the game of golf or for other recreational or leisure activity allowed by the facility;

(b) Travel to or from an area where "motor vehicles" or golf carts are parked or stored; or

(c) Cross public roads at designated points to access other parts of the golfing facility; or

(2) A private residential community, including its public roads upon which a motorized golf cart can legally travel, which is subject to the authority of a property owners association and contains an "insured's" residence.

B. Watercraft Liability

1. Coverages **E** and **F** do not apply to any "watercraft liability" if, at the time of an "occurrence", the involved watercraft is being:

a. Operated in, or practicing for, any prearranged or organized race, speed contest or other competition. This exclusion does not apply to a sailing vessel or a predicted log cruise;

b. Rented to others;

c. Used to carry persons or cargo for a charge; or

d. Used for any "business" purpose.

2. If Exclusion **B.1.** does not apply, there is still no coverage for "watercraft liability" unless, at the time of the "occurrence", the watercraft:

a. Is stored;

b. Is a sailing vessel, with or without auxiliary power, that is:

(1) Less than 26 feet in overall length; or

(2) 26 feet or more in overall length and not owned by an "insured"; or

c. Is not a sailing vessel and is powered by one or more engines or motors, including those that power a water jet pump, totaling:

(1) 25 horsepower or less; or

(2) More than 25 horsepower; and

(a) Not owned by an "insured"; or

(b) Are outboard engines or motors owned by an "insured" who acquired such engines or motors:

(i) During the policy period; or

(ii) Before the policy period, but only if you declare them at policy inception or your intent to insure them is reported to us in writing within 45 days after you acquire them.

The coverages in **(b)** above apply for the policy period.

Horsepower means the maximum power rating assigned to the engine or motor by the manufacturer.

C. Aircraft Liability

This Policy does not cover "aircraft liability".

D. Hovercraft Liability

This Policy does not cover "hovercraft liability".

E. Coverage E – Personal Liability And Coverage F – Medical Payments To Others

Coverages **E** and **F** do not apply to the following:

1. Expected Or Intended Injury

"Bodily injury" or "property damage" which is expected or intended by an "insured", even if the resulting "bodily injury" or "property damage":

a. Is of a different kind, quality or degree than initially expected or intended; or

b. Is sustained by a different person, entity or property than initially expected or intended.

However, this Exclusion **E.1.** does not apply to "bodily injury" or "property damage" resulting from the use of reasonable force by an "insured" to protect persons or property;

2. Business

a. "Bodily injury" or "property damage" arising out of or in connection with a "business" conducted from an "insured location" or engaged in by an "insured", whether or not the "business" is owned or operated by an "insured" or employs an "insured".

This Exclusion **E.2.** applies but is not limited to an act or omission, regardless of its nature or circumstance, involving a service or duty rendered, promised, owed or implied to be provided because of the nature of the "business".

b. With respect to other than "home-sharing host activities", this Exclusion **E.2.** does not apply to:

(1) The rental or holding for rental of an "insured location";

(a) On an occasional basis if used only as a residence;

(b) In part for use only as a residence, unless a single-family unit is intended for use by the occupying family to lodge more than two roomers or boarders; or

(c) In part, as an office, school, studio or private garage; and

(2) An "insured" under the age of 21 years involved in a part-time or occasional, self-employed "business" with no employees;

3. Professional Services

"Bodily injury" or "property damage" arising out of the rendering of or failure to render professional services;

4. Insured's Premises Not An Insured Location

"Bodily injury" or "property damage" arising out of a premises:

a. Owned by an "insured";

b. Rented to an "insured"; or

c. Rented to others by an "insured";

that is not an "insured location";

5. War

"Bodily injury" or "property damage" caused directly or indirectly by war, including the following and any consequence of any of the following:

a. Undeclared war, civil war, insurrection, rebellion or revolution;

b. Warlike act by a military force or military personnel; or

c. Destruction, seizure or use for a military purpose.

Discharge of a nuclear weapon will be deemed a warlike act even if accidental;

6. Communicable Disease

"Bodily injury" or "property damage" which arises out of the transmission of a communicable disease by an "insured";

7. Sexual Molestation, Corporal Punishment Or Physical Or Mental Abuse

"Bodily injury" or "property damage" arising out of sexual molestation, corporal punishment or physical or mental abuse; or

8. Controlled Substance

"Bodily injury" or "property damage" arising out of the use, sale, manufacture, delivery, transfer or possession by any person of:

a. A Controlled Substance as defined by the Federal Food and Drug Law at 21 U.S.C.A. Sections 811 and 812; or

b. Any "cannabis" regardless of whether such "cannabis" is considered a Controlled Substance.

Controlled Substances include but are not limited to cocaine, LSD and all narcotic drugs.

However, this exclusion does not apply to the legitimate use of prescription drugs by a person following the lawful orders of a licensed health care professional.

Exclusions **A.** "Motor Vehicle Liability", **B.** "Watercraft Liability", **C.** "Aircraft Liability", **D.** "Hovercraft Liability" and **E.4.** "Insured's" Premises Not An "Insured Location" do not apply to "bodily injury" to a "residence employee" arising out of and in the course of the "residence employee's" employment by an "insured".

F. Coverage E – Personal Liability

Coverage **E** does not apply to:

1. Liability:

a. For any loss assessment charged against you as a member of an association, corporation or community of property owners, except as provided in **D.** Loss Assessment under Section **II** – Additional Coverages;

b. Under any contract or agreement entered into by an "insured". However, this exclusion does not apply to written contracts:

(1) That directly relate to the ownership, maintenance or use of an "insured location"; or

(2) Where the liability of others is assumed by you prior to an "occurrence";

unless excluded in **a.** above or elsewhere in this Policy;

2. "Property damage" to property owned by an "insured". This includes costs or expenses incurred by an "insured" or others to repair, replace, enhance, restore or maintain such property to prevent injury to a person or damage to property of others, whether on or away from an "insured location";

3. "Property damage" to property rented to, occupied or used by or in the care of an "insured". This exclusion does not apply to "property damage" caused by fire, smoke or explosion;

4. "Bodily injury" to any person eligible to receive any benefits voluntarily provided or required to be provided by an "insured" under any:

a. Workers' compensation law;

b. Non-occupational disability law; or

c. Occupational disease law;

5. "Bodily injury" or "property damage" for which an "insured" under this Policy:

a. Is also an insured under a nuclear energy liability policy issued by the:

(1) Nuclear Energy Liability Insurance Association;

(2) Mutual Atomic Energy Liability Underwriters;

(3) Nuclear Insurance Association of Canada;

or any of their successors; or

b. Would be an insured under such a policy but for the exhaustion of its limit of liability; or

6. "Bodily injury" to you or an "insured" as defined under Definition **9.a.** or **b.**

This exclusion also applies to any claim made or suit brought against you or an "insured" to:

a. Repay; or

b. Share damages with;

another person who may be obligated to pay damages because of "bodily injury" to an "insured".

G. Coverage F – Medical Payments To Others

Coverage **F** does not apply to "bodily injury":

1. To a "residence employee" if the "bodily injury":

a. Occurs off the "insured location"; and

b. Does not arise out of or in the course of the "residence employee's" employment by an "insured";

2. To any person eligible to receive benefits voluntarily provided or required to be provided under any:

a. Workers' compensation law;

b. Non-occupational disability law; or

c. Occupational disease law;

3. From any:

a. Nuclear reaction;

b. Nuclear radiation; or

c. Radioactive contamination;

all whether controlled or uncontrolled or however caused; or

d. Any consequence of any of these; or

4. To:

a. A "home-sharing occupant"; or

b. Any person, other than a "residence employee" of an "insured", regularly residing on any part of the "insured location".

SECTION II – ADDITIONAL COVERAGES

We cover the following in addition to the limits of liability:

A. Claim Expenses

We pay:

1. Expenses we incur and costs taxed against an "insured" in any suit we defend;

2. Premiums on bonds required in a suit we defend, but not for bond amounts more than the Coverage **E** limit of liability. We need not apply for or furnish any bond;

3. Reasonable expenses incurred by an "insured" at our request, including actual loss of earnings (but not loss of other income) up to $250 per day, for assisting us in the investigation or defense of a claim or suit; and

4. Interest on the entire judgment which accrues after entry of the judgment and before we pay or tender, or deposit in court that part of the judgment which does not exceed the limit of liability that applies.

B. First Aid Expenses

We will pay expenses for first aid to others incurred by an "insured" for "bodily injury" covered under this Policy. We will not pay for first aid to an "insured".

C. Damage To Property Of Others

1. We will pay, at replacement cost, up to $5,000 per "occurrence" for "property damage" to property of others caused by an "insured".

2. We will not pay for "property damage":

a. To the extent of any amount recoverable under Section **I;**

b. Caused intentionally by an "insured" who is 13 years of age or older;

c. To property owned by an "insured";

d. To property owned by or rented to a tenant of an "insured" or a resident in your household; or

e. Arising out of:

(1) A "business" engaged in by an "insured";

(2) Any act or omission in connection with a premises owned, rented or controlled by an "insured", other than the "insured location"; or

(3) The ownership, maintenance, occupancy, operation, use, loading or unloading of aircraft, hovercraft, watercraft or "motor vehicles".

This Exclusion **e.(3)** does not apply to a "motor vehicle" that:

(a) Is designed for recreational use off public roads;

(b) Is not owned by an "insured"; and

(c) At the time of the "occurrence", is not required by law, or regulation issued by a government agency, to have been registered for it to be used on public roads or property.

D. Loss Assessment

1. We will pay up to $2,000 for your share of loss assessment charged against you, as owner or tenant of the "residence premises", during the policy period by a corporation or association of property owners, when the assessment is made as a result of:

a. "Bodily injury" or "property damage" not excluded from coverage under Section **II** – Exclusions; or

b. Liability for an act of a director, officer or trustee in the capacity as a director, officer or trustee, provided such person:

(1) Is elected by the members of a corporation or association of property owners; and

(2) Serves without deriving any income from the exercise of duties which are solely on behalf of a corporation or association of property owners.

2. Paragraph **I. Policy Period** under **Section II – Conditions** does not apply to this **Loss Assessment Coverage.**

3. Regardless of the number of assessments, the limit of $2,000 is the most we will pay for loss arising out of:

a. One accident, including continuous or repeated exposure to substantially the same general harmful condition; or

b. A covered act of a director, officer or trustee. An act involving more than one director, officer or trustee is considered to be a single act.

4. We do not cover assessments charged against you or a corporation or association of property owners by any governmental body.

SECTION II – CONDITIONS

A. Limit Of Liability

Our total liability under Coverage **E** for all damages resulting from any one "occurrence" will not be more than the Coverage **E** Limit Of Liability shown in the Declarations. This limit is the same regardless of the number of "insureds", claims made or persons injured. All "bodily injury" and "property damage" resulting from any one accident or from continuous or repeated exposure to substantially the same general harmful conditions shall be considered to be the result of one "occurrence".

Our total liability under Coverage **F** for all medical expense payable for "bodily injury" to one person as the result of one accident will not be more than the Coverage **F** Limit Of Liability shown in the Declarations.

B. Severability Of Insurance

This insurance applies separately to each "insured". This condition will not increase our limit of liability for any one "occurrence".

C. Duties After Occurrence

In case of an "occurrence", you or another "insured" will perform the following duties that apply. We have no duty to provide coverage under this Policy if your failure to comply with the following duties is prejudicial to us. You will help us by seeing that these duties are performed:

1. Give written notice to us or our agent as soon as is practical, which sets forth:

a. The identity of the Policy and the "named insured" shown in the Declarations;

b. Reasonably available information on the time, place and circumstances of the "occurrence"; and

c. Names and addresses of any claimants and witnesses;

2. Cooperate with us in the investigation, settlement or defense of any claim or suit;

3. Promptly forward to us every notice, demand, summons or other process relating to the "occurrence";

4. At our request, help us:

a. To make settlement;

b. To enforce any right of contribution or indemnity against any person or organization who may be liable to an "insured";

c. With the conduct of suits and attend hearings and trials; and

d. To secure and give evidence and obtain the attendance of witnesses;

5. With respect to **C.** Damage To Property Of Others under Section **II** – Additional Coverages, submit to us within 60 days after the loss a sworn statement of loss and show the damaged property, if in an "insured's" control;

6. No "insured" shall, except at such "insured's" own cost, voluntarily make payment, assume obligation or incur expense other than for first aid to others at the time of the "bodily injury".

D. Duties Of An Injured Person – Coverage F – Medical Payments To Others

1. The injured person or someone acting for the injured person will:

a. Give us written proof of claim, under oath if required, as soon as is practical; and

b. Authorize us to obtain copies of medical reports and records.

2. The injured person will submit to a physical exam by a doctor of our choice when and as often as we reasonably require.

E. Payment Of Claim – Coverage F – Medical Payments To Others

Payment under this coverage is not an admission of liability by an "insured" or us.

F. Suit Against Us

1. No action can be brought against us unless there has been full compliance with all of the terms under this Section **II.**

2. No one will have the right to join us as a party to any action against an "insured".

3. Also, no action with respect to Coverage **E** can be brought against us until the obligation of such "insured" has been determined by final judgment or agreement signed by us.

G. Bankruptcy Of An Insured

Bankruptcy or insolvency of an "insured" will not relieve us of our obligations under this Policy.

H. Other Insurance

This insurance is excess over other valid and collectible insurance except insurance written specifically to cover as excess over the limits of liability that apply in this Policy.

I. Policy Period

This Policy applies only to "bodily injury" or "property damage" which occurs during the policy period.

J. Concealment Or Fraud

We do not provide coverage to an "insured" who, whether before or after a loss, has:

1. Intentionally concealed or misrepresented any material fact or circumstance;

2. Engaged in fraudulent conduct; or

3. Made false statements;

relating to this insurance.

SECTIONS I AND II – CONDITIONS

A. Liberalization Clause

If we make a change which broadens coverage under this edition of our policy without additional premium charge, that change will automatically apply to your insurance as of the date we implement the change in your state, provided that this implementation date falls within 60 days prior to or during the policy period stated in the Declarations.

This Liberalization Clause does not apply to changes implemented with a general program revision that includes both broadenings and restrictions in coverage, whether that general program revision is implemented through introduction of:

1. A subsequent edition of this Policy; or

2. An amendatory endorsement.

B. Waiver Or Change Of Policy Provisions

A waiver or change of a provision of this Policy must be in writing by us to be valid. Our request for an appraisal or examination will not waive any of our rights.

C. Cancellation

1. You may cancel this Policy at any time by returning it to us or by letting us know in writing of the date cancellation is to take effect.

2. We may cancel this Policy only for the reasons stated below by letting you know in writing of the date cancellation takes effect. This cancellation notice may be delivered to you, or mailed to you at your mailing address shown in the Declarations. Proof of mailing will be sufficient proof of notice.

a. When you have not paid the premium, we may cancel at any time by letting you know at least 10 days before the date cancellation takes effect.

b. When this Policy has been in effect for less than 60 days and is not a renewal with us, we may cancel for any reason by letting you know at least 10 days before the date cancellation takes effect.

c. When this Policy has been in effect for 60 days or more, or at any time if it is a renewal with us, we may cancel:

(1) If there has been a material misrepresentation of fact which if known to us would have caused us not to issue the Policy; or

(2) If the risk has changed substantially since the Policy was issued.

This can be done by letting you know at least 30 days before the date cancellation takes effect.

d. When this Policy is written for a period of more than one year, we may cancel for any reason at anniversary by letting you know at least 30 days before the date cancellation takes effect.

3. When this Policy is canceled, the premium for the period from the date of cancellation to the expiration date will be refunded pro rata.

4. If the return premium is not refunded with the notice of cancellation or when this Policy is returned to us, we will refund it within a reasonable time after the date cancellation takes effect.

D. Nonrenewal

We may elect not to renew this Policy. We may do so by delivering to you, or mailing to you at your mailing address shown in the Declarations, written notice at least 30 days before the expiration date of this Policy. Proof of mailing will be sufficient proof of notice.

E. Assignment

Assignment of this Policy will not be valid unless we give our written consent.

F. Subrogation

An "insured" may waive in writing before a loss all rights of recovery against any person or organization. If not waived, we may require an assignment of rights of recovery for a loss to the extent that payment is made by us.

If an assignment is sought, an "insured" must sign and deliver all related papers and cooperate with us.

Subrogation does not apply to Coverage **F** or Paragraph **C. Damage To Property Of Others** under **Section II – Additional Coverages.**

G. Death

If any person named in the Declarations or the spouse, if a resident of the same household, dies, the following apply:

1. We insure the legal representative of the deceased but only with respect to the premises and property of the deceased covered under the Policy at the time of death; and

2. "Insured" includes:

a. An "insured" who is a member of your household at the time of your death, but only while a resident of the "residence premises"; and

b. With respect to your property, the person having proper temporary custody of the property until appointment and qualification of a legal representative.

COMMERCIAL PROPERTY
CP 10 10 10 12

CAUSES OF LOSS – BASIC FORM

Words and phrases that appear in quotation marks have special meaning. Refer to Section **E.** Definitions.

A. Covered Causes Of Loss

When Basic is shown in the Declarations, Covered Causes of Loss means the following:

1. Fire.

2. Lightning.

3. Explosion, including the explosion of gases or fuel within the furnace of any fired vessel or within the flues or passages through which the gases of combustion pass. This cause of loss does not include loss or damage by:

a. Rupture, bursting or operation of pressure-relief devices; or

b. Rupture or bursting due to expansion or swelling of the contents of any building or structure, caused by or resulting from water.

4. Windstorm or Hail, but not including:

a. Frost or cold weather;

b. Ice (other than hail), snow or sleet, whether driven by wind or not;

c. Loss or damage to the interior of any building or structure, or the property inside the building or structure, caused by rain, snow, sand or dust, whether driven by wind or not, unless the building or structure first sustains wind or hail damage to its roof or walls through which the rain, snow, sand or dust enters; or

d. Loss or damage by hail to lawns, trees, shrubs or plants which are part of a vegetated roof.

5. Smoke causing sudden and accidental loss or damage. This cause of loss does not include smoke from agricultural smudging or industrial operations.

6. Aircraft or Vehicles, meaning only physical contact of an aircraft, a spacecraft, a self-propelled missile, a vehicle or an object thrown up by a vehicle with the described property or with the building or structure containing the described property. This cause of loss includes loss or damage by objects falling from aircraft.

We will not pay for loss or damage caused by or resulting from vehicles you own or which are operated in the course of your business.

7. Riot or Civil Commotion, including:

a. Acts of striking employees while occupying the described premises; and

b. Looting occurring at the time and place of a riot or civil commotion.

8. Vandalism, meaning willful and malicious damage to, or destruction of, the described property.

We will not pay for loss or damage caused by or resulting from theft, except for building damage caused by the breaking in or exiting of burglars.

9. Sprinkler Leakage, meaning leakage or discharge of any substance from an Automatic Sprinkler System, including collapse of a tank that is part of the system.

If the building or structure containing the Automatic Sprinkler System is Covered Property, we will also pay the cost to:

a. Repair or replace damaged parts of the Automatic Sprinkler System if the damage:

(1) Results in sprinkler leakage; or

(2) Is directly caused by freezing.

b. Tear out and replace any part of the building or structure to repair damage to the Automatic Sprinkler System that has resulted in sprinkler leakage.

Automatic Sprinkler System means:

(1) Any automatic fire-protective or extinguishing system, including connected:

(a) Sprinklers and discharge nozzles;

(b) Ducts, pipes, valves and fittings;

(c) Tanks, their component parts and supports; and

(d) Pumps and private fire protection mains.

(2) When supplied from an automatic fire-protective system:

(a) Non-automatic fire-protective systems; and

(b) Hydrants, standpipes and outlets.

10. Sinkhole Collapse, meaning loss or damage caused by the sudden sinking or collapse of land into underground empty spaces created by the action of water on limestone or dolomite. This cause of loss does not include:

a. The cost of filling sinkholes; or

b. Sinking or collapse of land into man-made underground cavities.

11. Volcanic Action, meaning direct loss or damage resulting from the eruption of a volcano when the loss or damage is caused by:

a. Airborne volcanic blast or airborne shock waves;

b. Ash, dust or particulate matter; or

c. Lava flow.

With respect to coverage for Volcanic Action as set forth in **11.a.**, **11.b.** and **11.c.**, all volcanic eruptions that occur within any 168-hour period will constitute a single occurrence.

This cause of loss does not include the cost to remove ash, dust or particulate matter that does not cause direct physical loss or damage to the described property.

B. Exclusions

1. We will not pay for loss or damage caused directly or indirectly by any of the following. Such loss or damage is excluded regardless of any other cause or event that contributes concurrently or in any sequence to the loss.

a. Ordinance Or Law

The enforcement of or compliance with any ordinance or law:

(1) Regulating the construction, use or repair of any property; or

(2) Requiring the tearing down of any property, including the cost of removing its debris.

This exclusion, Ordinance Or Law, applies whether the loss results from:

(a) An ordinance or law that is enforced even if the property has not been damaged; or

(b) The increased costs incurred to comply with an ordinance or law in the course of construction, repair, renovation, remodeling or demolition of property, or removal of its debris, following a physical loss to that property.

b. Earth Movement

(1) Earthquake, including tremors and aftershocks and any earth sinking, rising or shifting related to such event;

(2) Landslide, including any earth sinking, rising or shifting related to such event;

(3) Mine subsidence, meaning subsidence of a man-made mine, whether or not mining activity has ceased;

(4) Earth sinking (other than sinkhole collapse), rising or shifting including soil conditions which cause settling, cracking or other disarrangement of foundations or other parts of realty. Soil conditions include contraction, expansion, freezing, thawing, erosion, improperly compacted soil and the action of water under the ground surface.

But if Earth Movement, as described in **b.(1)** through **(4)** above, results in fire or explosion, we will pay for the loss or damage caused by that fire or explosion.

(5) Volcanic eruption, explosion or effusion. But if volcanic eruption, explosion or effusion results in fire or Volcanic Action, we will pay for the loss or damage caused by that fire or Volcanic Action.

This exclusion applies regardless of whether any of the above, in Paragraphs **(1)** through **(5)**, is caused by an act of nature or is otherwise caused.

c. Governmental Action

Seizure or destruction of property by order of governmental authority.

But we will pay for loss or damage caused by or resulting from acts of destruction ordered by governmental authority and taken at the time of a fire to prevent its spread, if the fire would be covered under this Coverage Part.

d. Nuclear Hazard

Nuclear reaction or radiation, or radioactive contamination, however caused.

But if nuclear reaction or radiation, or radioactive contamination, results in fire, we will pay for the loss or damage caused by that fire.

e. Utility Services

The failure of power, communication, water or other utility service supplied to the described premises, however caused, if the failure:

(1) Originates away from the described premises; or

(2) Originates at the described premises, but only if such failure involves equipment used to supply the utility service to the described premises from a source away from the described premises.

Failure of any utility service includes lack of sufficient capacity and reduction in supply.

Loss or damage caused by a surge of power is also excluded, if the surge would not have occurred but for an event causing a failure of power.

But if the failure or surge of power, or the failure of communication, water or other utility service, results in a Covered Cause of Loss, we will pay for the loss or damage caused by that Covered Cause of Loss.

Communication services include but are not limited to service relating to Internet access or access to any electronic, cellular or satellite network.

f. War And Military Action

(1) War, including undeclared or civil war;

(2) Warlike action by a military force, including action in hindering or defending against an actual or expected attack, by any government, sovereign or other authority using military personnel or other agents; or

(3) Insurrection, rebellion, revolution, usurped power, or action taken by governmental authority in hindering or defending against any of these.

g. Water

(1) Flood, surface water, waves (including tidal wave and tsunami), tides, tidal water, overflow of any body of water, or spray from any of these, all whether or not driven by wind (including storm surge);

(2) Mudslide or mudflow;

(3) Water that backs up or overflows or is otherwise discharged from a sewer, drain, sump, sump pump or related equipment;

(4) Water under the ground surface pressing on, or flowing or seeping through:

(a) Foundations, walls, floors or paved surfaces;

(b) Basements, whether paved or not; or

(c) Doors, windows or other openings; or

(5) Waterborne material carried or otherwise moved by any of the water referred to in Paragraph **(1)**, **(3)** or **(4)**, or material carried or otherwise moved by mudslide or mudflow.

This exclusion applies regardless of whether any of the above, in Paragraphs **(1)** through **(5)**, is caused by an act of nature or is otherwise caused. An example of a situation to which this exclusion applies is the situation where a dam, levee, seawall or other boundary or containment system fails in whole or in part, for any reason, to contain the water.

But if any of the above, in Paragraphs **(1)** through **(5)**, results in fire, explosion or sprinkler leakage, we will pay for the loss or damage caused by that fire, explosion or sprinkler leakage (if sprinkler leakage is a Covered Cause of Loss).

h. "Fungus", Wet Rot, Dry Rot And Bacteria

Presence, growth, proliferation, spread or any activity of "fungus", wet or dry rot or bacteria.

But if "fungus", wet or dry rot or bacteria result in a Covered Cause of Loss, we will pay for the loss or damage caused by that Covered Cause of Loss.

This exclusion does not apply:

(1) When "fungus", wet or dry rot or bacteria result from fire or lightning; or

(2) To the extent that coverage is provided in the Additional Coverage, Limited Coverage For "Fungus", Wet Rot, Dry Rot And Bacteria, with respect to loss or damage by a cause of loss other than fire or lightning.

Exclusions **B.1.a.** through **B.1.h.** apply whether or not the loss event results in widespread damage or affects a substantial area.

2. We will not pay for loss or damage caused by or resulting from:

a. Artificially generated electrical, magnetic or electromagnetic energy that damages, disturbs, disrupts or otherwise interferes with any:

(1) Electrical or electronic wire, device, appliance, system or network; or

(2) Device, appliance, system or network utilizing cellular or satellite technology.

For the purpose of this exclusion, electrical, magnetic or electromagnetic energy includes but is not limited to:

(a) Electrical current, including arcing;

(b) Electrical charge produced or conducted by a magnetic or electromagnetic field;

(c) Pulse of electromagnetic energy; or

(d) Electromagnetic waves or microwaves.

But if fire results, we will pay for the loss or damage caused by that fire.

b. Rupture or bursting of water pipes (other than Automatic Sprinkler Systems) unless caused by a Covered Cause of Loss.

c. Leakage or discharge of water or steam from any part of a system or appliance containing water or steam (other than an Automatic Sprinkler System), unless the leakage or discharge occurs because the system or appliance was damaged by a Covered Cause of Loss. But we will not pay for loss or damage caused by or resulting from continuous or repeated seepage or leakage of water, or the presence or condensation of humidity, moisture or vapor, that occurs over a period of 14 days or more.

d. Explosion of steam boilers, steam pipes, steam engines or steam turbines owned or leased by you, or operated under your control.

But if explosion of steam boilers, steam pipes, steam engines or steam turbines results in fire or combustion explosion, we will pay for the loss or damage caused by that fire or combustion explosion.

e. Mechanical breakdown, including rupture or bursting caused by centrifugal force.

But if mechanical breakdown results in a Covered Cause of Loss, we will pay for the loss or damage caused by that Covered Cause of Loss.

f. Neglect of an insured to use all reasonable means to save and preserve property from further damage at and after the time of loss.

3. Special Exclusions

The following provisions apply only to the specified Coverage Forms:

a. Business Income (And Extra Expense) Coverage Form, Business Income (Without Extra Expense) Coverage Form, Or Extra Expense Coverage Form

We will not pay for:

(1) Any loss caused by or resulting from:

(a) Damage or destruction of "finished stock"; or

(b) The time required to reproduce "finished stock".

This exclusion does not apply to Extra Expense.

(2) Any loss caused by or resulting from direct physical loss or damage to radio or television antennas (including satellite dishes) and their lead-in wiring, masts or towers.

(3) Any increase of loss caused by or resulting from:

(a) Delay in rebuilding, repairing or replacing the property or resuming "operations", due to interference at the location of the rebuilding, repair or replacement by strikers or other persons; or

(b) Suspension, lapse or cancellation of any license, lease or contract. But if the suspension, lapse or cancellation is directly caused by the "suspension" of "operations", we will cover such loss that affects your Business Income during the "period of restoration" and any extension of the "period of restoration" in accordance with the terms of the Extended Business Income Additional Coverage and the Extended Period Of Indemnity Optional Coverage or any variation of these.

(4) Any Extra Expense caused by or resulting from suspension, lapse or cancellation of any license, lease or contract beyond the "period of restoration".

(5) Any other consequential loss.

b. Leasehold Interest Coverage Form

(1) Paragraph **B.1.a.**, Ordinance Or Law, does not apply to insurance under this Coverage Form.

(2) We will not pay for any loss caused by:

(a) Your cancelling the lease;

(b) The suspension, lapse or cancellation of any license; or

(c) Any other consequential loss.

c. Legal Liability Coverage Form

(1) The following exclusions do not apply to insurance under this Coverage Form:

(a) Paragraph **B.1.a.** Ordinance Or Law;

(b) Paragraph **B.1.c.** Governmental Action;

(c) Paragraph **B.1.d.** Nuclear Hazard;

(d) Paragraph **B.1.e.** Utility Services; and

(e) Paragraph **B.1.f.** War And Military Action.

(2) The following additional exclusions apply to insurance under this Coverage Form:

(a) Contractual Liability

We will not defend any claim or "suit", or pay damages that you are legally liable to pay, solely by reason of your assumption of liability in a contract or agreement. But this exclusion does not apply to a written lease agreement in which you have assumed liability for building damage resulting from an actual or attempted burglary or robbery, provided that:

(i) Your assumption of liability was executed prior to the accident; and

(ii) The building is Covered Property under this Coverage Form.

(b) Nuclear Hazard

We will not defend any claim or "suit", or pay any damages, loss, expense or obligation, resulting from nuclear reaction or radiation, or radioactive contamination, however caused.

C. Additional Coverage – Limited Coverage For "Fungus", Wet Rot, Dry Rot And Bacteria

1. The coverage described in **C.2.** and **C.6.** only applies when the "fungus", wet or dry rot or bacteria are the result of one or more of the following causes that occur during the policy period and only if all reasonable means were used to save and preserve the property from further damage at the time of and after that occurrence:

a. A Covered Cause of Loss other than fire or lightning; or

b. Flood, if the Flood Coverage Endorsement applies to the affected premises.

This Additional Coverage does not apply to lawns, trees, shrubs or plants which are part of a vegetated roof.

2. We will pay for loss or damage by "fungus", wet or dry rot or bacteria. As used in this Limited Coverage, the term loss or damage means:

a. Direct physical loss or damage to Covered Property caused by "fungus", wet or dry rot or bacteria, including the cost of removal of the "fungus", wet or dry rot or bacteria;

b. The cost to tear out and replace any part of the building or other property as needed to gain access to the "fungus", wet or dry rot or bacteria; and

c. The cost of testing performed after removal, repair, replacement or restoration of the damaged property is completed, provided there is a reason to believe that "fungus", wet or dry rot or bacteria are present.

3. The coverage described under **C.2.** of this Limited Coverage is limited to $15,000. Regardless of the number of claims, this limit is the most we will pay for the total of all loss or damage arising out of all occurrences of Covered Causes of Loss (other than fire or lightning) and Flood which take place in a 12-month period (starting with the beginning of the present annual policy period). With respect to a particular occurrence of loss which results in "fungus", wet or dry rot or bacteria, we will not pay more than a total of $15,000 even if the "fungus", wet or dry rot or bacteria continue to be present or active, or recur, in a later policy period.

4. The coverage provided under this Limited Coverage does not increase the applicable Limit of Insurance on any Covered Property. If a particular occurrence results in loss or damage by "fungus", wet or dry rot or bacteria, and other loss or damage, we will not pay more, for the total of all loss or damage, than the applicable Limit of Insurance on the affected Covered Property.

If there is covered loss or damage to Covered Property, not caused by "fungus", wet or dry rot or bacteria, loss payment will not be limited by the terms of this Limited Coverage, except to the extent that "fungus", wet or dry rot or bacteria cause an increase in the loss. Any such increase in the loss will be subject to the terms of this Limited Coverage.

5. The terms of this Limited Coverage do not increase or reduce the coverage provided under Paragraph **b.** of Covered Causes Of Loss **9.** Sprinkler Leakage.

6. The following, **6.a.** or **6.b.**, applies only if Business Income and/or Extra Expense Coverage applies to the described premises and only if the "suspension" of "operations" satisfies all terms and conditions of the applicable Business Income and/or Extra Expense Coverage Form:

a. If the loss which resulted in "fungus", wet or dry rot or bacteria does not in itself necessitate a "suspension" of "operations", but such "suspension" is necessary due to loss or damage to property caused by "fungus", wet or dry rot or bacteria, then our payment under Business Income and/or Extra Expense is limited to the amount of loss and/or expense sustained in a period of not more than 30 days. The days need not be consecutive.

b. If a covered "suspension" of "operations" was caused by loss or damage other than "fungus", wet or dry rot or bacteria but remediation of "fungus", wet or dry rot or bacteria prolongs the "period of restoration", we will pay for loss and/or expense sustained during the delay (regardless of when such a delay occurs during the "period of restoration"), but such coverage is limited to 30 days. The days need not be consecutive.

D. Limitation

We will pay for loss of animals only if they are killed or their destruction is made necessary.

E. Definitions

"Fungus" means any type or form of fungus, including mold or mildew, and any mycotoxins, spores, scents or by-products produced or released by fungi.

COMMERCIAL PROPERTY
CP 10 20 10 12

CAUSES OF LOSS – BROAD FORM

Words and phrases that appear in quotation marks have special meaning. Refer to Section **F.** Definitions.

A. Covered Causes Of Loss

When Broad is shown in the Declarations, Covered Causes of Loss means the following:

1. Fire.
2. Lightning.
3. Explosion, including the explosion of gases or fuel within the furnace of any fired vessel or within the flues or passages through which the gases of combustion pass. This cause of loss does not include loss or damage by:
   a. Rupture, bursting or operation of pressure-relief devices; or
   b. Rupture or bursting due to expansion or swelling of the contents of any building or structure, caused by or resulting from water.
4. Windstorm or Hail, but not including:
   a. Frost or cold weather;
   b. Ice (other than hail), snow or sleet, whether driven by wind or not;
   c. Loss or damage to the interior of any building or structure, or the property inside the building or structure, caused by rain, snow, sand or dust, whether driven by wind or not, unless the building or structure first sustains wind or hail damage to its roof or walls through which the rain, snow, sand or dust enters; or
   d. Loss or damage by hail to lawns, trees, shrubs or plants which are part of a vegetated roof.
5. Smoke causing sudden and accidental loss or damage. This cause of loss does not include smoke from agricultural smudging or industrial operations.
6. Aircraft or Vehicles, meaning only physical contact of an aircraft, a spacecraft, a self-propelled missile, a vehicle or an object thrown up by a vehicle with the described property or with the building or structure containing the described property. This cause of loss includes loss or damage by objects falling from aircraft.

   We will not pay for loss or damage caused by or resulting from vehicles you own or which are operated in the course of your business.
7. Riot or Civil Commotion, including:
   a. Acts of striking employees while occupying the described premises; and
   b. Looting occurring at the time and place of a riot or civil commotion.
8. Vandalism, meaning willful and malicious damage to, or destruction of, the described property.

   We will not pay for loss or damage caused by or resulting from theft, except for building damage caused by the breaking in or exiting of burglars.
9. Sprinkler Leakage, meaning leakage or discharge of any substance from an Automatic Sprinkler System, including collapse of a tank that is part of the system.

   If the building or structure containing the Automatic Sprinkler System is Covered Property, we will also pay the cost to:
   a. Repair or replace damaged parts of the Automatic Sprinkler System if the damage:
      (1) Results in sprinkler leakage; or
      (2) Is directly caused by freezing.
   b. Tear out and replace any part of the building or structure to repair damage to the Automatic Sprinkler System that has resulted in sprinkler leakage.

   Automatic Sprinkler System means:
      (1) Any automatic fire-protective or extinguishing system, including connected:
         (a) Sprinklers and discharge nozzles;
         (b) Ducts, pipes, valves and fittings;
         (c) Tanks, their component parts and supports; and
         (d) Pumps and private fire protection mains.
      (2) When supplied from an automatic fire-protective system:
         (a) Non-automatic fire-protective systems; and
         (b) Hydrants, standpipes and outlets.

10. Sinkhole Collapse, meaning loss or damage caused by the sudden sinking or collapse of land into underground empty spaces created by the action of water on limestone or dolomite. This cause of loss does not include:

a. The cost of filling sinkholes; or

b. Sinking or collapse of land into man-made underground cavities.

11. Volcanic Action, meaning direct loss or damage resulting from the eruption of a volcano when the loss or damage is caused by:

a. Airborne volcanic blast or airborne shock waves;

b. Ash, dust or particulate matter; or

c. Lava flow.

With respect to coverage for Volcanic Action as set forth in **11.a., 11.b.** and **11.c.,** all volcanic eruptions that occur within any 168-hour period will constitute a single occurrence.

This cause of loss does not include the cost to remove ash, dust or particulate matter that does not cause direct physical loss or damage to the described property.

12. Falling Objects

But we will not pay for loss or damage to:

a. Personal property in the open; or

b. The interior of a building or structure, or property inside a building or structure, unless the roof or an outside wall of the building or structure is first damaged by a falling object.

13. Weight Of Snow, Ice Or Sleet

But we will not pay for loss or damage to personal property outside of buildings or structures, or for loss or damage to lawns, trees, shrubs or plants which are part of a vegetated roof.

14. Water Damage

a. Water Damage, meaning accidental discharge or leakage of water or steam as the direct result of the breaking apart or cracking of a plumbing, heating, air conditioning or other system or appliance, that is located on the described premises and contains water or steam.

However, Water Damage does not include:

(1) Discharge or leakage from:

(a) An Automatic Sprinkler System;

(b) A sump or related equipment and parts, including overflow due to sump pump failure or excessive volume of water; or

(c) Roof drains, gutters, downspouts or similar fixtures or equipment;

(2) The cost to repair any defect that caused the loss or damage;

(3) Loss or damage caused by or resulting from continuous or repeated seepage or leakage of water, or the presence or condensation of humidity, moisture or vapor, that occurs over a period of 14 days or more; or

(4) Loss or damage caused by or resulting from freezing, unless:

(a) You do your best to maintain heat in the building or structure; or

(b) You drain the equipment and shut off the water supply if the heat is not maintained.

b. If coverage applies subject to **a.** above, and the building or structure containing the system or appliance is Covered Property, we will also pay the cost to tear out and replace any part of the building or structure to repair damage to the system or appliance from which the water or steam escapes. But we will not pay the cost to repair any defect that caused the loss or damage.

B. Exclusions

1. We will not pay for loss or damage caused directly or indirectly by any of the following. Such loss or damage is excluded regardless of any other cause or event that contributes concurrently or in any sequence to the loss.

a. Ordinance Or Law

The enforcement of or compliance with any ordinance or law:

(1) Regulating the construction, use or repair of any property; or

(2) Requiring the tearing down of any property including the cost of removing its debris.

This exclusion, Ordinance Or Law, applies whether the loss results from:

(a) An ordinance or law that is enforced even if the property has not been damaged; or

(b) The increased costs incurred to comply with an ordinance or law in the course of construction, repair, renovation, remodeling or demolition of property, or removal of its debris, following a physical loss to that property.

b. Earth Movement

(1) Earthquake, including tremors and aftershocks and any earth sinking, rising or shifting related to such event;

(2) Landslide, including any earth sinking, rising or shifting related to such event;

(3) Mine subsidence, meaning subsidence of a man-made mine, whether or not mining activity has ceased;

(4) Earth sinking (other than sinkhole collapse), rising or shifting including soil conditions which cause settling, cracking or other disarrangement of foundations or other parts of realty. Soil conditions include contraction, expansion, freezing, thawing, erosion, improperly compacted soil and the action of water under the ground surface.

But if Earth Movement, as described in **b.(1)** through **(4)** above, results in fire or explosion, we will pay for the loss or damage caused by that fire or explosion.

(5) Volcanic eruption, explosion or effusion. But if volcanic eruption, explosion or effusion results in fire, building glass breakage or Volcanic Action, we will pay for the loss or damage caused by that fire, building glass breakage or Volcanic Action.

This exclusion applies regardless of whether any of the above, in Paragraphs **(1)** through **(5),** is caused by an act of nature or is otherwise caused.

c. Governmental Action

Seizure or destruction of property by order of governmental authority.

But we will pay for loss or damage caused by or resulting from acts of destruction ordered by governmental authority and taken at the time of a fire to prevent its spread, if the fire would be covered under this Coverage Part.

d. Nuclear Hazard

Nuclear reaction or radiation, or radioactive contamination, however caused.

But if nuclear reaction or radiation, or radioactive contamination, results in fire, we will pay for the loss or damage caused by that fire.

e. Utility Services

The failure of power, communication, water or other utility service supplied to the described premises, however caused, if the failure:

(1) Originates away from the described premises; or

(2) Originates at the described premises, but only if such failure involves equipment used to supply the utility service to the described premises from a source away from the described premises.

Failure of any utility service includes lack of sufficient capacity and reduction in supply.

Loss or damage caused by a surge of power is also excluded, if the surge would not have occurred but for an event causing a failure of power.

But if the failure or surge of power, or the failure of communication, water or other utility service, results in a Covered Cause of Loss, we will pay for the loss or damage caused by that Covered Cause of Loss.

Communication services include but are not limited to service relating to Internet access or access to any electronic, cellular or satellite network.

f. War And Military Action

(1) War, including undeclared or civil war;

(2) Warlike action by a military force, including action in hindering or defending against an actual or expected attack, by any government, sovereign or other authority using military personnel or other agents; or

(3) Insurrection, rebellion, revolution, usurped power, or action taken by governmental authority in hindering or defending against any of these.

g. Water

(1) Flood, surface water, waves (including tidal wave and tsunami), tides, tidal water, overflow of any body of water, or spray from any of these, all whether or not driven by wind (including storm surge);

(2) Mudslide or mudflow;

(3) Water that backs up or overflows or is otherwise discharged from a sewer, drain, sump, sump pump or related equipment;

(4) Water under the ground surface pressing on, or flowing or seeping through:

(a) Foundations, walls, floors or paved surfaces;

(b) Basements, whether paved or not; or

(c) Doors, windows or other openings; or

(5) Waterborne material carried or otherwise moved by any of the water referred to in Paragraph **(1)**, **(3)** or **(4)**, or material carried or otherwise moved by mudslide or mudflow.

This exclusion applies regardless of whether any of the above, in Paragraphs **(1)** through **(5)**, is caused by an act of nature or is otherwise caused. An example of a situation to which this exclusion applies is the situation where a dam, levee, seawall or other boundary or containment system fails in whole or in part, for any reason, to contain the water.

But if any of the above, in Paragraphs **(1)** through **(5)**, results in fire, explosion or sprinkler leakage, we will pay for the loss or damage caused by that fire, explosion or sprinkler leakage (if sprinkler leakage is a Covered Cause of Loss).

h. "Fungus", Wet Rot, Dry Rot And Bacteria

Presence, growth, proliferation, spread or any activity of "fungus", wet or dry rot or bacteria.

But if "fungus", wet or dry rot or bacteria result in a Covered Cause of Loss, we will pay for the loss or damage caused by that Covered Cause of Loss.

This exclusion does not apply:

(1) When "fungus", wet or dry rot or bacteria result from fire or lightning; or

(2) To the extent that coverage is provided in the Additional Coverage, Limited Coverage For "Fungus", Wet Rot, Dry Rot And Bacteria, with respect to loss or damage by a cause of loss other than fire or lightning.

Exclusions **B.1.a.** through **B.1.h.** apply whether or not the loss event results in widespread damage or affects a substantial area.

2. We will not pay for loss or damage caused by or resulting from:

a. Artificially generated electrical, magnetic or electromagnetic energy that damages, disturbs, disrupts or otherwise interferes with any:

(1) Electrical or electronic wire, device, appliance, system or network; or

(2) Device, appliance, system or network utilizing cellular or satellite technology.

For the purpose of this exclusion, electrical, magnetic or electromagnetic energy includes but is not limited to:

(a) Electrical current, including arcing;

(b) Electrical charge produced or conducted by a magnetic or electromagnetic field;

(c) Pulse of electromagnetic energy; or

(d) Electromagnetic waves or microwaves.

But if fire results, we will pay for the loss or damage caused by that fire.

b. Explosion of steam boilers, steam pipes, steam engines or steam turbines owned or leased by you, or operated under your control.

But if explosion of steam boilers, steam pipes, steam engines or steam turbines results in fire or combustion explosion, we will pay for the loss or damage caused by that fire or combustion explosion.

c. Mechanical breakdown, including rupture or bursting caused by centrifugal force.

But if mechanical breakdown results in a Covered Cause of Loss, we will pay for the loss or damage caused by that Covered Cause of Loss.

d. Neglect of an insured to use all reasonable means to save and preserve property from further damage at and after the time of loss.

3. Special Exclusions

The following provisions apply only to the specified Coverage Forms:

a. Business Income (And Extra Expense) Coverage Form, Business Income (Without Extra Expense) Coverage Form, Or Extra Expense Coverage Form

We will not pay for:

(1) Any loss caused by or resulting from:

(a) Damage or destruction of "finished stock"; or

(b) The time required to reproduce "finished stock".

This exclusion does not apply to Extra Expense.

(2) Any loss caused by or resulting from direct physical loss or damage to radio or television antennas (including satellite dishes) and their lead-in wiring, masts or towers.

(3) Any increase of loss caused by or resulting from:

(a) Delay in rebuilding, repairing or replacing the property or resuming "operations", due to interference at the location of the rebuilding, repair or replacement by strikers or other persons; or

(b) Suspension, lapse or cancellation of any license, lease or contract. But if the suspension, lapse or cancellation is directly caused by the "suspension" of "operations", we will cover such loss that affects your Business Income during the "period of restoration" and any extension of the "period of restoration" in accordance with the terms of the Extended Business Income Additional Coverage and the Extended Period Of Indemnity Optional Coverage or any variation of these.

(4) Any Extra Expense caused by or resulting from suspension, lapse or cancellation of any license, lease or contract beyond the "period of restoration".

(5) Any other consequential loss.

b. Leasehold Interest Coverage Form

(1) Paragraph **B.1.a.**, Ordinance Or Law, does not apply to insurance under this Coverage Form.

(2) We will not pay for any loss caused by:

(a) Your cancelling the lease;

(b) The suspension, lapse or cancellation of any license; or

(c) Any other consequential loss.

c. Legal Liability Coverage Form

(1) The following exclusions do not apply to insurance under this Coverage Form:

(a) Paragraph **B.1.a.** Ordinance Or Law;

(b) Paragraph **B.1.c.** Governmental Action;

(c) Paragraph **B.1.d.** Nuclear Hazard;

(d) Paragraph **B.1.e.** Utility Services; and

(e) Paragraph **B.1.f.** War And Military Action.

(2) The following additional exclusions apply to insurance under this Coverage Form:

(a) **Contractual Liability**

We will not defend any claim or "suit", or pay damages that you are legally liable to pay, solely by reason of your assumption of liability in a contract or agreement. But this exclusion does not apply to a written lease agreement in which you have assumed liability for building damage resulting from an actual or attempted burglary or robbery, provided that:

(i) Your assumption of liability was executed prior to the accident; and

(ii) The building is Covered Property under this Coverage Form.

(b) **Nuclear Hazard**

We will not defend any claim or "suit", or pay any damages, loss, expense or obligation, resulting from nuclear reaction or radiation, or radioactive contamination, however caused.

C. Additional Coverage – Collapse

The coverage provided under this Additional Coverage, Collapse, applies only to an abrupt collapse as described and limited in **C.1.** through **C.7.**

1. For the purpose of this Additional Coverage, Collapse, abrupt collapse means an abrupt falling down or caving in of a building or any part of a building with the result that the building or part of the building cannot be occupied for its intended purpose.

2. We will pay for direct physical loss or damage to Covered Property, caused by abrupt collapse of a building or any part of a building that is insured under this Coverage Form or that contains Covered Property insured under this Coverage Form, if such collapse is caused by one or more of the following:

a. Fire; lightning; explosion; windstorm or hail; smoke; aircraft or vehicles; riot or civil commotion; vandalism; leakage from fire-extinguishing equipment; sinkhole collapse; volcanic action; breakage of building glass; falling objects; weight of snow, ice or sleet; water damage, meaning accidental discharge or leakage of water or steam as the direct result of the breaking apart or cracking of a plumbing, heating, air conditioning or other system or appliance (other than a sump system including its related equipment and parts), that is located on the described premises and contains water or steam; all only as insured against in this Coverage Part;

b. Building decay that is hidden from view, unless the presence of such decay is known to an insured prior to collapse;

c. Insect or vermin damage that is hidden from view, unless the presence of such damage is known to an insured prior to collapse;

d. Weight of people or personal property;

e. Weight of rain that collects on a roof;

f. Use of defective material or methods in construction, remodeling or renovation if the abrupt collapse occurs during the course of the construction, remodeling or renovation. However, if such collapse occurs after construction, remodeling or renovation is complete and is caused in part by a cause of loss listed in **2.a.** through **2.e.**, we will pay for the loss or damage even if use of defective material or methods, in construction, remodeling or renovation, contributes to the collapse.

This Additional Coverage, Collapse, does not limit the coverage otherwise provided under this Causes Of Loss form for the causes of loss listed in **2.a.**

3. This **Additional Coverage – Collapse** does **not** apply to:

a. A building or any part of a building that is in danger of falling down or caving in;

b. A part of a building that is standing, even if it has separated from another part of the building; or

c. A building that is standing or any part of a building that is standing, even if it shows evidence of cracking, bulging, sagging, bending, leaning, settling, shrinkage or expansion.

4. With respect to the following property:

a. Outdoor radio or television antennas (including satellite dishes) and their lead-in wiring, masts or towers;

b. Awnings, gutters and downspouts;

c. Yard fixtures;

d. Outdoor swimming pools;

e. Fences;

f. Piers, wharves and docks;

g. Beach or diving platforms or appurtenances;

h. Retaining walls; and

i. Walks, roadways and other paved surfaces;

if an abrupt collapse is caused by a cause of loss listed in **2.b.** through **2.f.** we will pay for loss or damage to that property only if:

(1) Such loss or damage is a direct result of the abrupt collapse of a building insured under this Coverage Form; and

(2) The property is Covered Property under this Coverage Form.

5. If personal property abruptly falls down or caves in and such collapse is **not** the result of abrupt collapse of a building, we will pay for loss or damage to Covered Property caused by such collapse of personal property only if:

a. The collapse of personal property was caused by a cause of loss listed in **2.a.** through **2.f.** above;

b. The personal property which collapses is inside a building; and

c. The property which collapses is not of a kind listed in **4.**, regardless of whether that kind of property is considered to be personal property or real property.

The coverage stated in this Paragraph **5.** does not apply to personal property if marring and/or scratching is the only damage to that personal property caused by the collapse.

6. This Additional Coverage, Collapse, does not apply to personal property that has not abruptly fallen down or caved in, even if the personal property shows evidence of cracking, bulging, sagging, bending, leaning, settling, shrinkage or expansion.

7. This Additional Coverage, Collapse, will not increase the Limits of Insurance provided in this Coverage Part.

8. The term Covered Cause of Loss includes the Additional Coverage, Collapse, as described and limited in **C.1.** through **C.7.**

D. Additional Coverage – Limited Coverage For "Fungus", Wet Rot, Dry Rot And Bacteria

1. The coverage described in **D.2.** and **D.6.** only applies when the "fungus", wet or dry rot or bacteria are the result of one or more of the following causes that occur during the policy period and only if all reasonable means were used to save and preserve the property from further damage at the time of and after that occurrence:

   a. A Covered Cause of Loss other than fire or lightning; or

   b. Flood, if the Flood Coverage Endorsement applies to the affected premises.

   This Additional Coverage does not apply to lawns, trees, shrubs or plants which are part of a vegetated roof.

2. We will pay for loss or damage by "fungus", wet or dry rot or bacteria. As used in this Limited Coverage, the term loss or damage means:

   a. Direct physical loss or damage to Covered Property caused by "fungus", wet or dry rot or bacteria, including the cost of removal of the "fungus", wet or dry rot or bacteria;

   b. The cost to tear out and replace any part of the building or other property as needed to gain access to the "fungus", wet or dry rot or bacteria; and

   c. The cost of testing performed after removal, repair, replacement or restoration of the damaged property is completed, provided there is a reason to believe that "fungus", wet or dry rot or bacteria are present.

3. The coverage described under **D.2.** of this Limited Coverage is limited to $15,000. Regardless of the number of claims, this limit is the most we will pay for the total of all loss or damage arising out of all occurrences of Covered Causes of Loss (other than fire or lightning) and Flood which take place in a 12-month period (starting with the beginning of the present annual policy period). With respect to a particular occurrence of loss which results in "fungus", wet or dry rot or bacteria, we will not pay more than a total of $15,000 even if the "fungus", wet or dry rot or bacteria continue to be present or active, or recur, in a later policy period.

4. The coverage provided under this Limited Coverage does not increase the applicable Limit of Insurance on any Covered Property. If a particular occurrence results in loss or damage by "fungus", wet or dry rot or bacteria, and other loss or damage, we will not pay more, for the total of all loss or damage, than the applicable Limit of Insurance on the affected Covered Property.

   If there is covered loss or damage to Covered Property, not caused by "fungus", wet or dry rot or bacteria, loss payment will not be limited by the terms of this Limited Coverage, except to the extent that "fungus", wet or dry rot or bacteria cause an increase in the loss. Any such increase in the loss will be subject to the terms of this Limited Coverage.

5. The terms of this Limited Coverage do not increase or reduce the coverage provided under Paragraph **b.** of Covered Cause Of Loss **9.** Sprinkler Leakage, or Paragraph **b.** of Covered Causes Of Loss **14.** Water Damage, or under the Additional Coverage, Collapse.

6. The following, **6.a.** or **6.b.**, applies only if Business Income and/or Extra Expense Coverage applies to the described premises and only if the "suspension" of "operations" satisfies all terms and conditions of the applicable Business Income and/or Extra Expense Coverage Form:

   a. If the loss which resulted in "fungus", wet or dry rot or bacteria does not in itself necessitate a "suspension" of "operations", but such "suspension" is necessary due to loss or damage to property caused by "fungus", wet or dry rot or bacteria, then our payment under Business Income and/or Extra Expense is limited to the amount of loss and/or expense sustained in a period of not more than 30 days. The days need not be consecutive.

b. If a covered "suspension" of "operations" was caused by loss or damage other than "fungus", wet or dry rot or bacteria but remediation of "fungus", wet or dry rot or bacteria prolongs the "period of restoration", we will pay for loss and/or expense sustained during the delay (regardless of when such a delay occurs during the "period of restoration"), but such coverage is limited to 30 days. The days need not be consecutive.

E. Limitation

We will pay for loss of animals only if they are killed or their destruction is made necessary.

F. Definitions

"Fungus" means any type or form of fungus, including mold or mildew, and any mycotoxins, spores, scents or by-products produced or released by fungi.

COMMERCIAL PROPERTY
CP 10 30 10 12

CAUSES OF LOSS – SPECIAL FORM

Words and phrases that appear in quotation marks have special meaning. Refer to Section **G.** Definitions.

A. Covered Causes Of Loss

When Special is shown in the Declarations, Covered Causes of Loss means direct physical loss unless the loss is excluded or limited in this policy.

B. Exclusions

1. We will not pay for loss or damage caused directly or indirectly by any of the following. Such loss or damage is excluded regardless of any other cause or event that contributes concurrently or in any sequence to the loss.

a. Ordinance Or Law

The enforcement of or compliance with any ordinance or law:

(1) Regulating the construction, use or repair of any property; or

(2) Requiring the tearing down of any property, including the cost of removing its debris.

This exclusion, Ordinance Or Law, applies whether the loss results from:

(a) An ordinance or law that is enforced even if the property has not been damaged; or

(b) The increased costs incurred to comply with an ordinance or law in the course of construction, repair, renovation, remodeling or demolition of property, or removal of its debris, following a physical loss to that property.

b. Earth Movement

(1) Earthquake, including tremors and aftershocks and any earth sinking, rising or shifting related to such event;

(2) Landslide, including any earth sinking, rising or shifting related to such event;

(3) Mine subsidence, meaning subsidence of a man-made mine, whether or not mining activity has ceased;

(4) Earth sinking (other than sinkhole collapse), rising or shifting including soil conditions which cause settling, cracking or other disarrangement of foundations or other parts of realty. Soil conditions include contraction, expansion, freezing, thawing, erosion, improperly compacted soil and the action of water under the ground surface.

But if Earth Movement, as described in **b.(1)** through **(4)** above, results in fire or explosion, we will pay for the loss or damage caused by that fire or explosion.

(5) Volcanic eruption, explosion or effusion. But if volcanic eruption, explosion or effusion results in fire, building glass breakage or Volcanic Action, we will pay for the loss or damage caused by that fire, building glass breakage or Volcanic Action.

Volcanic Action means direct loss or damage resulting from the eruption of a volcano when the loss or damage is caused by:

(a) Airborne volcanic blast or airborne shock waves;

(b) Ash, dust or particulate matter; or

(c) Lava flow.

With respect to coverage for Volcanic Action as set forth in **(5)(a)**, **(5)(b)** and **(5)(c)**, all volcanic eruptions that occur within any 168-hour period will constitute a single occurrence.

Volcanic Action does not include the cost to remove ash, dust or particulate matter that does not cause direct physical loss or damage to the described property.

This exclusion applies regardless of whether any of the above, in Paragraphs **(1)** through **(5)**, is caused by an act of nature or is otherwise caused.

c. Governmental Action

Seizure or destruction of property by order of governmental authority.

But we will pay for loss or damage caused by or resulting from acts of destruction ordered by governmental authority and taken at the time of a fire to prevent its spread, if the fire would be covered under this Coverage Part.

d. Nuclear Hazard

Nuclear reaction or radiation, or radioactive contamination, however caused.

But if nuclear reaction or radiation, or radioactive contamination, results in fire, we will pay for the loss or damage caused by that fire.

e. Utility Services

The failure of power, communication, water or other utility service supplied to the described premises, however caused, if the failure:

(1) Originates away from the described premises; or

(2) Originates at the described premises, but only if such failure involves equipment used to supply the utility service to the described premises from a source away from the described premises.

Failure of any utility service includes lack of sufficient capacity and reduction in supply.

Loss or damage caused by a surge of power is also excluded, if the surge would not have occurred but for an event causing a failure of power.

But if the failure or surge of power, or the failure of communication, water or other utility service, results in a Covered Cause of Loss, we will pay for the loss or damage caused by that Covered Cause of Loss.

Communication services include but are not limited to service relating to Internet access or access to any electronic, cellular or satellite network.

f. War And Military Action

(1) War, including undeclared or civil war;

(2) Warlike action by a military force, including action in hindering or defending against an actual or expected attack, by any government, sovereign or other authority using military personnel or other agents; or

(3) Insurrection, rebellion, revolution, usurped power, or action taken by governmental authority in hindering or defending against any of these.

g. Water

(1) Flood, surface water, waves (including tidal wave and tsunami), tides, tidal water, overflow of any body of water, or spray from any of these, all whether or not driven by wind (including storm surge);

(2) Mudslide or mudflow;

(3) Water that backs up or overflows or is otherwise discharged from a sewer, drain, sump, sump pump or related equipment;

(4) Water under the ground surface pressing on, or flowing or seeping through:

(a) Foundations, walls, floors or paved surfaces;

(b) Basements, whether paved or not; or

(c) Doors, windows or other openings; or

(5) Waterborne material carried or otherwise moved by any of the water referred to in Paragraph **(1)**, **(3)** or **(4)**, or material carried or otherwise moved by mudslide or mudflow.

This exclusion applies regardless of whether any of the above, in Paragraphs **(1)** through **(5)**, is caused by an act of nature or is otherwise caused. An example of a situation to which this exclusion applies is the situation where a dam, levee, seawall or other boundary or containment system fails in whole or in part, for any reason, to contain the water.

But if any of the above, in Paragraphs **(1)** through **(5)**, results in fire, explosion or sprinkler leakage, we will pay for the loss or damage caused by that fire, explosion or sprinkler leakage (if sprinkler leakage is a Covered Cause of Loss).

h. "Fungus", Wet Rot, Dry Rot And Bacteria

Presence, growth, proliferation, spread or any activity of "fungus", wet or dry rot or bacteria.

But if "fungus", wet or dry rot or bacteria result in a "specified cause of loss", we will pay for the loss or damage caused by that "specified cause of loss".

This exclusion does not apply:

(1) When "fungus", wet or dry rot or bacteria result from fire or lightning; or

(2) To the extent that coverage is provided in the Additional Coverage, Limited Coverage For "Fungus", Wet Rot, Dry Rot And Bacteria, with respect to loss or damage by a cause of loss other than fire or lightning.

Exclusions **B.1.a.** through **B.1.h.** apply whether or not the loss event results in widespread damage or affects a substantial area.

2. We will not pay for loss or damage caused by or resulting from any of the following:

a. Artificially generated electrical, magnetic or electromagnetic energy that damages, disturbs, disrupts or otherwise interferes with any:

(1) Electrical or electronic wire, device, appliance, system or network; or

(2) Device, appliance, system or network utilizing cellular or satellite technology.

For the purpose of this exclusion, electrical, magnetic or electromagnetic energy includes but is not limited to:

(a) Electrical current, including arcing;

(b) Electrical charge produced or conducted by a magnetic or electromagnetic field;

(c) Pulse of electromagnetic energy; or

(d) Electromagnetic waves or microwaves.

But if fire results, we will pay for the loss or damage caused by that fire.

b. Delay, loss of use or loss of market.

c. Smoke, vapor or gas from agricultural smudging or industrial operations.

d.(1) Wear and tear;

(2) Rust or other corrosion, decay, deterioration, hidden or latent defect or any quality in property that causes it to damage or destroy itself;

(3) Smog;

(4) Settling, cracking, shrinking or expansion;

(5) Nesting or infestation, or discharge or release of waste products or secretions, by insects, birds, rodents or other animals.

(6) Mechanical breakdown, including rupture or bursting caused by centrifugal force. But if mechanical breakdown results in elevator collision, we will pay for the loss or damage caused by that elevator collision.

(7) The following causes of loss to personal property:

(a) Dampness or dryness of atmosphere;

(b) Changes in or extremes of temperature; or

(c) Marring or scratching.

But if an excluded cause of loss that is listed in **2.d.(1)** through **(7)** results in a "specified cause of loss" or building glass breakage, we will pay for the loss or damage caused by that "specified cause of loss" or building glass breakage.

e. Explosion of steam boilers, steam pipes, steam engines or steam turbines owned or leased by you, or operated under your control. But if explosion of steam boilers, steam pipes, steam engines or steam turbines results in fire or combustion explosion, we will pay for the loss or damage caused by that fire or combustion explosion. We will also pay for loss or damage caused by or resulting from the explosion of gases or fuel within the furnace of any fired vessel or within the flues or passages through which the gases of combustion pass.

f. Continuous or repeated seepage or leakage of water, or the presence or condensation of humidity, moisture or vapor, that occurs over a period of 14 days or more.

g. Water, other liquids, powder or molten material that leaks or flows from plumbing, heating, air conditioning or other equipment (except fire protective systems) caused by or resulting from freezing, unless:

(1) You do your best to maintain heat in the building or structure; or

(2) You drain the equipment and shut off the supply if the heat is not maintained.

h. Dishonest or criminal act (including theft) by you, any of your partners, members, officers, managers, employees (including temporary employees and leased workers), directors, trustees or authorized representatives, whether acting alone or in collusion with each other or with any other party; or theft by any person to whom you entrust the property for any purpose, whether acting alone or in collusion with any other party.

This exclusion:

(1) Applies whether or not an act occurs during your normal hours of operation;

(2) Does not apply to acts of destruction by your employees (including temporary employees and leased workers) or authorized representatives; but theft by your employees (including temporary employees and leased workers) or authorized representatives is not covered.

i. Voluntary parting with any property by you or anyone else to whom you have entrusted the property if induced to do so by any fraudulent scheme, trick, device or false pretense.

j. Rain, snow, ice or sleet to personal property in the open.

k. Collapse, including any of the following conditions of property or any part of the property:

(1) An abrupt falling down or caving in;

(2) Loss of structural integrity, including separation of parts of the property or property in danger of falling down or caving in; or

(3) Any cracking, bulging, sagging, bending, leaning, settling, shrinkage or expansion as such condition relates to **(1)** or **(2)** above.

But if collapse results in a Covered Cause of Loss at the described premises, we will pay for the loss or damage caused by that Covered Cause of Loss.

This exclusion, **k.**, does not apply:

(a) To the extent that coverage is provided under the Additional Coverage, Collapse; or

(b) To collapse caused by one or more of the following:

(i) The "specified causes of loss";

(ii) Breakage of building glass;

(iii) Weight of rain that collects on a roof; or

(iv) Weight of people or personal property.

l. Discharge, dispersal, seepage, migration, release or escape of "pollutants" unless the discharge, dispersal, seepage, migration, release or escape is itself caused by any of the "specified causes of loss". But if the discharge, dispersal, seepage, migration, release or escape of "pollutants" results in a "specified cause of loss", we will pay for the loss or damage caused by that "specified cause of loss".

This exclusion, **l.**, does not apply to damage to glass caused by chemicals applied to the glass.

m. Neglect of an insured to use all reasonable means to save and preserve property from further damage at and after the time of loss.

3. We will not pay for loss or damage caused by or resulting from any of the following, **3.a.** through **3.c.** But if an excluded cause of loss that is listed in **3.a.** through **3.c.** results in a Covered Cause of Loss, we will pay for the loss or damage caused by that Covered Cause of Loss.

a. Weather conditions. But this exclusion only applies if weather conditions contribute in any way with a cause or event excluded in Paragraph **1.** above to produce the loss or damage.

b. Acts or decisions, including the failure to act or decide, of any person, group, organization or governmental body.

c. Faulty, inadequate or defective:

(1) Planning, zoning, development, surveying, siting;

(2) Design, specifications, workmanship, repair, construction, renovation, remodeling, grading, compaction;

(3) Materials used in repair, construction, renovation or remodeling; or

(4) Maintenance;

of part or all of any property on or off the described premises.

4. Special Exclusions

The following provisions apply only to the specified Coverage Forms:

a. Business Income (And Extra Expense) Coverage Form, Business Income (Without Extra Expense) Coverage Form, Or Extra Expense Coverage Form

We will not pay for:

(1) Any loss caused by or resulting from:

(a) Damage or destruction of "finished stock"; or

(b) The time required to reproduce "finished stock".

This exclusion does not apply to Extra Expense.

(2) Any loss caused by or resulting from direct physical loss or damage to radio or television antennas (including satellite dishes) and their lead-in wiring, masts or towers.

(3) Any increase of loss caused by or resulting from:

(a) Delay in rebuilding, repairing or replacing the property or resuming "operations", due to interference at the location of the rebuilding, repair or replacement by strikers or other persons; or

(b) Suspension, lapse or cancellation of any license, lease or contract. But if the suspension, lapse or cancellation is directly caused by the "suspension" of "operations", we will cover such loss that affects your Business Income during the "period of restoration" and any extension of the "period of restoration" in accordance with the terms of the Extended Business Income Additional Coverage and the Extended Period Of Indemnity Optional Coverage or any variation of these.

(4) Any Extra Expense caused by or resulting from suspension, lapse or cancellation of any license, lease or contract beyond the "period of restoration".

(5) Any other consequential loss.

b. Leasehold Interest Coverage Form

(1) Paragraph **B.1.a.**, Ordinance Or Law, does not apply to insurance under this Coverage Form.

(2) We will not pay for any loss caused by:

(a) Your cancelling the lease;

(b) The suspension, lapse or cancellation of any license; or

(c) Any other consequential loss.

c. Legal Liability Coverage Form

(1) The following exclusions do not apply to insurance under this Coverage Form:

(a) Paragraph **B.1.a.** Ordinance Or Law;

(b) Paragraph **B.1.c.** Governmental Action;

(c) Paragraph **B.1.d.** Nuclear Hazard;

(d) Paragraph **B.1.e.** Utility Services; and

(e) Paragraph **B.1.f.** War And Military Action.

(2) The following additional exclusions apply to insurance under this Coverage Form:

(a) Contractual Liability

We will not defend any claim or "suit", or pay damages that you are legally liable to pay, solely by reason of your assumption of liability in a contract or agreement. But this exclusion does not apply to a written lease agreement in which you have assumed liability for building damage resulting from an actual or attempted burglary or robbery, provided that:

(i) Your assumption of liability was executed prior to the accident; and

(ii) The building is Covered Property under this Coverage Form.

(b) Nuclear Hazard

We will not defend any claim or "suit", or pay any damages, loss, expense or obligation, resulting from nuclear reaction or radiation, or radioactive contamination, however caused.

5. Additional Exclusion

The following provisions apply only to the specified property:

Loss Or Damage To Products

We will not pay for loss or damage to any merchandise, goods or other product caused by or resulting from error or omission by any person or entity (including those having possession under an arrangement where work or a portion of the work is outsourced) in any stage of the development, production or use of the product, including planning, testing, processing, packaging, installation, maintenance or repair. This exclusion applies to any effect that compromises the form, substance or quality of the product. But if such error or omission results in a Covered Cause of Loss, we will pay for the loss or damage caused by that Covered Cause of Loss.

C. Limitations

The following limitations apply to all policy forms and endorsements, unless otherwise stated:

1. We will not pay for loss of or damage to property, as described and limited in this section. In addition, we will not pay for any loss that is a consequence of loss or damage as described and limited in this section.

   a. Steam boilers, steam pipes, steam engines or steam turbines caused by or resulting from any condition or event inside such equipment. But we will pay for loss of or damage to such equipment caused by or resulting from an explosion of gases or fuel within the furnace of any fired vessel or within the flues or passages through which the gases of combustion pass.

   b. Hot water boilers or other water heating equipment caused by or resulting from any condition or event inside such boilers or equipment, other than an explosion.

   c. The interior of any building or structure, or to personal property in the building or structure, caused by or resulting from rain, snow, sleet, ice, sand or dust, whether driven by wind or not, unless:

      (1) The building or structure first sustains damage by a Covered Cause of Loss to its roof or walls through which the rain, snow, sleet, ice, sand or dust enters; or

      (2) The loss or damage is caused by or results from thawing of snow, sleet or ice on the building or structure.

   d. Building materials and supplies not attached as part of the building or structure, caused by or resulting from theft.

      However, this limitation does not apply to:

      (1) Building materials and supplies held for sale by you, unless they are insured under the Builders Risk Coverage Form; or

      (2) Business Income Coverage or Extra Expense Coverage.

   e. Property that is missing, where the only evidence of the loss or damage is a shortage disclosed on taking inventory, or other instances where there is no physical evidence to show what happened to the property.

   f. Property that has been transferred to a person or to a place outside the described premises on the basis of unauthorized instructions.

   g. Lawns, trees, shrubs or plants which are part of a vegetated roof, caused by or resulting from:

      (1) Dampness or dryness of atmosphere or of soil supporting the vegetation;

      (2) Changes in or extremes of temperature;

      (3) Disease;

      (4) Frost or hail; or

      (5) Rain, snow, ice or sleet.

2. We will not pay for loss of or damage to the following types of property unless caused by the "specified causes of loss" or building glass breakage:

   a. Animals, and then only if they are killed or their destruction is made necessary.

   b. Fragile articles such as statuary, marbles, chinaware and porcelains, if broken. This restriction does not apply to:

      (1) Glass; or

      (2) Containers of property held for sale.

   c. Builders' machinery, tools and equipment owned by you or entrusted to you, provided such property is Covered Property.

      However, this limitation does not apply:

      (1) If the property is located on or within 100 feet of the described premises, unless the premises is insured under the Builders Risk Coverage Form; or

      (2) To Business Income Coverage or to Extra Expense Coverage.

3. The special limit shown for each category, **a.** through **d.**, is the total limit for loss of or damage to all property in that category. The special limit applies to any one occurrence of theft, regardless of the types or number of articles that are lost or damaged in that occurrence. The special limits are (unless a higher limit is shown in the Declarations):
   a. $2,500 for furs, fur garments and garments trimmed with fur.
   b. $2,500 for jewelry, watches, watch movements, jewels, pearls, precious and semiprecious stones, bullion, gold, silver, platinum and other precious alloys or metals. This limit does not apply to jewelry and watches worth $100 or less per item.
   c. $2,500 for patterns, dies, molds and forms.
   d. $250 for stamps, tickets, including lottery tickets held for sale, and letters of credit.

   These special limits are part of, not in addition to, the Limit of Insurance applicable to the Covered Property.

   This limitation, **C.3.**, does not apply to Business Income Coverage or to Extra Expense Coverage.
4. We will not pay the cost to repair any defect to a system or appliance from which water, other liquid, powder or molten material escapes. But we will pay the cost to repair or replace damaged parts of fire-extinguishing equipment if the damage:
   a. Results in discharge of any substance from an automatic fire protection system; or
   b. Is directly caused by freezing.

   However, this limitation does not apply to Business Income Coverage or to Extra Expense Coverage.

D. Additional Coverage – Collapse

The coverage provided under this Additional Coverage, Collapse, applies only to an abrupt collapse as described and limited in **D.1.** through **D.7.**

1. For the purpose of this Additional Coverage, Collapse, abrupt collapse means an abrupt falling down or caving in of a building or any part of a building with the result that the building or part of the building cannot be occupied for its intended purpose.
2. We will pay for direct physical loss or damage to Covered Property, caused by abrupt collapse of a building or any part of a building that is insured under this Coverage Form or that contains Covered Property insured under this Coverage Form, if such collapse is caused by one or more of the following:
   a. Building decay that is hidden from view, unless the presence of such decay is known to an insured prior to collapse;
   b. Insect or vermin damage that is hidden from view, unless the presence of such damage is known to an insured prior to collapse;
   c. Use of defective material or methods in construction, remodeling or renovation if the abrupt collapse occurs during the course of the construction, remodeling or renovation.
   d. Use of defective material or methods in construction, remodeling or renovation if the abrupt collapse occurs after the construction, remodeling or renovation is complete, but only if the collapse is caused in part by:
      (1) A cause of loss listed in **2.a.** or **2.b.**;
      (2) One or more of the "specified causes of loss";
      (3) Breakage of building glass;
      (4) Weight of people or personal property; or
      (5) Weight of rain that collects on a roof.
3. This **Additional Coverage – Collapse** does **not** apply to:
   a. A building or any part of a building that is in danger of falling down or caving in;
   b. A part of a building that is standing, even if it has separated from another part of the building; or
   c. A building that is standing or any part of a building that is standing, even if it shows evidence of cracking, bulging, sagging, bending, leaning, settling, shrinkage or expansion.
4. With respect to the following property:
   a. Outdoor radio or television antennas (including satellite dishes) and their lead-in wiring, masts or towers;

b. Awnings, gutters and downspouts;

c. Yard fixtures;

d. Outdoor swimming pools;

e. Fences;

f. Piers, wharves and docks;

g. Beach or diving platforms or appurtenances;

h. Retaining walls; and

i. Walks, roadways and other paved surfaces;

if an abrupt collapse is caused by a cause of loss listed in **2.a.** through **2.d.**, we will pay for loss or damage to that property only if:

(1) Such loss or damage is a direct result of the abrupt collapse of a building insured under this Coverage Form; and

(2) The property is Covered Property under this Coverage Form.

5. If personal property abruptly falls down or caves in and such collapse is **not** the result of abrupt collapse of a building, we will pay for loss or damage to Covered Property caused by such collapse of personal property only if:

a. The collapse of personal property was caused by a cause of loss listed in **2.a.** through **2.d.**;

b. The personal property which collapses is inside a building; and

c. The property which collapses is not of a kind listed in **4.**, regardless of whether that kind of property is considered to be personal property or real property.

The coverage stated in this Paragraph **5.** does not apply to personal property if marring and/or scratching is the only damage to that personal property caused by the collapse.

6. This Additional Coverage, Collapse, does not apply to personal property that has not abruptly fallen down or caved in, even if the personal property shows evidence of cracking, bulging, sagging, bending, leaning, settling, shrinkage or expansion.

7. This Additional Coverage, Collapse, will not increase the Limits of Insurance provided in this Coverage Part.

8. The term Covered Cause of Loss includes the Additional Coverage, Collapse, as described and limited in **D.1.** through **D.7.**

E. Additional Coverage – Limited Coverage For "Fungus", Wet Rot, Dry Rot And Bacteria

1. The coverage described in **E.2.** and **E.6.** only applies when the "fungus", wet or dry rot or bacteria are the result of one or more of the following causes that occur during the policy period and only if all reasonable means were used to save and preserve the property from further damage at the time of and after that occurrence:

a. A "specified cause of loss" other than fire or lightning; or

b. Flood, if the Flood Coverage Endorsement applies to the affected premises.

This Additional Coverage does not apply to lawns, trees, shrubs or plants which are part of a vegetated roof.

2. We will pay for loss or damage by "fungus", wet or dry rot or bacteria. As used in this Limited Coverage, the term loss or damage means:

a. Direct physical loss or damage to Covered Property caused by "fungus", wet or dry rot or bacteria, including the cost of removal of the "fungus", wet or dry rot or bacteria;

b. The cost to tear out and replace any part of the building or other property as needed to gain access to the "fungus", wet or dry rot or bacteria; and

c. The cost of testing performed after removal, repair, replacement or restoration of the damaged property is completed, provided there is a reason to believe that "fungus", wet or dry rot or bacteria are present.

3. The coverage described under **E.2.** of this Limited Coverage is limited to $15,000. Regardless of the number of claims, this limit is the most we will pay for the total of all loss or damage arising out of all occurrences of "specified causes of loss" (other than fire or lightning) and Flood which take place in a 12-month period (starting with the beginning of the present annual policy period). With respect to a particular occurrence of loss which results in "fungus", wet or dry rot or bacteria, we will not pay more than a total of $15,000 even if the "fungus", wet or dry rot or bacteria continue to be present or active, or recur, in a later policy period.

4. The coverage provided under this Limited Coverage does not increase the applicable Limit of Insurance on any Covered Property. If a particular occurrence results in loss or damage by "fungus", wet or dry rot or bacteria, and other loss or damage, we will not pay more, for the total of all loss or damage, than the applicable Limit of Insurance on the affected Covered Property.

   If there is covered loss or damage to Covered Property, not caused by "fungus", wet or dry rot or bacteria, loss payment will not be limited by the terms of this Limited Coverage, except to the extent that "fungus", wet or dry rot or bacteria cause an increase in the loss. Any such increase in the loss will be subject to the terms of this Limited Coverage.

5. The terms of this Limited Coverage do not increase or reduce the coverage provided under Paragraph **F.2.** (Water Damage, Other Liquids, Powder Or Molten Material Damage) of this Causes Of Loss form or under the Additional Coverage, Collapse.

6. The following, **6.a.** or **6.b.**, applies only if Business Income and/or Extra Expense Coverage applies to the described premises and only if the "suspension" of "operations" satisfies all terms and conditions of the applicable Business Income and/or Extra Expense Coverage Form:

   a. If the loss which resulted in "fungus", wet or dry rot or bacteria does not in itself necessitate a "suspension" of "operations", but such "suspension" is necessary due to loss or damage to property caused by "fungus", wet or dry rot or bacteria, then our payment under Business Income and/or Extra Expense is limited to the amount of loss and/or expense sustained in a period of not more than 30 days. The days need not be consecutive.

   b. If a covered "suspension" of "operations" was caused by loss or damage other than "fungus", wet or dry rot or bacteria but remediation of "fungus", wet or dry rot or bacteria prolongs the "period of restoration", we will pay for loss and/or expense sustained during the delay (regardless of when such a delay occurs during the "period of restoration"), but such coverage is limited to 30 days. The days need not be consecutive.

F. Additional Coverage Extensions

1. Property In Transit

This Extension applies only to your personal property to which this form applies.

a. You may extend the insurance provided by this Coverage Part to apply to your personal property (other than property in the care, custody or control of your salespersons) in transit more than 100 feet from the described premises. Property must be in or on a motor vehicle you own, lease or operate while between points in the coverage territory.

b. Loss or damage must be caused by or result from one of the following causes of loss:

(1) Fire, lightning, explosion, windstorm or hail, riot or civil commotion, or vandalism.

(2) Vehicle collision, upset or overturn. Collision means accidental contact of your vehicle with another vehicle or object. It does not mean your vehicle's contact with the roadbed.

(3) Theft of an entire bale, case or package by forced entry into a securely locked body or compartment of the vehicle. There must be visible marks of the forced entry.

c. The most we will pay for loss or damage under this Extension is $5,000.

This Coverage Extension is additional insurance. The Additional Condition, Coinsurance, does not apply to this Extension.

2. Water Damage, Other Liquids, Powder Or Molten Material Damage

If loss or damage caused by or resulting from covered water or other liquid, powder or molten material damage loss occurs, we will also pay the cost to tear out and replace any part of the building or structure to repair damage to the system or appliance from which the water or other substance escapes. This Coverage Extension does not increase the Limit of Insurance.

3. Glass

a. We will pay for expenses incurred to put up temporary plates or board up openings if repair or replacement of damaged glass is delayed.

b. We will pay for expenses incurred to remove or replace obstructions when repairing or replacing glass that is part of a building. This does not include removing or replacing window displays.

This Coverage Extension **F.3.** does not increase the Limit of Insurance.

G. Definitions

1. "Fungus" means any type or form of fungus, including mold or mildew, and any mycotoxins, spores, scents or by-products produced or released by fungi.

2. "Specified causes of loss" means the following: fire; lightning; explosion; windstorm or hail; smoke; aircraft or vehicles; riot or civil commotion; vandalism; leakage from fire-extinguishing equipment; sinkhole collapse; volcanic action; falling objects; weight of snow, ice or sleet; water damage.

a. Sinkhole collapse means the sudden sinking or collapse of land into underground empty spaces created by the action of water on limestone or dolomite. This cause of loss does not include:

(1) The cost of filling sinkholes; or

(2) Sinking or collapse of land into man-made underground cavities.

b. Falling objects does not include loss or damage to:

(1) Personal property in the open; or

(2) The interior of a building or structure, or property inside a building or structure, unless the roof or an outside wall of the building or structure is first damaged by a falling object.

c. Water damage means:

(1) Accidental discharge or leakage of water or steam as the direct result of the breaking apart or cracking of a plumbing, heating, air conditioning or other system or appliance (other than a sump system including its related equipment and parts), that is located on the described premises and contains water or steam; and

(2) Accidental discharge or leakage of water or waterborne material as the direct result of the breaking apart or cracking of a water or sewer pipe that is located off the described premises and is part of a municipal potable water supply system or municipal sanitary sewer system, if the breakage or cracking is caused by wear and tear.

But water damage does not include loss or damage otherwise excluded under the terms of the Water Exclusion. Therefore, for example, there is no coverage under this policy in the situation in which discharge or leakage of water results from the breaking apart or cracking of a pipe which was caused by or related to weather-induced flooding, even if wear and tear contributed to the breakage or cracking. As another example, and also in accordance with the terms of the Water Exclusion, there is no coverage for loss or damage caused by or related to weather-induced flooding which follows or is exacerbated by pipe breakage or cracking attributable to wear and tear.

To the extent that accidental discharge or leakage of water falls within the criteria set forth in **c.(1)** or **c.(2)** of this definition of "specified causes of loss," such water is not subject to the provisions of the Water Exclusion which preclude coverage for surface water or water under the surface of the ground.

COMMERCIAL PROPERTY
CP 10 40 10 12

THIS ENDORSEMENT CHANGES THE POLICY. PLEASE READ IT CAREFULLY.

EARTHQUAKE AND VOLCANIC ERUPTION ENDORSEMENT

This endorsement modifies insurance provided under the following:

COMMERCIAL PROPERTY COVERAGE PART
STANDARD PROPERTY POLICY

A. When this endorsement is attached to the Standard Property Policy, the terms Coverage Part and Coverage Form in this endorsement are replaced by the term Policy.

B. This endorsement applies to the Covered Property and Coverages for which an Earthquake – Volcanic Eruption Limit Of Insurance is shown in the Declarations.

C. Additional Covered Causes Of Loss

1. The following are added to the Covered Causes Of Loss:

a. Earthquake.

b. Volcanic Eruption, meaning the eruption, explosion or effusion of a volcano.

All Earthquake shocks or Volcanic Eruptions that occur within any 168-hour period will constitute a single Earthquake or Volcanic Eruption. The expiration of this policy will not reduce the 168-hour period.

2. If the Declarations indicate that this endorsement covers Earthquake – Sprinkler Leakage Only, then the Covered Causes of Loss in Paragraph **C.1.** of this endorsement do not apply, and the following apply instead:

a. Sprinkler Leakage resulting from Earthquake.

b. Sprinkler Leakage resulting from Volcanic Eruption. Volcanic Eruption means the eruption, explosion or effusion of a volcano.

All Earthquake shocks or Volcanic Eruptions that occur within any 168-hour period will constitute a single Earthquake or Volcanic Eruption. The expiration of this policy will not reduce the 168-hour period.

D. Exclusions, Limitations And Related Provisions

1. The Exclusions and Limitation(s) sections of the Causes Of Loss Form (and the Exclusions section of the Mortgageholders Errors And Omissions Coverage Form and the Standard Property Policy) apply to coverage provided under this endorsement, except as provided in **D.2.** and **D.3.** below.

2. To the extent that the Earth Movement Exclusion might conflict with coverage provided under this endorsement, the Earth Movement Exclusion does not apply.

3. The exclusion of collapse, in the Causes Of Loss – Special Form and Mortgageholders Errors And Omissions Coverage Form, does not apply to collapse caused by Earthquake or Volcanic Eruption.

4. The Additional Coverage – Collapse, in the Causes Of Loss – Broad Form, Causes Of Loss – Special Form and Mortgageholders Errors And Omissions Coverage Form, does not apply to the coverage provided under this endorsement. This endorsement includes coverage for collapse caused by Earthquake or Volcanic Eruption.

5. We will not pay for loss or damage caused directly or indirectly by tidal wave or tsunami, even if attributable to an Earthquake or Volcanic Eruption.

6. We will not pay for loss or damage caused by or resulting from any Earthquake or Volcanic Eruption that begins before the inception of this insurance.

7. The Ordinance Or Law Exclusion in this Coverage Part continues to apply with respect to any loss under this Coverage Part including any loss under this endorsement, unless Ordinance Or Law Coverage is added by endorsement.

8. We will not pay for loss of or damage to exterior masonry veneer (except stucco) on wood frame walls caused by or resulting from Earthquake or Volcanic Eruption. The value of such veneer will not be included in the value of Covered Property or the amount of loss when applying the Property Damage Deductible applicable to this endorsement.

This limitation, **D.8.**, does not apply if:

a. The Declarations indicate that the "Including Masonry Veneer" option applies or the premises description in the Declarations specifically states "Including Masonry Veneer"; or

b. Less than 10% of the total outside wall area is faced with masonry veneer (excluding stucco).

9. Under this Coverage Part, as set forth under Property Not Covered in the Coverage Form to which this endorsement is attached, land is not covered property, nor is the cost of excavations, grading, backfilling or filling. Therefore, coverage under this endorsement does not include the cost of restoring or remediating land.

E. Property Damage Deductible

1. The provisions of Section **E.3.** of this endorsement are applicable to all Coverage Forms except:

a. Business Income (And Extra Expense) Coverage Form;

b. Business Income (Without Extra Expense) Coverage Form;

c. Extra Expense Coverage Form.

2. If the Declarations indicate that this endorsement covers Earthquake – Sprinkler Leakage Only, then the Deductible set forth in Section **E.3.** of this endorsement does not apply to such coverage. The applicable Deductible for such coverage is the same Deductible that applies to Fire.

3. The Deductible, if any, in this Coverage Part is replaced by the following with respect to Earthquake and Volcanic Eruption:

a. All Policies

(1) The Deductible provisions apply to each Earthquake or Volcanic Eruption.

(2) Separate Deductibles are calculated for, and apply to, each building, personal property at each building and personal property in the open. Deductibles are separately calculated and applied even if:

(a) Two or more buildings sustain loss or damage;

(b) Personal property at two or more buildings sustains loss or damage; and/or

(c) A building and the personal property in that building sustain loss or damage.

(3) We will not pay for loss or damage until the amount of loss or damage exceeds the applicable Deductible. We will then pay the amount of loss or damage in excess of that Deductible, up to the applicable Limit of Insurance, after any reduction required by any of the following: Coinsurance Condition, Agreed Value Optional Coverage, Additional Condition – Need For Adequate Insurance or Additional Condition – Need For Full Reports.

(4) When property is covered under the Coverage Extension for Newly Acquired or Constructed Property: In determining the amount, if any, that we will pay for loss or damage, we will deduct an amount equal to a percentage of the value of the property at time of loss. The applicable percentage for Newly Acquired or Constructed Property is the highest percentage shown in the Declarations for any described premises.

(5) If there is loss or damage caused by Earthquake or Volcanic Eruption, and loss or damage caused by a Cause of Loss (e.g., fire) that is covered by means of an exception to the Earth Movement Exclusion, then the only applicable Deductible provisions are those stated in this endorsement.

b. Calculation Of The Deductible – Specific Insurance Other Than Builders Risk

(1) Property Not Subject To Value Reporting Forms

In determining the amount, if any, that we will pay for loss or damage, we will deduct an amount equal to a percentage (as shown in the Declarations, concerning the Earthquake – Volcanic Eruption Deductible) of the Limit of Insurance applicable to the property that has sustained loss or damage.

(2) Property Subject To Value Reporting Forms

In determining the amount, if any, that we will pay for loss or damage, we will deduct an amount equal to a percentage (as shown in the Declarations, concerning the Earthquake – Volcanic Eruption Deductible) of the value of the property that has sustained loss or damage. The value to be used is the latest value shown in the most recent Report of Values on file with us.

However:

(a) If the most recent Report of Values shows less than the full value of the property on the report dates, we will determine the deductible amount as a percentage of the full value as of the report dates.

(b) If the first Report of Values is not filed with us prior to loss or damage, we will determine the deductible amount as a percentage of the applicable Limit of Insurance.

c. Calculation Of The Deductible – Blanket Insurance Other Than Builders Risk

(1) Property Not Subject To Value Reporting Forms

In determining the amount, if any, that we will pay for loss or damage, we will deduct an amount equal to a percentage (as shown in the Declarations, concerning the Earthquake – Volcanic Eruption Deductible) of the value of the property that has sustained loss or damage. The value to be used is that shown in the most recent Statement of Values on file with us.

(2) Property Subject To Value Reporting Forms

In determining the amount, if any, that we will pay for property that has sustained loss or damage, we will deduct an amount equal to a percentage (as shown in the Declarations, concerning the Earthquake – Volcanic Eruption Deductible) of the value of that property as of the time of loss or damage.

d. Calculation Of The Deductible – Builders Risk Insurance

(1) Builders Risk Other Than Reporting Form

In determining the amount, if any, that we will pay for property that has sustained loss or damage, we will deduct an amount equal to a percentage (as shown in the Declarations, concerning the Earthquake – Volcanic Eruption Deductible) of the actual cash value of that property as of the time of loss or damage.

(2) Builders Risk Reporting Form

In determining the amount, if any, that we will pay for loss or damage, we will deduct an amount equal to a percentage (as shown in the Declarations, concerning the Earthquake – Volcanic Eruption Deductible) of the value of the property that has sustained loss or damage. The value to be used is the actual cash value shown in the most recent Report of Values on file with us.

However:

(a) If the most recent Report of Values shows less than the actual cash value of the property on the report date, we will determine the deductible amount as a percentage of the actual cash value as of the report date.

(b) If the first Report of Values is not filed with us prior to loss or damage, we will determine the deductible amount as a percentage of the actual cash value of the property as of the time of loss or damage.

F. Examples – Application Of Deductible In E.3.:

EXAMPLE 1 – SPECIFIC INSURANCE (E.3.b.(1))

The amount of loss to the damaged building is $60,000.

The value of the damaged building at time of loss is $100,000. The Coinsurance percentage shown in the Declarations is 80%; the minimum Limit of Insurance needed to meet the Coinsurance requirement is $80,000 (80% of $100,000).

The **actual** Limit of Insurance on the damaged building is $70,000.

The Deductible is 5%.

Step **(1)**: $70,000 ÷ $80,000 = .875

Step **(2)**: $60,000 X .875 = $52,500

Step **(3)**: $70,000 X 5% = $3,500

Step **(4)**: $52,500 – $3,500 = $49,000

The most we will pay is $49,000. The remainder of the loss, $11,000, is not covered due to the Coinsurance penalty for inadequate insurance (steps **(1)** and **(2)**) and the application of the Deductible (steps **(3)** and **(4)**).

EXAMPLE 2 – SPECIFIC INSURANCE (E.3.b.(1))

The amounts of loss to the damaged property are $60,000 (building) and $40,000 (business personal property in building).

The value of the damaged building at time of loss is $100,000. The value of the business personal property in that building is $80,000. The Coinsurance percentage shown in the Declarations is 80%; the minimum Limits of Insurance needed to meet the Coinsurance requirement are $80,000 (80% of $100,000) for the building and $64,000 (80% of $80,000) for the business personal property.

The **actual** Limits of Insurance on the damaged property are $80,000 on the building and $64,000 on the business personal property (therefore no Coinsurance penalty).

The Deductible is 10%.

Building 1

Step **(1)**: $80,000 X 10% = $8,000

Step **(2)**: $60,000 – $8,000 = $52,000

Business Personal Property

Step **(1)**: $64,000 X 10% = $6,400

Step **(2)**: $40,000 – $6,400 = $33,600

The most we will pay is $85,600. That portion of the total loss not covered due to application of the Deductible is $14,400.

EXAMPLE 3 – BLANKET INSURANCE (E.3.c.(1))

The sum of the values of Building 1 ($500,000), Building 2 ($500,000) and Building 3 ($1,000,000), as shown in the most recent Statement of Values on file with us, is $2,000,000.

The Coinsurance percentage shown in the Declarations is 90%; the minimum Blanket Limit of Insurance needed to meet the Coinsurance requirement is $1,800,000 (90% of $2,000,000).

The **actual** Blanket Limit of Insurance covering Buildings 1, 2, and 3, shown in the Declarations, is $1,800,000 (therefore no Coinsurance penalty).

Buildings 1 and 2 have sustained damage; the amounts of loss to these buildings are $40,000 (Building 1) and $60,000 (Building 2).

The Deductible is 5%.

Building 1

Step **(1)**: $500,000 X 5% = $25,000

Step **(2)**: $40,000 – $25,000 = $15,000

Building 2

Step **(1)**: $500,000 X 5% = $25,000

Step **(2)**: $60,000 – $25,000 = $35,000

The most we will pay is $50,000. That portion of the total loss not covered due to application of the Deductible is $50,000.

EXAMPLE 4 – BLANKET INSURANCE (E.3.c.(1))

The sum of the values of Building 1 ($500,000), Building 2 ($500,000), Business Personal Property at Building 1 ($250,000) and Business Personal Property at Building 2 ($250,000), as shown in the most recent Statement of Values on file with us, is $1,500,000.

The Coinsurance percentage shown in the Declarations is 90%; the minimum Blanket Limit of Insurance needed to meet the Coinsurance requirement is $1,350,000 (90% of $1,500,000).

The **actual** Blanket Limit of Insurance covering Buildings 1 and 2 and Business Personal Property at Buildings 1 and 2, shown in the Declarations, is $1,350,000. Therefore there is no Coinsurance penalty.

Building 1 and Business Personal Property at Building 1 have sustained damage; the amounts of loss are $95,000 (Building) and $5,000 (Business Personal Property).

The Deductible is 10%.

Building

Step **(1)**: $500,000 X 10% = $50,000

Step **(2)**: $95,000 – $50,000 = $45,000

Business Personal Property

Step **(1)**: $250,000 X 10% = $25,000

The loss, $5,000, does not exceed the deductible.

The most we will pay is $45,000. The remainder of the building loss, $50,000, is not covered due to application of the Deductible. There is no loss payment for the business personal property.

G. Business Income And Extra Expense Period Of Restoration

This Section **G.** is applicable only to the Coverage Forms specified below:

1. Business Income (And Extra Expense) Coverage Form;

2. Business Income (Without Extra Expense) Coverage Form;

3. Extra Expense Coverage Form.

The "period of restoration" definition stated in the Coverage Form, or in any endorsement amending the beginning of the "period of restoration", applies to each Earthquake or Volcanic Eruption. A single Earthquake or Volcanic Eruption is defined in Section **C.** of this endorsement.

Sample Bylaws

Bylaws Of The [Name Of Condominium]

ARTICLE I. Name, Location, and Applicability

The Bylaws of The *[name of condominium]* located at *[location of condominium]*, City of *[name of city]*, *[name of county]*, *[name of state]*, are applicable to all present and future owners, mortgagees, lessees, occupants, employees, guests, or any other persons who may use the facilities in any manner.

ARTICLE II. General

Section 1. *Purpose*: These Bylaws provide for the organization of the Condominium and provide the means through which Unit Owners may express their opinions, wishes, and take action with regard to electing a Condominium Board to administer, manage, and operate the Condominium. The Property has been submitted to the provisions of the Condominium Act by the recording of the Declaration in the County Clerk's Office, of which Declaration these Bylaws form a part.

Section 2. *Applicability*: These Bylaws are applicable to the Property and to the use and occupancy thereof. All present and future Unit Owners, mortgagees, lessees, sublessees, and occupants of Units, and employees and guests of Unit Owners, as well as all other Persons who may use the Property, are and shall be subject to the Declaration, these Bylaws, and the Rules and Regulations, as each of the same may be amended from time to time. The acceptance of a deed or other instrument of conveyance, or the succeeding to title to, or the execution of a lease or sublease for, or the act of occupancy of, a Unit shall constitute an agreement that the provisions of the Declaration, these Bylaws, and the Rules and Regulations, as each of the same may be amended from time to time, are accepted and ratified, and will be complied with.

ARTICLE III. Condominium Board

Section 1. *General*: The affairs of the Condominium shall be governed by the Condominium Board. In exercising its powers and performing its duties under the Declaration and these Bylaws, the Condominium Board shall act as, and shall be, the Agent of the Unit Owners, subject to, and in accordance with, the terms of the Declaration and these Bylaws. The Condominium Board shall also have the status conferred upon it under, or pursuant to, the terms of the Condominium Act.

Section 2. *Number*: The first Condominium Board to be elected by the Unit Owners shall consist of four (4) persons to serve at the first annual meeting. From and after the first annual meeting of the Unit Owners, the Condominium Board shall consist of four (4) individuals to be elected by the Residential Unit Owners. Except for members designated or elected by Sponsor pursuant to the terms hereof, all members of the Condominium Board shall be either: (i) individual Unit Owners; (ii) individual Permitted Mortgagees; (iii) officers, directors, shareholders, partners, fiduciaries, or any other entities that are Unit Owners or Permitted Mortgagees; or (iv) adult Family Members of any of the foregoing.

Section 3. *Terms of Office*: The term of office of the three (3) members of the Condominium Board designated by Sponsor prior to the first annual meeting of the Unit Owners shall expire when the nine (9) individuals to be elected at such meeting are so elected and qualified. The term of office of each of the four (4) individuals elected and qualified at the first annual meeting of the Unit Owners shall be fixed at a term of office of one year. At each annual meeting of the Unit Owners subsequent to the first such meeting, four (4) members of the Condominium Board shall be elected to serve a term of office fixed at one year.

Section 4. *Nomination and Election*:

A. Prior to any meeting of the Condominium which has as one of its purposes the election of members of the Condominium Board, the President shall appoint a nominating committee of not less than three (3) members. The nominating committee shall meet and select the persons to be nominated for election to the Board of Managers at the forthcoming meeting. The Committee shall report its nominees to the Condominium Board who shall promptly notify the Unit Owners at least twenty (20) days prior to the date of the meeting.

B. Any Unit Owner in good standing may nominate one or more candidates to the Condominium Board by a petition in writing signed by them presented to the Chairman of the nominating committee or to the Secretary of the Condominium, and thereupon the names of such candidates shall be added to the official ballot with a note distinguishing same from the nominations presented by the nominating committee.

C. Before balloting for a member of the Condominium Board, the President of the Condominium shall appoint two inspectors of election who shall collect, receive, canvass, and report the votes cast at such election. The inspectors shall not be candidates.

D. A typed or printed ballot shall be prepared by the Condominium Board and delivered to each Unit Owner. The ballot shall list the nominees designated by the nominating committee in alphabetical order. The names of additional nominees (if any) shall be listed separately on the same ballot, likewise in alphabetical order.

E. On any matter of voting not covered herein, the retiring Condominium Board may prescribe additional rules and regulations. Likewise, the retiring Condominium Board shall determine any dispute.

F. No Unit Owner who has failed to pay *[his/her]* common charges shall be eligible for election as a member of the Board of Managers.

G. Members of the Condominium Board shall be deemed installed at the next meeting of the Board after their election.

H. Members of the Condominium Board elected or appointed to fill any vacancies due to death, resignation, disqualification, or removal shall serve for the remaining unexpired term of the member replaced.

I. If the number of members of the Condominium Board shall have been increased, they shall be elected in the manner prescribed at the meeting where such increase has been adopted.

Section 5. *Removal and Restrictions*:

A. During the initial period when the Sponsor is in control of the Condominium Board, it may remove a member or members of said Board. It shall be entitled to appoint new members in their place and stead.

B. A member of the Condominium Board duly elected by the Unit Owners may be removed upon five (5) days' written notice by a majority vote of the Board or by a majority vote of the Unit Owners at a special meeting called for that purpose.

C. A member of the Condominium Board may resign at any time by giving written notice to the Board, the President, or the Secretary.

Unless otherwise specified in the letter of resignation, the resignation shall take effect immediately upon receipt thereof by the Board or by the officers designated to receive the same and acceptance of the resignation shall not be necessary to make it effective. A resignation will not relieve the member resigning from *[his/her]* liability by reason of malfeasance or negligence while in office.

Section 6. *Quorum*: A majority of the Condominium Board shall constitute a quorum for the transaction of business or for any specific item of business. If at any meeting there is less than a quorum present, the majority of those present may adjourn the meeting from time to time until a quorum is present. At an adjourned meeting any business which would have been transacted at the meeting originally called may be transacted without further notice.

Section 7. *Action of the Board*: A quorum being present, a vote of the majority of those present shall constitute the action of the Board except as to those matters where the law and the Condominium documents require a different vote.

Section 8. *Vacancies in the Board*: Vacancies in the Board may be filled until the date of the next annual meeting of the Unit Owners by a majority of the remaining members of the Board at a meeting called for that purpose though less than a quorum.

Section 9. *Time and Place of Board Meetings*: A meeting of the Condominium Board shall be held immediately following the annual meeting of the Unit Owners. Thereafter the Board shall meet at least once in three (3) months at the office of the Condominium or at such other place or places as it may determine. A special meeting of the Condominium Board may be called by the President or Vice President on two (2) days' notice given either in writing, in person, by telephone, or by wire to each member. Such special meeting must be called on the demand or request of two (2) members of the Board.

Section 10. *Notice of Meetings and Waivers*: Regular meetings once established may thereafter be held without notice at the time and at the place agreed upon by the Board. If the time or the place of the regular meeting be changed by circumstances beyond the control of the Board, notice of the change shall be given in the same manner as for a special meeting. Notice of a meeting need not be given to any member who submits a waiver of notice, whether such waiver be before or after the meeting.

Section 11. *Presiding Officer*: The President or, in [his/her] absence, the Vice President, or if both be absent, then a Chairman selected and chosen by the Board, shall preside at all meetings of the Condominium Board and of the Condominium.

Section 12. *Powers and Duties of the Board*: The Condominium Board shall have the powers and duties necessary for the administration of the affairs of the Condominium and may engage the services of a manager or managing agent or both to assist it in promoting the interests of the Condominium. Such powers and duties shall include, but not be limited to, the following:

A. Preparation and adoption of an annual budget which may include reserve funds against the replacement of equipment and/or the repurchase of Units.

B. Maintenance of accurate records and books of account showing receipts and expenditures in connection with the operation of the property which shall be available for examination by Unit Owners at reasonable times.

C. Establishment and collection of the common charges from Unit Owners. In the event that payment is not made within fifteen (15) days after the due date, the Board may make a reasonable additional administrative charge for late payment.

D. Operation, care, upkeep, and maintenance of the Common Elements.

E. Employment and dismissal of the personnel necessary for the maintenance and operation of the Common Elements, including the services of a manager or managing agent or both; establishment of compensation for said employees.

F. Opening of bank accounts on behalf of the Condominium and designating the signatories required therefor.

G. Purchase or leasing or otherwise acquiring in the name of the Condominium Board, or its designee, corporate or otherwise, on behalf of all Unit Owners, Units or other interests in property offered for sale or lease or surrendered by their owners to the Condominium Board.

H. Purchase of Units at foreclosure or other judicial sales in the name of the Condominium Board, or its designee, corporate or otherwise, on behalf of all Unit Owners.

I. Selling, leasing, mortgaging, or otherwise dealing with Units acquired by, and subleasing Units leased by, the Condominium

Board or its designee, corporate or otherwise, on behalf of all Unit Owners.

J. Making and terminating all leases, licenses, and concession agreements, and establishing charges, fees, and rents.

K. Organization of corporations to act as designees of the Condominium Board in acquiring title to or lease of Units or other interests in property on behalf of all Unit Owners.

L. Purchase of insurance for the Property as hereinafter set forth and to adjust and settle claims arising thereunder.

M. Taking possession of any abandoned Unit to prevent damage to the other Units or to the Common Elements.

N. Paragraphs B, D, E, F, and M of this Section may be delegated to a manager or managing agent or both.

O. Borrow money on behalf of the Condominium when required in connection with the operation, maintenance, repair, restoration, improvement, alteration and replacement of the Common Elements; provided, however, that: (a) the affirmative consent of at least 75% of the members of the Condominium Board shall be required for the borrowing of any sum in excess of $5,000 in any one fiscal year (regardless of the balance of any loans outstanding from previous fiscal years); (b) no lien to secure repayment of any sum borrowed may be created on any Unit or its Appurtenant Interests without the consent of the owner of such Unit; and (c) the documentation executed in connection with any such borrowing shall provide that, if any sum borrowed by the Condominium Board pursuant to this subparagraph O shall not be repaid by the Condominium Board, any Unit Owner who pays to the creditor thereunder such proportion of the then outstanding indebtedness represented or secured thereby as such Unit Owner's Common Interest, as applicable, bears to the aggregate Common Interest of all Unit Owners, as applicable, shall be entitled to obtain from the creditor a release of any judgment or other lien that the said creditor shall have filed, or shall have the right to file, against such Unit Owner's Unit.

P. To use the Common Charges and Special Assessments collected from Unit Owners, as well as all other funds held by the Condominium Board or received in connection with the operation of the Property, for the administration of the Condominium, including, without limitation: (a) the payment of Common Expenses and (b) the making of restorations, additions, alterations, and improvements to the General Common Elements and the Residential Common Elements.

Q. To make, or to contract with others for the making of, repairs, maintenance, additions, and improvements to, and alterations, restoration, and replacements of, the Property after damage or destruction by fire or other casualty, or as a result of condemnation or eminent domain proceedings, all in accordance with the terms of these Bylaws.

R. To adopt and amend the Rules and Regulations and to levy and authorize collection of fines against Unit Owners for violations of the same.

S. To enforce by legal means the terms, covenants, and conditions contained in the Condominium Documents and to bring, or defend against, any proceedings that may be instituted on behalf of, or against, the Unit Owners.

T. To carry out any other duties imposed upon the Condominium Board pursuant to the Declaration and these Bylaws.

U. Doing any and all things which prudent operation of the Condominium would require, including enforcement of the provisions of the Condominium documents by legal action when deemed necessary.

Section 13. *Liability of the Condominium Board*: The members of the Condominium Board shall not be liable to the Unit Owners for any mistake of judgment, negligence, or otherwise, except for their own individual willful misconduct or bad faith. The Unit Owners shall indemnify and hold harmless each of the members of the Condominium Board on behalf of the Condominium unless any such contract shall have been made in bad faith or contrary to the provisions of the Declaration or these Bylaws. It is intended that the members of the Condominium Board shall have no personal liability with respect to any contract made by them in good faith on behalf of the Condominium. It is understood and permissible for the Condominium Board to contract with the Sponsor, its principals, employees, affiliates, or successors, and/or members of the Condominium Board, and they shall not be charged with self-dealing by virtue thereof. It is also intended that the liability, if any, of a Unit Owner arising out of any contract made in good faith by the Condominium Board or out of the aforesaid indemnity in favor of the members of the Condominium Board shall be limited to such proportion of the total liability thereunder as *[his/ her]* interest in the Common Elements bears to the interests of all Unit Owners in the Common Elements.

Section 14. *Limitations on the Powers of the Board*: Notwithstanding anything to the contrary contained in these Bylaws, the Condominium Board shall not take any of the following actions unless 75% of all members thereof shall approve the same in writing or by vote at a duly constituted meeting called for such purpose;

(i) increase the number, or change the type, of employees;

(ii) provide for new or additional services;

(iii) impose any Common Charge or Special Assessment for the purpose of making any capital or major improvement, alteration, or addition to the Common Elements or to any Unit, unless required by Law; or

(iv) establish any reserves, including, without limitation, a reserve for contingencies, repairs, improvements, or replacements, other than a reserve for contingencies to be used within a period of twelve months from the date such reserve is established, not exceeding 5% of the budgeted operating expenses for the ensuing twelve (12) months of operation.

ARTICLE IV. Meetings

Section 1. *Place*: The Unit Owners of the condominium shall hold meetings at the principal office of the Condominium or at such place within the City of *[name of city]*, County of *[name of county]*, State of *[name of state]*, as the Condominium Board shall authorize.

Section 2. *First Meeting*: The first meeting of the Unit Owners of the Condominium shall be held within sixty (60) days after notice from the Sponsor that it intends to relinquish control of the Condominium Board, but in no event later than two (2) years from the date of the Declaration. At such time, the Condominium Board shall resign and the Unit Owners, including the Sponsor, shall elect a new Condominium Board.

Section 3. *Annual Meetings*: Thereafter, the annual meetings of the Unit Owners of the Condominium shall be held at a date and time selected by the Condominium Board. At such annual meetings, the Unit Owners shall elect a Condominium Board of the Condominium, and may transact such other business as may properly come before the meeting.

Section 4. *Special Meetings*: Special meetings of the Unit Owners may be called by the President, Vice President, Secretary, or by a majority of the Condominium Board, and must be called by such officers upon receipt of a written request from five (5) or more of the Unit Owners. Such written request shall state the purpose or purposes of the proposed meeting. Business transacted at a special meeting shall be confined to the purposes stated in the notice.

Section 5. *Fixing Record Date*: For the purpose of determining the Unit Owners entitled to notice of any meeting of the Condominium, or any adjournment thereof, or for the purpose of any other action, the Condominium Board shall fix in advance a date as the record date for such determination. Such date shall not be more than thirty (30) nor less than three (3) days before the date of the meeting.

Section 6. *Notice*: Notice of meetings of the Unit Owners of the Condominium shall be in writing. Notice of the meetings other than the annual meeting shall indicate and state that it is being issued by or at the direction of the person or persons calling the meeting. Such notice shall be mailed or delivered not less than five (5) nor more than twenty (20) days prior to the date of the meeting. Notice of all meetings at which disposition is to be made of assets or granting of rights or easements in the Condominium property must also be given to the holders of the first mortgages on the Units.

Section 7. *Waiver of Notice*: Notice of meetings need not be given to any Unit Owner who signs a waiver of notice either in person or by proxy whether before or after the meeting. The attendance of any Unit Owner at a meeting, in person or by proxy, without protesting prior to the conclusion of the meeting the lack of proper notice of such meeting, shall constitute a waiver of notice of the meeting by *[him/her]*.

Section 8. *Quorum of Unit Owners*: A quorum at Unit Owners' meeting shall consist of persons holding three (3) or more Units, entitled to vote thereon. The subsequent joinder of a Unit Owner in the action taken at a meeting by signing and concurring in the minutes thereof shall constitute the presence of such persons for the purpose of determining a quorum. When a quorum is once present to organize the meeting, it cannot be broken by the subsequent withdrawal of a Unit Owner or Owners. The Unit Owners present may adjourn the meeting despite the absence of a quorum.

Section 9. *Voting*: An Owner is entitled to one vote for each 25% Common Interest attributable to *[his/her]* Unit owned, provided *[he/she]* is not in arrears in the payment of *[his/her]* common charges, in person or by proxy, except where the percentage of interest may be required by law, in which event *[he/she]* shall be entitled to vote *[his/her]* Unit's proportionate interest in the Condominium. The Condominium Board may issue certificates to Unit Owners showing the right to vote. A Unit which has been acquired by the Condominium Board in its own name or in the name of its agent, designee, or nominee on behalf of all of the Unit Owners shall not be entitled to vote as long as it continues to be so held.

Section 10. *Proxies*: A vote may be cast in person or by proxy. To be valid, proxies must be fully signed and acknowledged by the Unit Owner and must, together with the Unit Owner's certificate showing *[he/she]* is entitled to vote, be filed with the Secretary at least 24 hours before the appointed time of the meeting. A proxy may be revoked by the Unit Owner by appearance in person at the meeting and there and then filing with the Secretary at that time notice of the revocation.

Section 11. *Order of Business*: The usual order of business at the annual meeting of the Unit Owners of the Condominium shall be:

(a) Calling the roll and certifying of proxies.

(b) Proof of notice of the meeting or certification as to waivers.

(c) Reading and disposal of unapproved minutes.

(d) Reports of the officers of the Condominium.

(e) Reports of the Condominium Board.

(f) Reports of Committees.

(g) Appointment of inspectors of election.

(h) Election of Condominium Board.

(i) Unfinished business.

(j) New business.

(k) Adjournment.

Section 12. The order of business at all other meetings of the Unit Owners shall as far as practical conform to the order of business at the annual meeting insofar as the special purpose of the meeting will permit.

ARTICLE V. Officers

Section 1. *Election of Officers*: At the first meeting of the Condominium Board following the annual meeting of the Condominium, the Board shall, by a majority vote, elect a President, Secretary, Treasurer, and such Vice President and assistants to the Secretary and Treasurer as they deem necessary. The President shall be selected from the members of the Condominium Board. All officers shall serve for a term of one year or until successors shall have been selected.

Section 2. *President*: Shall be the Chief Executive officer of the Condominium and Chairman of the Condominium Board. *[He/She]* shall have all of the powers and duties usually vested in a President of a Condominium, including the power to appoint committees as *[he/she]* may, with the consent of the Condominium Board, deem appropriate and all the powers and duties incident to the president of a stock corporation organized under the Business Corporation Law of the State of *[name of state]*. *[He/She]* shall exercise such other powers and duties as shall be prescribed by the Board. *[He/She]* shall see that all orders and resolutions of the Board shall be carried into effect. *[He/She]* may delegate some of *[his/her]* duties to Vice Presidents elected.

Section 3. *Vice President*: Shall perform all duties delegated to *[him/her]* by the President. *[He/She]* shall serve as chairman of such committees as the Condominium Board shall deem appropriate. If there is more than one Vice President, they shall exercise the powers and perform the duties of the President in *[his/her]* absence or disability in the order of their appointment. The Vice President may hold office as Secretary or Treasurer.

Section 4. *Secretary*: Shall keep a record of all actions of the Board and all meetings of the Unit Owners.

[He/She] shall attend to the giving of all notices. *[He/She]* shall prepare and have available at each meeting of the Unit Owners a list in alphabetical order of the names of the Unit Owners entitled to vote as set forth in ARTICLE IV, Section 9, and their percentage of common interest. *[He/She]* shall perform all other duties incident to the office of Secretary of the Condominium as may be required by the President of the Condominium Board.

Section 5. *Treasurer*: Shall keep the financial records of the Condominium and shall keep books of account and shall have custody of funds, securities, and evidences of indebtedness. *[He/She]* shall perform all other duties incident to a Treasurer of a Condominium as prescribed by the Board.

[He/She] shall deposit all moneys and other valuables in the name of and to the credit of the Condominium in such depositories as may be designated by the Board. *[He/She]* shall disburse the funds of the Condominium as may be ordered and authorized by the Board and shall preserve proper vouchers for such disbursements. *[He/She]* shall render an annual report at the annual meeting of the Unit Owners. The Treasurer and the President shall, as prescribed by the Board, report on the operation of the Condominium property and the payment of the common expenses and the determination and collection of the common charges.

Section 6. *Assistant Secretary and/or Assistant Treasurer*: Shall perform the duties respectively of the Secretary or Treasurer in the absence or incapacity of either or both of such officers.

Section 7. *Compensation*: No fees shall be paid to any officers of the Condominium during the period when it is controlled by the Sponsor. Thereafter their compensation, if any, shall be fixed by the Board. This provision shall not preclude the Board from employing a manager as an employee of the Condominium nor preclude the contracting with *[him/her]* for *[his/her]* full time service.

Section 8. *Removal*: All officers and employees of the Condominium may be removed with or without cause by a majority vote of the Condominium Board.

Section 9. *Vacancies*: Any vacancy in an office shall be filled by a majority vote of the Condominium Board at any regular meeting of the Condominium Board or at a special meeting thereof called for such purpose.

Section 10. *Qualification*: The President, Vice President, and the Treasurer shall be elected from among the members of the Condominium Board. The officers of the Condominium Board need not be Unit Owners and need not have any interest in the Condominium.

ARTICLE VI. Operation of the Property

Section 1. Fiscal Management:

A. A record of receipts and expenditures shall be maintained in a set of accounting books in which there shall be an account for each Unit. Such account shall designate the name and address of the Owner or Owners, the amount of common charges against the Owners, the dates they become due, the amounts paid upon the account, and the balance due thereon. In making up the common charges due, the Unit is treated as such and no division shall be made because the Unit is held by more than one person.

B. The Condominium Board shall adopt a budget for each year which shall contain estimates of the cost of performing the various functions of the Condominium and shall include among its items:

(i) Common expenses budget:

(a) Maintenance and operation of common elements.

(b) Utility services.

(c) Casualty insurance.

(d) Liability insurance.

(e) Administration.

(f) Reserves, including but not limited to funds for future repairs and replacements to property and equipment, and for the repurchase of Units and/or mortgages as authorized by the Declaration.

(g) Any other item which the Board finds necessary to include therein.

(ii) The proposed common charges.

(iii) Copies of the proposed budget shall be transmitted to each member promptly after adoption. If the budget is substantially amended, a copy thereof shall be furnished each member concerned.

(iv) The depository of the Condominium shall be such bank or banks as shall be designated from time to time by the Condominium Board. The moneys of the Condominium shall be deposited therein.

(v) An audit of the accounts of the Condominium shall be made annually by a certified public accountant and a copy of the report shall be furnished to each Unit Owner not later than ninety (90) days after the end of the fiscal year for which it is made.

Section 2. *Maintenance, Repairs, Replacements, Improvements*:

A. *By the Condominium Board*: It shall be the sole responsibility of the Condominium Board to maintain, repair, or replace common elements located either inside or outside of the Units. The cost thereof shall be a common expense unless the work shall have been necessitated by the negligence, misuse, or neglect of a Unit Owner responsible therefor. Any such work shall be substantially in accordance with the filed plans and specifications under which the building was constructed. If the cost of such work may exceed $10,000, it shall be done under the supervision of a qualified architect or engineer.

B. *By the Unit Owner*:

(i) All other maintenance, repairs, and replacements to Units shall be made by the respective Unit Owner, including painting, wall papering, decorating, or work of any kind on the interior surfaces of the walls, ceilings, or floors and floor covering at *[his/her]* own expense.

(ii) The fixtures and equipment installed in each Unit, including but not limited to the following: air conditioning units, plumbing fixtures, including wash basins, sinks, showers, bathtubs, and water closets; electric fixtures, appliances, and outlets; bathroom and kitchen cabinets and equipment; fireplaces in those Units where installed; are all the property of each Unit Owner to be maintained, repaired, or replaced by *[him/her]* at *[his/her]* own expense.

(iii) It shall be the responsibility of the Unit Owner, at *[his/her]* own cost and expense, to maintain, repair, or replace common elements of which *[he/she]* has exclusive use, including but not limited to patio or deck, doors leading to and from *[his/her]* Unit, garbage pail, window panes, and screens. Nevertheless, the Unit Owner shall not make any changes in structure, design, or color of common elements without the written consent of the Condominium Board.

C. *Access*: The Condominium Board or its designee shall have the right of access to any Unit during reasonable hours of the day, and in the event of emergencies at any time, for the purpose of making inspections, repairs, replacements, or improvements to the Common Elements within a Unit, and to remedy conditions of the Unit itself which could result in damage to other portions of the Building, whether Units or Common Elements, or to abate any violation of law, orders, rules, or regulations of governmental authorities having jurisdiction.

D. *Improvements to the Common Elements*:

(i) When, in the opinion of the Condominium Board, additions, alterations, or improvements in excess of $10,000 are advisable to the Common Elements, the consent of two-thirds of the Unit Owners shall be required.

(ii) When, in the sole opinion of the Condominium Board, the aforesaid addition, alteration, or improvement is general in character, the cost therefor shall be a common expense.

E. *Restrictive Provisions*: No Unit Owner shall make any structural modifications or changes or do any work which would jeopardize the soundness or safety of the property, reduce the value thereof, or impair any easement or hereditament, nor may any Unit Owner add any material structure or excavate any additional basement, crawl space, or cellar nor do any work on the exterior of a building, erect a fence, move or replace shrubs, or change the landscaping in any way, without in every such case the consent of all of the Unit Owners affected being first obtained. When, in the sole opinion of the Condominium Board, a Unit Owner is in violation of this provision, *[he/she]* shall cause any such work, whether within *[his/her]* Unit or within the Common Elements, to be stopped, and *[he/she]* shall refrain from recommencing or continuing the same.

Section 3. *Insurance*:

A. *The Condominium Board shall obtain and maintain, to the extent available*: fire insurance with extended coverage in the minimum amount of $*[dollar amount of fire insurance coverage]*, vandalism and malicious mischief endorsements insuring the Condominium building, including all of the apartment Units, and the bathroom and kitchen equipment and appliances initially installed therein by the sponsor, covering the interest of the Condominium organization, the Condominium Board, and all Unit Owners and their mortgagees, as their interests may appear, in an amount equal to not less than 80% of the full replacement value of the building; water damage insurance; and such other insurance as the Condominium Board may determine.

B. The proceeds of all policies of physical damage insurance shall be payable to the Condominium Board to be applied for the purpose of repairing, restoring, or rebuilding the building unless otherwise determined by the Unit Owners, as hereinafter set forth, and the Board shall arrange for such repair or work. If the insurance proceeds are insufficient to cover the cost of such work, the balance of the cost will be assessed among all Unit Owners in proportion to their respective interests in the Common Elements.

C. All policies of physical damage insurance shall contain waivers of subrogation and of any reduction of pro rata liability of the insurer as a result of any insurance carried by Unit Owners or of any invalidity arising from any acts of the insured or any Unit Owners and shall provide that such policies may not be canceled or substantially modified without at least ten (10) days' prior written notice to the named insured, including all first mortgagees of Units.

D. The Condominium Board shall also obtain and maintain to the extent obtainable: (1) fidelity insurance covering all members of the board, officers, or employees of the Condominium who handle Condominium funds; (2) workmen's compensation insurance; and (3) in order to limit the liability of Unit Owners for personal injury and tort, public liability insurance covering each member of the Condominium Board and Unit Owners (as a group) in such limits as the Condominium Board may deem proper.

E. The public liability insurance policy to be maintained until otherwise determined by the Condominium Board will be in a single limit of $500,000 covering all claims for bodily injury or property damage arising out of any one occurrence in the Common Elements. The public liability insurance shall also cover cross liability claims of one insured against another, but said policy will not cover the liability of a Unit Owner arising from an occurrence within *[his/her]* own Unit. Unit Owners who want such additional protection may obtain same, at their own cost and expense.

F. The Condominium Board shall review insurance limits on all types of insurance carried at least once in each year and shall obtain insurance coverage in such amounts as may be deemed necessary. The cost of all insurance shall be paid by the Board of Managers and shall constitute a common expense.

G. Unit Owners shall not be prohibited from carrying other insurance for their own benefit, provided such policies contain waivers of subrogation and further provided that the liability of the carriers issuing insurance procured by the Condominium Board shall not be affected or diminished by reason of any Unit Owner's other insurance.

Section 4. *Repair or Reconstruction after Fire or Other Casualty*:

A. In the event of damage to or destruction of a building as a result of fire or other casualty (unless 75% or more of the building is destroyed or substantially damaged and 75% or more of the Unit Owners do not duly and promptly resolve to proceed with repair or restoration), the Condominium Board shall arrange for the prompt repair, replacement, and restoration of the building and damaged Units (including fixtures and equipment the same or equal to those installed by the Sponsor but not including any wall, ceiling, floor, or other decorations or coverings, or any furniture, furnishings, fixtures, or equipment installed by Unit Owners in the Units), and the Condominium Board or the Insurance Trustee, as the case may be, shall disburse the proceeds of all insurance policies to the contractors engaged in such repair and restoration in appropriate progress payments. The cost of repair, replacement, and restoration in excess of the insurance proceeds, if any, shall constitute a common expense and the Condominium Board may assess all the Unit Owners for such deficit as part of the common charges.

B. If 75% or more of a building is destroyed or substantially damaged and 75% or more of the Unit Owners do not promptly resolve to proceed with the repair or restoration thereof, the Condominium property shall be subject to an action for partition at the suit of any Unit Owner or lienor, as if owned in common, in which event the net proceeds of sale, together with the net proceeds of insurance policies (or if there shall have been a repair or restoration pursuant to the first paragraph of this Section 5, and the amount of insurance proceeds shall have exceeded the cost of such repair or restoration, then the excess of such insurance proceeds) shall be divided by the Condominium Board or the Insurance Trustee, as the case may be, among all the Unit Owners in proportion to their respective common interests, after first paying out of the share of each Unit Owner the amount of any unpaid liens on *[his/her]* Unit, in the order of the priority of such liens.

Section 5. *Transfer of Units*:

A. The Unit Owner has the right to sell or lease *[his/her]* Unit, providing *[he/she]* gives thirty (30) days' notice of the terms of a bona fide sale or lease to the Condominium Board and obtains its approval for the sale or lease. The failure of the Condominium Board to act within such thirty (30)-day period shall be deemed to constitute approval. If the Board disapproves of the transaction, it shall, within fifteen (15) days after making its decision known, produce a purchaser or lessee approved by it who will accept the transaction upon terms as favorable to the seller or landlord as the terms stated in the notice to the Board. If the Board does not produce such a purchaser or lessee, as the case may be, within the aforesaid fifteen (15) days, the Unit Owner shall have the right to effectuate such sale or lease on the terms submitted as more specifically set forth herein. The Condominium Board, or its designee, may elect to purchase or lease such Unit on behalf of all the Unit Owners in the manner set forth herein.

B. A Unit Owner intending to make a transfer, sale, or lease shall give notice to the Condominium Board by registered or certified mail. *[He/She]* shall furnish the name and address of the intended grantee or lessee. *[He/She]* shall furnish a copy of the proposed contract of sale or lease and a statement of social and financial reference concerning the transferee or lessee, together with such other information as the Board may reasonably require. The notice shall constitute a representation, warranty, and offer to sell or lease to any purchaser or lessee produced by the Board.

C. If the Board produces a purchaser or a lessee willing and able to buy or lease in accordance with the offer, a binding contract shall be deemed to have come into existence and the Unit Owner shall be bound to consummate the transaction with such purchaser or lessee furnished by the Board in accordance with the terms thereof.

D. The action by the Board consenting to a sale or lease shall be in recordable form signed by any officer of the Condominium and attested to by the Secretary thereof. The Unit Owner, purchaser, or lessee may demand and shall be entitled to receive from the Board, without charge, a certificate in recordable form setting forth either the action of the Board in consenting or that records of the Condominium disclose no action by the Board within a thirty (30)-day period after receipt of notice.

E. In addition to any other remedy which the Condominium may have as to any sale, voluntary transfer, conveyance, or lease which the Condominium Board deems is unauthorized by the terms of the Declaration and these Bylaws, it may issue a certificate to this effect in recordable form to be recorded with the Recording Officer.

F. The provisions of this Section shall not apply to any sale or lease to a spouse, children, parents, brothers or sisters, or any one of them, or to a Unit owned by the Sponsor, or to the acquisition or sale of a Unit and its appurtenant interests by a mortgagee herein authorized who shall acquire title thereto by foreclosure or by deed in lieu of foreclosure.

G. Any contract to sell a Residential Unit together with its Appurtenant Interest and any lease of a Residential Unit (Sale Agreement or Lease Agreement) shall contain the following language: "THIS AGREEMENT AND THE RIGHTS AND OBLIGATIONS OF THE PARTIES HEREUNDER ARE HEREBY MADE EXPRESSLY SUBJECT TO THE RIGHTS, IF ANY, OF THE CONDOMINIUM BOARD OF THE *[NAME OF CONDOMINIUM]* WITH RESPECT TO THE TRANSACTION EMBODIED HEREIN PURSUANT TO THE TERMS OF THE BY-LAWS OF THE SAID CONDOMINIUM, AS THE SAME MAY HAVE BEEN AMENDED." Promptly after any such bona fide contract of sale or lease shall be fully executed, the Residential Unit Owner executing the same (Offeree Unit Owner) shall send written notice thereof to the Condominium Board by certified or registered mail, return receipt requested, which notice shall be accompanied by a fully executed, original counterpart of the contract of sale or the lease, as the case may be, containing all of the terms offered in good faith by the prospective purchaser or tenant (Outside Offerer).

H. Each lease of a Residential Unit shall be in the then current form of apartment lease recommended by the *[designation of party]*, subject to such modifications as may be approved in writing by the Condominium Board. Each such lease shall provide that:

(i) such lease may not be amended, modified, or extended without the prior written consent of the Condominium Board in each instance;

(ii) the tenant thereunder shall not assign *[his/her]* interest in such lease or sublet the premises demised thereunder or any part thereof without the prior written consent of the Condominium Board in each instance; and

(iii) the Condominium Board shall have the power to terminate such lease and/or to bring summary proceedings to evict the tenant in the name of the landlord thereunder in the event of: (a) a default by the tenant in the performance of its obligations under such lease; or (b) a foreclosure of the lien.

I. No Unit Owner shall execute any deed or other instrument conveying title to *[his/her]* Unit without including therein its Appurtenant Interests, it being the intention to prevent any severance of such combined ownership.

J. No Unit Owner shall be permitted to convey or lease *[his/her]* Unit unless *[he/she]* shall have paid in full to the Condominium Board all unpaid Common Charges and Special Assessments theretofore assessed against such Unit and shall have satisfied all unpaid liens, other than that of Permitted Mortgages, levied against such Unit. However, where the payment of such unpaid Common Charges and/or Special Assessments is made by the grantee or provided for out of the proceeds of the sale, a sale may take place notwithstanding the foregoing.

K. Any Unit Owner shall be free to convey or transfer *[his/her]* Unit, together with its Appurtenant Interests, by gift, or to devise the same by will or to have the same pass by intestacy, without restriction.

Section 6. *Mortgages:*

A. A Unit Owner who mortgages *[his/her]* Unit shall notify the Condominium Board of the name and address of *[his/her]* mortgagee and shall file a conformed copy of the note and mortgage with the Condominium Board.

B. The Condominium Board, whenever so requested in writing by a mortgagee of a Unit, shall promptly report any then unpaid common charges due from or any other default by the Owner of the mortgaged Unit.

C. The Condominium Board, when giving notice to a Unit Owner of a default in paying common charges or other default, shall send a copy of such notice to each holder of a mortgage covering such Unit whose name and address have theretofore been furnished to the Condominium Board.

Section 7. *Foreclosure of mortgage or other liens*:

A. Upon the happening of a default under the terms of the mortgage or other liens which would permit the holder to declare the entire principal sum due, notice of the intention of the holder to do so shall be given to the Condominium Board but the failure to give such notice shall not prevent the holder from instituting a foreclosure action and joining the Condominium Board as a party defendant herein.

B. The Condominium Board shall have the following rights, powers, and privileges with respect to mortgages or other liens in default:

(i) By and with the consent of the holder thereto, to remedy the defaults existing under the terms of a mortgage and to put the same in good standing.

(ii) To acquire by assignment either before or after the institution of foreclosure action from the holder of said mortgage or other lien in the name of the Board or in the name of their designated nominee with all the powers and rights of the holder against the defaulting Unit Owner, including the right to foreclose the same for the benefit of the remaining Unit Owners.

(iii) To accept from the defaulting Unit Owner a deed transferring the Unit and its common interest and with the consent of the holder of the mortgage or other lien to remedy the defaults existing under the terms thereof for the benefit of the other Unit Owners.

(iv) To continue any pending action or to institute an action to foreclose any mortgage or other lien taken by assignment under subdivision B-2 hereof, or to take a deed in lieu of foreclosure of the mortgage. In no event shall a Unit Owner be relieved from liability already incurred for past due common expenses and charges nor be relieved from personal liability on the bond, note, or other obligation by reason of any conveyance made under subdivision B-3 hereof, or under this subdivision.

C. The Condominium Board shall be a necessary party in every action brought to foreclose any mortgage or other lien affecting a Unit. The Condominium Board shall be entitled to bid at any sale, whether the action be in its name or they be a defendant therein, and to purchase any Unit at such sale for such amount as shall be approved by a majority of the Board, taking into consideration the amount due the plaintiff, the costs and disbursements, and all other charges affecting the Unit. The Board shall not, however, be limited in its bidding to such amount or total, but may bid any higher sum that it finds necessary in order to protect the interests of the other Unit Owners.

Section 8. *Other Defaults*:

A. Failure of present and future owners, lessees, and occupants of Units to comply with the terms of the Declaration, Bylaws, and Rules and Regulations as they may be amended from time to time, and the resolutions and decisions duly adopted pursuant thereto shall be ground for an action to recover sums due, for damages or injunctive relief or both, by the Condominium Board on behalf of one or more of the Unit Owners, or by a Unit Owner in *[his/her]* own behalf. In any case of flagrant or repeated violation by a Unit Owner, *[he/she]* may be required by the Condominium Board to give sufficient surety or sureties for *[his/her]* future compliance therewith.

B. Each Unit Owner shall be liable for the expense of any maintenance, repair, or replacement rendered necessary by [his/her] act, neglect, or carelessness to the extent that such expense is not met by the proceeds of insurance carried by the Condominium Board. Such liability shall include any increase in fire insurance rates occasioned by use, misuse, occupancy, or abandonment of a Unit or its appurtenances. Nothing herein contained, however, shall be construed so as to modify any waiver by insurance companies of rights of subrogation.

C. In any proceeding arising because of an alleged default by a Unit Owner, the prevailing party shall be entitled to recover the costs of the proceedings and such reasonable attorney's fees as may be determined by the Court.

D. The failure of the Condominium Board or of a Unit Owner to enforce any right, provision, covenant, or condition of the Condominium documents shall not constitute a waiver of the right of the Condominium Board or Unit Owner to enforce same in the future.

E. All rights, remedies, and privileges granted to the Condominium Board, its designated agent, or a Unit Owner pursuant to any terms, provisions, covenants, or conditions of the Declaration and Bylaws shall be deemed to be cumulative, and the exercise of any one or more shall not be deemed to constitute an election of remedies nor shall it preclude the party thus exercising the same from exercising such other and additional rights, remedies, or privileges as may be granted to such party by the Declaration, Bylaws, or at law or in equity.

Section 9. *Condemnation*: In the event of a taking in condemnation or by eminent domain of part or all of the Common Elements, the award made for such taking shall be payable to the Condominium. If 75% or more of the Unit Owners duly and promptly approve the repair and restoration of such Common Elements, the Condominium Board shall arrange for the repair and restoration of such Common Elements, and the Condominium Board shall disburse the proceeds of such award to the contractors engaged in such repair and restoration in appropriate progress payments. In the event that 75% or more of Unit Owners do not duly and promptly approve the repair and restoration of such Common Elements, or if the award exceeds the cost of such repair or restoration, the Board of Managers shall disburse the net proceeds among all Unit Owners in proportion to their respective common interests after first paying out of the share of each Unit Owner the amount of any unpaid liens on *[his/her]* Unit, in the order of the priority of such liens. As used in this Section, the words "promptly approve" shall mean not more than sixty (60) days from the date of such taking.

Section 10. *Use of the Property*:

A. No nuisance shall be allowed on the Property, nor shall any use or practice be allowed that either is a source of annoyance to its residents or interferes with the peaceful possession or proper use of the Property by its residents or occupants. No immoral, improper, offensive, or unlawful use shall be made of the Property or any portion thereof, and all valid Laws relating to any portion of the Property shall be complied with at the sole cost and expense of the respective Unit Owners or the Condominium, whoever shall have the obligation to maintain or repair such part of the Property.

B. Nothing shall be done or kept in any Residential Unit or in any of the Common Elements that would increase the rate of insurance for the Property, except upon the prior written consent of the Condominium Board. No Unit Owner shall permit anything to be done or kept in a Unit or in the Common Elements that will result in the cancellation of insurance on the property or the contents thereof, or that would be in violation of any Law. No waste shall be committed in the Common Elements.

C. Nothing shall be done in any Unit or in, on, or to the Common Elements that will impair the structural integrity of the Property or will structurally change the Building, except as is otherwise provided in the Declaration or in these Bylaws. In no event shall interior partitions contributing to the support of any Unit or the Common Elements be altered or removed.

Section 11. *Use of the Units*:

A. In order to provide for congenial occupancy of the Property and for the protection of the values of the Units, the use of Units shall be restricted to, and shall be in accordance with, the terms contained herein.

B. Each Residential Unit shall be used only as a residence, and not more than one family may occupy a Residential Unit at any one time. Notwithstanding the foregoing, Sponsor (or, when there are no longer any Unsold Residential Units, the Condominium Board) may, in its sole discretion, permit Persons other than those set forth above to occupy a Residential Unit. In no event, however, shall a portion of a Residential Unit (as opposed to the entire Residential Unit) be sold, conveyed, leased, or subleased, and no transient occupant (other than a guest permitted under this paragraph B) may be accommodated therein.

C. Notwithstanding anything to the contrary contained in this Section, Sponsor may, without the consent of either the Condominium Board or the Unit Owners:

(i) grant permission for the use of any Unsold Residential Unit as a professional or business office or for any other purpose, provided that the nature and manner of such use complies with Law and the user thereof complies with all applicable governmental regulations; and

(ii) use any one or more Unsold Residential Units as models and offices for the sales, promotions, rental, management, and operation of the Unsold Residential Units or for any other purpose, subject only to compliance

Section 12. *Use of the Common Elements*:

A. The Common Elements may be used only for the furnishing of the services and facilities, and for the other uses for which they are reasonably suited and capable.

B. The terms of paragraph A of this Section shall not apply to Sponsor for as long as there are any Unsold Residential Units. Sponsor shall have the right, without charge or limitation, to:

(i) erect and maintain signs, of any size or content determined by Sponsor on or about any portion of the Common

Elements chosen by Sponsor including, without limitation, on the exterior walls of the Building or adjacent to the main entrance thereof;

(ii) have its employees, contractors, subcontractors, and sales agents present on the Property; and

(iii) do all things necessary or appropriate, including the use of the Common Elements, to sell, lease, manage, or operate Unsold Residential Units, to complete any work or repairs to the Building expressly undertaken by Sponsor, and to comply with Sponsor's obligations under the Plan and the Condominium Documents. In no event, however, shall Sponsor be entitled to use any Common Elements in such a manner as will unreasonably interfere with the use of any Unit for its permitted purposes.

ARTICLE VII. Common Charges

Section 1. *Determination of Common Expenses and Fixing of Common Charges*:

A. From time to time, but not less frequently than once a year, the Condominium Board shall: (i) prepare and adopt a budget for the Condominium; (ii) determine the aggregate amount of Common Charges necessary to be charged to the Unit Owners in order to meet the Common Expenses; and (iii) allocate and assess such Common Charges amongst the Unit Owners, pro rata, in accordance with their respective Common Interests or Residential Common Interests, as applicable (except as otherwise provided in the Declaration or in these Bylaws). The Condominium Board shall advise all Unit Owners promptly thereafter in writing of the amount of Common Charges payable by each of them, not later than ten (10) days next preceding the date upon which the first installment of newly-determined Common Charges is due, shall furnish copies of the budget (in a reasonably itemized form) upon which such Common Charges are based to all Unit Owners and to their respective Permitted Mortgagees. The Condominium Board may, at its sole discretion, from time to time, increase or decrease the amount of Common Charges allocated to the Units and payable by the Unit Owners and may modify its prior determination of the Common Expenses for any fiscal year or portion thereof; however, no such revised determination of Common Expenses shall have a retroactive effect on the amount of Common Charges payable by Unit Owners for any period prior to the date of such new determination.

B. The failure or delay of the Condominium Board to prepare or adopt a budget or to determine the Common Expenses for any fiscal year or portion thereof shall not be deemed a waiver or modification in any respect of the covenants and provisions hereof or a release of any Unit Owner from the obligation to pay Common Charges. In such event, the Common Charges that were computed an the basis of the Common Expenses last determined for any fiscal year or portion thereof shall continue thereafter to be the Common Charges payable by the Unit Owners until a new determination of the Common Expenses shall be made.

C. In addition to the foregoing duty to determine the amount of and assess Common Charges, the Condominium Board shall have the right to levy Special Assessments to meet the Common Expenses. All Special Assessments relative to the Common Elements shall be levied against all Unit Owners in proportion to their respective Common Interests and all Special Assessments relative to the Common Elements shall be levied against all Residential Unit Owners in proportion to their respective Common Interests. Special Assessments may be payable either in one lump sum or in installments, as the Condominium Board shall determine; provided, however, that the Condominium Board shall give each Unit Owner not less than fifteen (15) days' written notice prior to the date upon which such Special Assessment, or the first installment thereof, shall be due and payable, which notice shall set forth, in reasonable detail, the nature and purpose thereof. The Condominium Board shall have all rights and remedies for the collection of Special Assessments as are provided herein for the collection of Common Charges.

Section 2. *Payment of Common Charges*:

A. All Unit Owners (including Sponsor with respect to Unsold Residential Units for as long as the same are owned thereby) shall be obligated to pay Common Charges and Special Assessments assessed by the Condominium Board pursuant to the terms of Section 1 hereof at such time or times (but not less than annually) as the Condominium Board shall determine. Unless otherwise determined by the Condominium Board, Common Charges shall be payable in installments on the first day of every month in advance. To the extent permitted by Law, the Condominium Board shall have a lien on each Unit, on behalf of all Unit Owners, for unpaid Common Charges and Special Assessments assessed against such Unit. Such lien, however, shall be subordinate, to the extent required by Law, to any liens for real estate taxes assessed against such Unit.

B. No Unit Owner shall be liable for the payment of any part of the Common Charges and any Special Assessments assessed against [his/her] Unit subsequent to a sale, transfer, or other conveyance by [him/her] of such Unit, together with its Appurtenant Interests.

C. Any Unit Owner may convey [his/her] Unit, together with its Appurtenant Interests, to the Condominium Board or to its designee, corporate or otherwise, on behalf of all Unit Owners, without being compensated therefor, and, in such event, be exempt from the payment of Common Charges and Special Assessments thereafter accruing; provided, however, that: (i) all Common Charges and any Special Assessments then due and payable with respect to such Unit have been paid; (ii) such Unit is free and clear of all liens and encumbrances other than a Permitted First Mortgage and the statutory lien for unpaid Common Charges and Special Assessments; and (iii) no violation of any provisions of the Condominium Documents then exists with respect to such Unit. However, in no event shall Sponsor be permitted to convey any Unsold Residential Unit to the Condominium Board and thereby exempt itself from Common Charges and any Special Assessments attributable to such Residential Unit thereafter accruing unless the aggregate Common Interests then appertaining to the Unsold Residential Units constitute 15% or less of the total Residential Common Interests then appertaining to all Residential Units, at least five (5) years shall have elapsed from the date of the First Closing, and, at the time of conveyance, Sponsor shall pay to the Condominium Board an amount equal to the product of the then current monthly Common Charges for the Unsold Residential Unit(s) being conveyed, multiplied by 24.

D. No Unit Owner shall be exempted from liability for the payment of Common Charges or Special Assessments by waiving the use or enjoyment of any or all of the Common Elements or by abandoning [his/her] Unit (except with respect to a conveyance of the same to the Condominium Board, without compensation). No Unit Owner shall be entitled to a diminution or abatement in the Common Charges or Special Assessments payable thereby for any inconvenience or discomfort arising from: (i) the failure or interruption of any utility or other services; (ii) the making of repairs or improvements to the Common Elements or any Unit; or (iii) any action taken by the Condominium Board or the officers of the Condominium to comply with Law.

ARTICLE VIII. Miscellaneous

Section 1. *Invalidity*: The invalidity of any part of these Bylaws shall not impair or affect in any manner the validity, enforceability, or effect of the balance of these Bylaws.

Section 2. *Captions*: The captions herein are inserted only as a matter of convenience and for reference, and in no way define, limit, or describe the scope of these Bylaws, or the intent of any provision thereof.

Section 3. *Gender*: The use of the masculine gender in these Bylaws shall be deemed to include the feminine gender and the use of the singular shall be deemed to include the plural, whenever the context so requires.

Section 4. *Parliamentary Rules*: Roberts' Rules of Order (latest edition) shall govern the conduct or proceedings except where the Declaration, Bylaws, or the laws of the State of *[name of state]* require a different method of procedure.

Section 5. *Fiscal Year*: The fiscal year shall begin on such date in each year as the Board of Managers shall establish.

Section 6. *Execution of Instruments*: All instruments of the Condominium shall be signed, executed, and acknowledged under seal by such officer or officers as the Board of Managers shall designate.

Section 7. *Conflicts*: These Bylaws are set forth to comply with the requirements of *[designation of citation]* of the Real Property Law of the State of *[name of state]*. In case any of these Bylaws conflict with the provisions of said statute or of the Declaration, the provisions of said statute or of the Declaration, as the case may be, shall control.

Section 8. *Amendments*: These Bylaws may be modified or amended by the vote of 75% in number and in common interest of all Unit Owners at a meeting duly held for such purpose, but only with the written approval of the holders of the mortgages constituting first liens thereon. However, no amendments shall affect or impair the validity or priority of the interests of holders of recorded mortgages encumbering the Units. For as long as the Sponsor remains the owner of one or more Units, these Bylaws may not be amended so as to adversely affect the Sponsor without its consent.

Rules and Regulations of the *[name of condominium]*

1. The sidewalks, entrance passages, public halls, elevators, vestibules, corridors, and stairways of or appurtenant to the Building

shall not be obstructed or used for any purpose other than ingress to and egress from the Units.

2. No baby carriages, velocipedes, bicycles, scooters, or similar vehicle shall be allowed to stand in the public halls, passageways, or other public areas of the Building.

3. No article (including, but not limited to, garbage cans, bottles, or mats) shall be placed or stored in any of the halls or on any of the staircases or fire tower landings of the Building, nor shall any fire exit thereof be obstructed in any manner.

4. No refuse from the Residential Units shall be sent to the cellar of the Building, except at such times and in such manner as the Condominium Board or the Managing Agent may direct. Nothing shall be hung or shaken from any doors or windows, or placed upon the window sills, of the Building, and no Unit Owner shall sweep or throw, or permit to be swept or thrown, any dirt, debris, or other substance therefrom.

5. There shall be no playing or lounging in the entrances, passages, public halls, elevators, vestibules, corridors, stairways, or fire towers of the Building, except in recreational areas or other areas designated as such in the Declaration or by the Condominium Board.

6. The Condominium Board or the Managing Agent may, from time to time, curtail or relocate any portion of the Common Elements devoted to storage, recreation, or service purposes in the Building.

7. Nothing shall be done or kept in any Unit or in the Common Elements that will increase the rate of insurance of the Building or the contents thereof. No Unit Owner shall permit anything to be done or kept in [his/her] Unit or in the Common Elements that will result in the cancellation of insurance on the Building, or the contents thereof, or that would be in violation of any Law. No Unit Owner or any of [his/her] Family Members, agents, servants, employees, licensees, or visitors shall, at any time, bring into or keep in [his/her] Unit any inflammable, combustible, or explosive fluid, material, chemical, or substance, except as shall be necessary and appropriate for the permitted uses of such Unit.

8. No Unit Owner shall make, cause, or permit any unusual, disturbing, or objectionable noises or odors to be produced upon or to

emanate from *[his/her]* Unit or permit anything to be done therein that will interfere with the rights, comforts, or conveniences of the other Unit Owners. No Residential Unit Owner shall play upon or suffer to be played upon any musical instrument, or shall operate or permit to be operated a phonograph, radio, television set, or other loudspeaker in such Residential Unit Owner's Residential Unit between midnight and the following 8:00 a.m., if the same shall disturb or annoy other occupants of the Building, and in no event shall any Residential Unit Owner practice or suffer to be practiced either vocal or instrumental music between the hours of 10:00 p.m. and the following 9:00 a.m. No construction, repair work, or other installation involving noise shall be conducted in any Unit except on weekdays (not including legal holidays) and only between the hours of 8:00 a.m. and 5:00 p.m., unless such construction or repair work is necessitated by an emergency.

9. In the event that any Residential Unit shall be used for home occupation purposes in conformance with the Declaration and the Bylaws, no patients, clients, or other invitees shall be permitted to wait in any lobby, public hallway, or vestibule.

10. Unless expressly authorized by the Condominium Board in each instance, not less than 80% of the floor area of each Residential Unit (excepting only kitchens, pantries, bathrooms, closets, and foyers) must be covered with rugs, carpeting, or equally effective noise-reducing material.

11. In no event, however, shall any exterior glass surface of any windows at the Property be colored or painted.

12. No ventilator or air conditioning device shall be installed in any Residential Unit without the prior written approval of the Condominium Board, which approval may be granted or refused in the sole discretion of the Condominium Board.

13. No radio or television aerial shall be attached to or hung from the exterior of the Building, and no sign, notice, advertisement, or illumination (including, without limitation, "For Sale," "For Lease," or "For Rent" signs) shall be inscribed or exposed on or at any window or other part of the Building, except such as are permitted pursuant to the terms of Declaration and/or the Bylaws or shall have been approved in writing by the Condominium Board or the Managing Agent. Nothing shall be projected from any window of a Unit without similar approval.

14. All radio, television, or other electrical equipment of any kind or nature installed or used in each Unit shall fully comply with all rules, regulations, requirements, or recommendations of the *[specification of board of fire underwriters]* and the public authorities having jurisdiction, and the Unit Owner alone shall be liable for any damage or injury caused by any radio, television, or other electrical equipment.

15. Water closets and other water apparatus in the Building shall not be used for any purpose other than those of which they were designated, and no sweepings, rubbish, rags, or any other article shall be thrown into same. Any damage resulting from misuse of any water closets or other apparatus in a Unit shall be repaired and paid for by the owner of such Unit.

16. Each Unit Owner shall keep *[his/her]* Unit in a good state of preservation, condition, repair, and cleanliness in accordance with the terms of the Bylaws.

17. The agents of the Condominium Board or the Managing Agent, and any contractor or workman authorized by the Condominium Board of the Managing Agent, may enter any room or Unit at any reasonable hour of the day, on at least one day's prior notice, to the Unit Owner, for the purpose of inspecting such Unit for the presence of any vermin, insects, or other pests and for the purpose of taking such measures as may be necessary to control or exterminate any such vermin, insects, or other pests; however, such entry, inspection, and extermination shall be done in a reasonable manner so as not to unreasonably interfere with the use of such Unit for its permitted purposes.

18. The Condominium Board or the Managing Agent may retain a passkey to each Residential Unit. If any lock is altered or a new lock is installed, the Condominium Board or the Managing Agent shall be provided with a key thereto immediately upon such alteration or installation. If the Residential Unit Owner is not personally present to open and permit any entry to *[his/her]* Residential Unit at any time when an entry therein is necessary or permissible, then the Condominium Board or Managing Agent may forcibly enter such Residential Unit without liability for damages or trespass by reason thereof (if, during such entry, reasonable care is given to such Residential Unit Owner's property).

19. No occupant of the Building shall send any employee of the Condominium or of the Managing Agent out of the Building on any private business.

20. Any consent or approval given under these Rules and Regulations may be amended, modified, added to, or repealed at any time by resolution of the Condominium Board. Furthermore, any such consent or approval may, in the discretion of the Condominium Board or the Managing Agent, be conditional in nature.

21. Complaints regarding the service of the Condominium shall be made in writing to the Condominium Board or to the Managing Agent.

Index